THE BOOK OF ZECHARIAH AND ITS INFLUENCE

The book bearing the title of 'Zechariah' is, in its present form, an amalgam of oracles and prophecies stemming from Zechariah himself as well as others. It became part of Jewish scripture, was revered and valued, and was a particular favourite of a number of early Christian writers. Often cited by New Testament writers, this book of one of the most important of the 'minor prophets' is itself deeply indebted to earlier Jewish prophetic texts and has been an important resource for later writers, Jewish and Christian, as they sought to tap their own 'Biblical' material.

The amalgam of oracles and prophecies presented in the book of Zechariah offers an ideal thematic focus for the leading scholars in this volume who explore areas of the Hebrew Bible, post-Biblical Jewish literature, and early Christian literature and history (in the New Testament and beyond). The essays examine the book of Zechariah itself as well as its subsequent interpretation by a number of other writers, Jewish and Christian. The essays raise important issues in relation to the influence of Biblical texts in subsequent literature and also the broad area of 'intertextuality' and the way in which later texts relate to and use earlier texts in their sacred tradition.

The Book of Zechariah and its Influence

Edited by
Christopher Tuckett
University of Oxford, UK

Routledge
Taylor & Francis Group
LONDON AND NEW YORK

First published 2003 by Ashgate Publishing

Reissued 2018 by Routledge
2 Park Square, Milton Park, Abingdon, Oxon OX14 4RN
711 Third Avenue, New York, NY 10017, USA

Routledge is an imprint of the Taylor & Francis Group, an informa business

Typeset in Times New Roman by N²productions

ISBN 13: 978-1-138-70864-8 (hbk)
ISBN 13: 978-1-138-70860-0 (pbk)
ISBN 13: 978-1-315-19846-0 (ebk)

Contents

Preface

The essays in this volume were all first presented as papers at a colloquium arranged between the Biblical Studies sections of the Faculties of Theology in the University of Oxford, UK, and the University of Leiden, The Netherlands. The colloquium took place in Oxford in January 2002.

The subject chosen for the colloquium was the book of Zechariah from the Hebrew Bible/'Old Testament' and its subsequent influence in later literature, both Jewish and Christian. At one level, the choice of subject was pragmatic, to enable a wide range of scholars covering study of the Hebrew Bible, post-Biblical Jewish literature, and early Christian literature and history (in the New Testament and beyond) to come together with a common theme. It was however clear from the very beginning that the choice of the book of Zechariah as the common focus for the colloquium proved to be particularly apt and fruitful, raising as it did many issues of concern common to a wide range of interests within the broad fields covered by participants of the colloquium.

The book of Zechariah itself is widely accepted as being composite: the first eight chapters (may) represent oracles stemming from a prophet in the early post-exilic period. As such, the text witnesses to ideas and beliefs current in a particularly significant time in Jewish history, with hopes and expectations raised and articulated concerning (a) future figure(s) who would perhaps bring a change in the nation's fortunes. Certainly Zechariah's prophecy about the 'branch' (Zech 3) represents one important phase in the developing beliefs within Judaism about eschatological 'messianic' figures, beliefs which became influential in both Judaism and Christianity. Another aspect of these chapters, namely the precise nature of the charge against the priests in this section, is discussed fully in the essay of Tiemeyer (Chapter 1).

At some stage, the collection of the oracles of Zechariah himself were supplemented by further oracles, now included in what we call chapters 9–14 of the book of Zechariah. How, when and why all this happened is not clear. Nor is it clear whether the chapters should be regarded as a unitary set of oracles, stemming (at however many stages removed) from a single prophetic figure. Often called 'Deutero-Zechariah' or 'Second Zechariah', these oracles are clearly rather different from those contained in 'Proto-Zechariah' (i.e. Zech 1–8).

The book now bearing the title 'Zechariah' is thus in its present form an amalgam of oracles and prophecies stemming from more than one person. How far each section of the book is also composite is debated. To what extent should the oracles be interpreted individually and in (some degree of) isolation from each other? How much unity should one seek to find the longer sections of the present work? To what extent is any attempt to find an over-arching theme or plan in a longer section of the book simply imposing an artificial unity or literary plan on what is essentially highly disparate material? These issues are raised here in relation to one particular oracle by the essay of Tromp (Chapter 4) in his discussion of Zech 10:1–2. Tromp argues that one should not necessarily look for, and impose, an artificial unity on material which may be highly disparate; and in the case of Zech 10:1–2, he makes a strong case for seeing this as an oracle which is completely independent of its present immediate literary context in Zech 9–10. The general issue is clearly an important one. The trend among many Biblical scholars today is to adopt a 'literary' approach to Biblical texts, sometimes bracketing off historical questions and analysing the text in its present form and assuming that the text has a literary integrity of its own with a structure and plan which can be clearly identified. In such an enterprise it then becomes extremely important to determine how much literary unity in a text one might look for and/or expect to find.

In due course, the book of Zechariah became part of Jewish scripture. As such, it was revered and valued by all those who based their religious beliefs, wholly or in part, on Jewish scripture. This in turn had various consequences. Within Judaism, the book underwent the same kind of experience as other books in that it was in due course translated into other languages as well as being paraphrased in Targums and being the focus of commentaries etc. In relation to translations, the book was of course translated into Greek in the so-called Septuagint. All translation from one language to another can involve a degree of interpretation as well, and the translation of Jewish scriptural books from Hebrew to Greek is no exception. The LXX translators evidently felt free (or forced) to make a number of interpretative 'translations' in working with individual texts; in addition, the inevitable semi-conscious process of the influence of other literature available at the time had an effect on the language used to translate the work. In this volume, the topic is treated in some detail in the essay of van der Kooij (Chapter 5) who shows (on the basis of parallel terminology in other texts) how one particular passage from Zechariah, the prediction of the royal figure in 9:9–10, was probably interpreted by the LXX translator as a reference to Simon Maccabaeus.

Jewish scripture was also highly valued within early Christianity, and it is clear that the book of Zechariah was a particular favourite of a number of early Christian writers. The book is often cited by New Testament writers who clearly saw a significant number of oracles, mostly from Deutero-Zechariah, 'fulfilled' in the story about Jesus and/or the early church. The precise extent of this is debated: Foster's essay (Chapter 6) in particular focuses on the gospel of Matthew and questions how far many possible 'allusions' to the text of Zechariah are in fact intended to be such and how far they simply represent coincidence in language. Nevertheless it is clear that certainly a number of early Christians responsible for the gospel traditions saw significant parts of the story of Jesus as a fulfilment of the oracles of Deutero-Zechariah. Different aspects of this are developed here in the essays of Foster (on Matthew) (Chapter 6), de Jonge (arguing for influence of Zechariah at a pre-Markan stage of the tradition, but Mark being unaware of this) (Chapter 7), and by Tuckett (on the significance of the explicit reference to the 'pierced one' in John) (Chapter 9).

Perhaps slightly surprisingly, Zechariah does not seem to be echoed quite so strongly in the New Testament epistles. However, there is one notable allusion to Zechariah in the text of the small epistle of Jude which has always formed a notorious crux. Many of the problems concerning this allusion, especially the precise text form of the allusion, are dealt with in detail in the essay of Hollander (Chapter 10). Hollander also suggests that the text of Zechariah may be alluded elsewhere in Jude, though without necessarily any verbal identity between the Greek of Jude and the Greek of the LXX of Zechariah. Such an argument raises important issues about how one may determine whether there is an allusion to an earlier work: clearly the presence or absence of verbal identity is a factor. But in the case of the NT referring to texts of the Hebrew Bible, one must not forget that 'the LXX' was not necessarily the only Greek form of the text of these Jewish writings and hence one cannot rely solely on the detailed wording of the LXX to determine the issue one way or the other.

Jewish scripture remained an important resource for Christians in the post-NT period as well. However, its potential value may have varied, depending on whether one was addressing Jews or non-Jews. Some of the work of the second-century Christian apologists is particularly interesting in this respect. In this volume, Boccabello (Chapter 11) takes the example of Justin Martyr whose extant works include both an *Apology* (presumably addressed primarily to a Gentile readership) and a *Dialogue* (with the Jewish figure of Trypho). Boccabello shows well how Justin's use of material from Zechariah varies, depending on which audience he is addressing. Thus the 'influence' of a book from Jewish scripture was felt to be important when addressing non-Jews from a Christian perspective, even if the finer points of detail in the text were taken up only when debating with a Jewish conversation partner.

The phenomenon of one writer quoting, or alluding to, an earlier text is of course well known in relation to NT writers referring to the 'OT'. Much recent research on some of the later Jewish Biblical texts have however highlighted the way in which many of these writings are themselves indebted to earlier texts. Indeed modern literary study of the phenomenon of 'intertextuality' has shown the ways in which *all* literary texts gain force and meaning by being part of a complex network of interrelationships with other texts. In this respect the book of Zechariah itself is particularly interesting, especially 'Deutero-Zechariah', i.e. Zech 9–14. The relatively late date of these oracles certainly means that this section of the book postdates many other parts of the Jewish scriptures. But it has also become clear in recent years that this section of Zechariah is deeply indebted to other (earlier) Jewish scriptural text and represents at times a rich collage of allusions or 'quotations'. (The dividing line between 'quotations' and 'allusions' is not always easy to draw.) This aspect of Deutero-Zechariah is addressed especially here by the essays of Mason and Collins (Chapters 2 and 3). Mason raises the questions of *why* the author of these oracles shows so much continuity with earlier language and feels driven to reproduce so many 'quotations'. Collins discusses the issue of how far there is continuity and how much there is discontinuity in this activity, and how perhaps it is precisely the differences from earlier texts that are important and highlight the points being made by the author(s) of the oracles concerned.

All the papers engendered valuable discussion and debate, and they are here offered to a wider public to enable such discussion to be furthered. The colloquium was made possible by the generosity of the Faculty Board of Theology in Oxford, and the meeting was kindly hosted by St Benet's Hall. Particular thanks are extended to the Master of St Benet's, Dom Henry Wansbrough, for his welcome to visitors to Oxford and in hosting the meeting at St Benet's.

Christopher Tuckett
Oxford, October 2002

Contributors

Jeremy S. Boccabello is a research student at Wolfson College, University of Oxford.

Terry Collins is Tutor and Lecturer in Hebrew Texts and Old Testament Studies, University of Oxford.

Henk Jan de Jonge is ordinary Professor of New Testament and Early Christian Literature, University of Leiden.

Paul Foster is a research student at The Queen's College, University of Oxford.

Harm W. Hollander is Lecturer in New Testament Studies in the University of Leiden.

Rex Mason is Emeritus Fellow at Regent's Park College, Oxford and was University Lecturer in Old Testament & Hebrew, University of Oxford.

John Muddiman is George Caird Fellow at Mansfield College, Oxford, and Lecturer in New Testament Studies, University of Oxford.

Lena-Sofia Tiemeyer was a research student in Oxford and is currently a lecturer in Hebrew and Jewish Studies, University of Birmingham.

Johannes Tromp is Lecturer for Ancient Israelite Religion and Early Judaism, University of Leiden.

Christopher M. Tuckett is Professor of New Testament Studies, University of Oxford and a Fellow of Pembroke College, Oxford.

Arie van der Kooij is Professor of Old Testament Studies, University of Leiden.

Chapter 1

The Guilty Priesthood (Zech 3)

Lena-Sofia Tiemeyer

In this article,[1] I shall propose a new interpretation of Zech 3. Inspired by the statement in Hag 2:14 where all the Judahites, including the priesthood and their sacrifices, are declared impure, I suggest that Zech 3 is an attempt to rectify that very situation. By describing the miraculous cleansing of the high priest (vv. 3–5), followed by the celebration of the Day of Atonement (v. 9), the author of Zech 3 depicts Joshua's renewed ability to atone for the sins of the people. Prior to this, the people of Judah had lacked the possibility to become free of guilt due to the priests' impurity and their subsequent inability to bring atonement. The cleansing of Joshua thus solves the impasse reached in Hag 2:10–14.

Concerning the source of the priests' impurity, there are reasons to suspect that Joshua together with the rest of the clergy were unclean due to their idolatry or unorthodox worship of YHWH.

THE TEXTUAL HISTORY OF ZECH 3

The secondary character of Zech 3:8b, 10

The inner unity of Zech 3 is often questioned. Many exegetes regard vv. 8–10, or any smaller unit thereof, as a later interpolation.[2] This view depends largely on the clause כי הנני מביא את־עבדי צמח in 8b. The צמח (branch) can either be identified with Zerubbabel or with a future saviour:

1 An identification as Zerubbabel is difficult since the verb מביא implies that at the time of the composition of Zech 3, Joshua was in Judah but 'the branch', who would according to this be Zerubbabel, was still to arrive. There is little reason to doubt that the two leaders arrived together in Judah (Ezra 2:2; Neh 7:7). Further, Ezra 3:2ff. states that both Joshua and Zerubbabel were present in Judah *before* the work on the temple was begun in 520 BCE. Therefore, the idea that Zerubbabel's coming is yet to take place at the time of the vision in Zech 3 is difficult to accept.[3] It is possible to argue that what is envisioned here is Zerubbabel's coming into more *power/status* than he had previously enjoyed,[4] but such an interpretation stands on very shaky ground since the phrase הנני מביא seems to involve more than a rise in the social structure. The alternative, in order to keep the identification with Zerubbabel, is to question the date in 1:7 and to claim that Zechariah began his ministry in Jerusalem *before* Zerubbabel's arrival

but *after* Joshua's.[5] This, however, does not solve any problems unless one also doubts the credibility of the account in Ezra 3:2ff., as well as the integral nature of Zech 4:14, both of which indicate that the *two* leaders were in Judah at the time when the visions were written down.[6]

2 The second possibility is to interpret עבדי צמח as a symbol expressing Messianic expectations. However, when Haggai uses the word עבדי (Hag 2:23), he identifies him with Zerubbabel. Furthermore, Zech 4:6b–10a emphasizes that it is Zerubbabel who in Zechariah's eyes is the one figure upon whom his hopes are set.[7] Lastly, Zech 6:12–13 speaks about the צמח who will build the temple, something which fits the already present Zerubbabel better than a future Messianic figure.[8] Hence, interpreting עבדי צמח as a Messianic symbol while at the same time arguing for Zecharian authorship of 3:8b is doubtful.[9]

In view of this, discarding the assumption that Joshua was present in Judah *before* Zerubbabel, together with the proposition that all of Zech 3 stems from a time earlier than 520 BCE, it follows that v. 8b must be later than the other references to Zerubbabel or to the branch in Zech 1–6. Therefore, I propose that Zech 3:8b was added later when Zerubbabel was no longer an important presence in Judah. At that time, the expression צמח had ceased to indicate him as a person, and instead had come to carry Messianic connotations, expressing the people's hope of the coming of a future saviour. This addition changes the overall content of the vision. As I shall argue below, v. 9 spoke originally of the Day of Atonement. However, as Rudolph points out, the addition of v. 8b gives the removal of the sin of the land an eschatological character and turns it into a description of the general removal of all sin in the day when the Messiah comes.[10]

Concerning verses 8a and 9, it has been argued that there is a change of both location and characters, beginning in v. 8a, which indicates a break in the literary flow.[11] In response to this, Rose argues convincingly that the inclusion of the other priests is in itself not convincing evidence for the secondary character of v. 8a: given that the high priest is the head of a larger body of people, it should not be surprising that his colleagues are included at one point.[12] Concerning the apparent change of location, I follow Perowne's suggestion that the expression הישבים לפניך should be understood less as an indication of the *geographical placement* of the other priests and rather as an indication of their *subordinate rank*.[13] Hence, they are not necessarily present physically in the vision.

In the case of v. 9, it is noted primarily by Sellin that this verse would be rendered incomprehensible without the background of the removal of Joshua's sin in 3:3–5. Hence, it can never have existed independently of 3:1–7.[14] Thus, the interpretation that all of vv. 8–10 form a separate oracle is difficult to substantiate. Finally, 3:10, with its imagery of peaceful relaxation under the vine and the fig tree, would be a fitting ending to the removal of the sin of the land in v. 9. However, its eschatological flavour makes it more likely that it belongs together with v. 8b.

The integral character of Zech 3:6–7

While Beuken accepts the integral character of Zech 3:8–10, he casts doubts upon the originality of vv. 6–7. He suggests that they stem from a time when the Davidic heir had lost his importance and the high priest had seized almost royal authority. Hence, by portraying Joshua with authority, a later author sought to create a contrast to the picture, prevalent elsewhere in Zech 1–8, of a superior Zerubbabel.[15] Beuken's basic assumption is, however, difficult to accept:

1 The angel of the Lord *admonishes* (ויעד – v. 6) Joshua, the root עוד often carrying connotations of warning and admonishing.
2 The tasks and privileges assigned to Joshua in v. 7, centred mainly around the temple,[16] do not contradict those of Zerubbabel described elsewhere in Zech 1–8.
3 Zerubbabel is not the only focal point of Zech 1–8. As Jeremias points out, such an interpretation is only possible if we accept the secondary character of Zech 4:14. If, however, this latter verse is original, the focus on Joshua here in Zech 3 does not contradict the idea of Joshua's and Zerubbabel's dual leadership.[17]

In conclusion, there is little reason to doubt the integral character of vv. 6–7.

JOSHUA'S GUILT (ZECH 3:3–5)

In this section, the issue of Joshua's guilt will be addressed.

1 Firstly, the question arises whether Joshua is personally guilty or whether his guilt represents that of the priesthood or even that of the whole province of Judah. I will argue that the whole clergy, including the high priest, are guilty.[18] Even so, their guilt is linked with that of the people in that it has rendered the priests unfit to offer up sacrifices of atonement.
2 Secondly, I will suggest that their guilt[19] is due to their worship of gods other than YHWH, a claim supported by the use of the metaphor of the brand (v. 2).
3 Thirdly, there is in my view a link between the removal of Joshua's personal guilt and that of the Judahites.

1 Joshua, together with the rest of the priesthood, is guilty

Joshua is personally guilty

Verse 4ba (ראה העברתי מעליך עונך) states that it is Joshua's sin which is being removed. The very clarity of the expression, pointing unequivocally to Joshua as a person, has given rise to the suggestion, made by exegetes who maintain that Joshua is guilty only in his role as representative of the people, that v. 4ba is a later interpolation.[20] LXX may support a secondary character of v. 4ba, due to its rendering of the infinite absolute (הלבש) as a parallel to the imperative (הסירו) which possibly indicates that the translators considered the clause in between as a parenthesis.[21]

Barthélemy, however, argues that an infinite absolute is natural after העברתי, the subject of והלבש being the speaker rather than the people commanded to undress Joshua.[22] Taking both claims into account, the evidence is not sufficient to warrant an exclusion of v. 4ba.

Joshua's fellow priests are guilty

In 3:8, men labelled רעיך הישבים לפניך appear. The expression הישבים לפניך is a clue to their identification in that it stresses their inferior position compared with Joshua:[23] in Ezek 8:1; 14:1; 20:1, the elders *sit before* Ezekiel, acknowledging their inferior knowledge, and in Gen 43:33, Joseph's brothers *sit before* him. Hence, we may assume that the רעיך were men below Joshua on the social ladder. 2 Kings 4:38; 6:1 further support an identification of these men with the clergy in particular.[24] Although these verses speak of disciples of *prophets* sitting before the prophet, they nevertheless show that men sharing a profession *sit before* their master. In view of this, I follow the scholarly majority who identify the רעיך הישבים לפניך with Joshua's fellow priests.[25]

These priests are described as אנשי מופת, an expression the meaning of which is not transparent. A מופת is normally a 'sign' or a 'token' of future events, often parallel with the word אות (1 Kings 13:1–5; Isa 8:18; 20:2–6; Ezek 12:6, 11; 24:24, 27). Hence, the אנשי מופת are people who signify and demonstrate a coming event. Even so, it is still not clear *what* they signify.[26] In the final version of the text, these priests are signs of the coming of the branch.[27] However, having argued in favour of the secondary character of v. 8b, I agree with Sellin that their presence more likely indicates the removal of the sin of the land (v. 9).[28] Furthermore, Rudolph's suggestion that the priests, in their function as carriers of sin, guarantee this atonement[29] carries conviction. It takes into account both Joshua's purification as well as the subsequent atonement of the land: the cleansed Joshua can now perform the rituals of the Day of Atonement and as such is a sign of the cleansing of the whole country. Also, following the purification of the high priest, Joshua is in a position to render the other priests clean, and to enable them to function in their sacrificial duties. As such, all the priests are a sign of God's mercy which, surpassing justice, enables them to purify the land (vv. 8a, 9): 'indeed, they are signs, for behold, [...] I will erase the sins of that land in one day'.

The clergy's impurity has rendered the Judahites perpetually unclean

This leads us to the question to what extent Joshua represents the people. As already alluded to by Rudolph (n. 29), there may be a link between Joshua's impurity and his high priestly office of carrying the sins of the people.

Zech 3:1–2 does not provide us with any information about the content of the prosecutor's[30] accusation. As a result, there are several theories concerning what it might have been. Common to most of these suggestions is the observation that the prosecutor's case is *justified* and represents *justice*,[31] while God offers *undeserved mercy*.[32] There are hence no indications that Joshua is falsely accused. On the contrary, his dirty clothes (vv. 3–4) in particular point to his actual guilt.

When rebuking the prosecutor, God is called הבחר בירושלם. Because of this, God's relationship with Jerusalem is often understood to indicate that the accusation against Joshua concerned the whole community.[33] In my opinion, God's choosing of Jerusalem in 3:2 is certainly the *reason* for His mercy: God rebukes the prosecutor *because* He has chosen Jerusalem, understanding the syntactic relation between v. 2aa and v. 2ab as result + cause.[34] The focus of Zech 3, however, remains on Joshua alone. In other words, the purification of Joshua *as an individual* must in some way be connected with the situation of the people of Judah. The Judahites needed God's mercy because of Joshua's impure state. This fits with my proposition that Joshua had to be cleansed before he could atone for the people.[35] So, despite the justice of the prosecutor's claim, God, in His mercy and because of His election of Jerusalem, cleansed Joshua.

Conclusion

To sum up, no strict separation should be made between Joshua as an individual and in his role as high priest:

1 The statement ראה העברתי מעליך עונך (v. 4) stresses that it is *Joshua's* guilt which is removed.
2 The expression אתה ורעיך (v. 8) emphasizes that Joshua shares the guilt of the *priesthood.*
3 The priests are a sign of the coming removal of the sin of the *land.*
4 The stress on the election of Jerusalem suggests that the impurity of the land, that is its people, is connected with, and in fact stems from, the impurity of the high priest.

2 The origin of Joshua's guilt

'Like a brand saved from the fire'

There are several hints in Zech 3 at the origin of Joshua's guilt. One of the more significant ones is the expression הלוא זה אוד מצל מאש (v. 2) which is often understood as an allusion to Joshua's exilic experience: Joshua is likened to a brand who escaped the fire of Babylon, his exilic background being the reason for his present state of uncleanness.[36] In support of this interpretation, Sellin claims that fire symbolizes the exile in Isa 9:18; 48:10; 52:11; Ezek 22:21; Am 5:6. However, the cited passages do not tally with this interpretation: Isa 9:18 probably speaks about a civil war (cf. 9:21) and Isa 48:10 refers to cleansing through suffering. If we adhere to the generally accepted view that Deutero-Isaiah spoke to the people in Babylon, then this verse would speak about the exile. However, if a Judahite setting of Isa 40–55 is maintained,[37] 48:10 is more likely to refer to the destruction of Jerusalem. Ezek 22:17–22 speaks about the gathering of the people of Israel *to Jerusalem* where God will throw them into the fire. Finally, while the larger context of Am 5:6 speaks about the exile (v. 5), the fire most likely symbolizes the preceding destruction (of Bethel). Adding to Sellin's quoted references, Jeremias[38] cites Hos 9:3–4; Ezek 4:12–14;

36:25, 29, which, in his opinion, support the view that the exile was impure. However, Hos 9:3–4 speaks about the uncleanness of *Assyria* rather than *Babylon*. Additionally, what is unclean is not Assyria itself but the *food* that Ephraim will have to eat there. Ezek 4:12–14 *supports* the idea that the exile in itself was not impure: God commands Ezekiel to eat food cooked in an unclean manner in order to symbolize the unclean food that the exiles in Babylon will be consuming. In response to this, Ezekiel, *being one of the exiles*, refuses, having hitherto never eaten anything unclean. This shows that the exile itself was not unclean, only actions which the expatriates might commit there. Lastly, although Ezek 36:25, 29 speak about the cleansing of the people coming out of exile, their focus is on the reason for their uncleanness, i.e. their *idolatry*. Apart from the instances already quoted, Isa 52:11 mentions that in leaving Babylon (צאו משם) those who carry the vessels of God (נשאי כלי ה׳) are commanded not to touch anything unclean and to purify themselves. The expression נשאי כלי ה׳ is probably a reference to priests responsible for the cult and its artifacts. Thus, this verse seemingly states that the priests coming out of the exile were in need of purification. Assuming that they obeyed the command, however, this would actually have ensured their purity upon their arrival in Judah.

To sum up, the quoted examples show that the *exile in itself* did not make a person unclean. Rather, each person had a choice: to stay pure, or to participate in unclean rites and accordingly contract uncleanness. Thus, while the exiles could easily contract impurity during their time in Babylon, this depended more upon their own choice to assimilate with the people around them than upon the very fact that they lived in the Diaspora.[39]

A smaller group of scholars argues that the fire in the metaphor refers to the destruction of Jerusalem in 586 BCE. For example, Mitchell sees Joshua as the representative of the survivors,[40] while Rudolph argues that Joshua the individual, in his position as the grandchild of the high priest Seraiah, was saved in order to preserve the high priestly office.[41]

Rudolph's interpretation stresses Joshua as an individual. The idea that the fire is a divine punitive act correlates well with the situation described in Am 4:11, where the similar expression כאוד מצל משרפה is attested (below). Lacking any reference within the text to either the destruction of Jerusalem or to the family history of Joshua, however, neither interpretation can be regarded as final.

Therefore, a new interpretation of the declaration הלוא זה אוד מצל מאש is needed. The clue is found within Zech 3 itself, more exactly in the preceding statement הבחר בירושלם. Both expressions form part of the angel's retort to the prosecutor. As seen already, God's election of Jerusalem is one reason for His mercy towards Joshua. In view of this, I propose that the statement הלוא זה אוד מצל מאש similarly refers to God's saving mercy. The prosecutor's case is justified, and without God's love for His city Joshua would be condemned and given over to God's punishment. It is from this just, divine punitive 'fire' that Joshua is saved 'like a brand'. Because of God's compassion alone, Joshua is miraculously cleansed and reinstalled in his office, rather than being left in his filthy clothes, unable to serve as priest.

The choice of the specific metaphor הלוא זה אוד מצל מאש may further allude to the origin of Joshua's sin. This expression is reminiscent of the metaphor כאוד מצל משרפה in Am 4:11 which refers to the survivors of the last and most dire of a sequence of five punishments[42] which were sent because of the people's participation in sacrifices performed in Gilgal and Bethel (4:4 – באו בית־אל ופשעו הגלגל הרבו לפשע). Barstad, focusing on the word פשע which describes those activities, argues that it is often used in prophetic writings as a technical term for the participation of the Israelites in non-YHWH-istic or unorthodox YHWH-istic rites (Isa 1:29–31; 43:27; 46:8; 48:8; 59:13; 66:24; Jer 2:8, 29; 3:13; 33:8; Ezek 2:3; 18:31; 20:38; Hos 14:10; Zeph 3:11 and their immediate context). In addition, Barstad points out that the cults performed at Bethel and Gilgal were most likely either non-YHWH-istic or syncretistic (Am 3:3, 14; 5:5–6; 7:10ff.; 1 Kings 13:1–32; 2 Kings 23:15–20). Hence, he suggests that Am 4:4–5 should be interpreted against a similar background of cult criticism, accusing the people of offering illegitimate sacrifices or of being involved in idol worship.[43]

In my view, assuming that Am 4:4–5 was familiar to the author of Zech 3:2, it is possible that the latter, by using the similar expression אוד מצל מאש, sought to convey that Joshua and the rest of the Judahite priesthood were guilty of similar sins.

Joshua's clothes

In addition to the expression הלוא זה אוד מאש, the metaphor of dirty versus clean clothes in Zech 3:3–5 supports my suggestion that Joshua is unclean because of idolatry or unorthodox worship of YHWH. The stripping of Joshua's filthy garments and the dressing in מחלצות are symbolic actions which are linked with his cleansing from guilt. The adjective צאם carries overtones of ritual impurity while the noun מחלצות stresses Joshua's new, pure state.

i. בגדים צאים

The word צאים, vocalized as an adjective, occurs only in Zech 3:3, 4. Elsewhere, the same consonantal form, pointed as a feminine noun צאה, is attested in Deut 23:14; Ezek 4:12 (*sere*, *kamats*) and in 2 Kings 18:27 // Isa 36:12; Isa 4:4; 28:8 and Prov 30:12 (*holem*, *kamats*). Common to these instances is the notion of filth. Further, Isa 4:4 and Prov 30:12 probably refer to *ritual impurity*. In addition, Isa 4:4 depicts the defiled persons being cleansed through burning (ברוח בער)[44] which is reminiscent of the fire image of the expression זה אוד מצל מאש.[45]

The reference to צאים has been understood in many different ways, for example as shabby,[46] or as a sign of mourning,[47] while yet others, especially those scholars who understand the metaphor of the brand scorched by fire as a picture of the Diaspora, see Joshua's dirty clothes as yet another image of what they perceive to be the impurity of exile.[48] In this section, I shall focus on the interpretation that Joshua's dirty clothes symbolize his and his sons' marriages to foreign women.

In TJ (ויהושע הוו ליה בנין דנסבין להון נשין דלא כשרן לכהונתא)[49] and in many traditional commentaries,[50] Joshua's filthy garments are linked with his sons' marriages to foreign women (cf. Ezra 9:2; 10:18–19). This interpretation has, however, been correctly criticized.[51] One reason is the chronological difference of approximately 70 years between the cleansing of Joshua in Zech 3 (around 520 BCE) and the events reported in Ezra 9–10 (around 450 BCE). Hence, it is extremely unlikely that Joshua's sons were married to foreign women in 520 BCE and were still alive to divorce them 70 years later. Accordingly, while the record in Ezra 9–10 cannot describe events taking place while Joshua was high priest, it probably tells of tendencies in the priestly families in Judah at the time of Ezra. Furthermore, the heads of priestly families recorded in the list in Ezra 10:18–22 (Joshua, Immer, Harim, Pashur) are the same as those in the list in Ezra 2:36–39 / Neh 7:39–42 (Jediah, Joshua, Immer, Pashur, Harim). This suggests that either the first generation of priests, Joshua's contemporaries, or their descendants, *later* arranged for their sons to marry foreign women.

In the light of this, I suggest that the priests having married outside Israel around 450 BCE gave rise to the interpretation that Joshua's sin, although 70 years earlier, was connected with intermarriage, a tradition which would later find its way into the Targum. Hence, while Joshua's guilt in Zech 3 had originally nothing to do with foreign wives, it nevertheless mirrors a later reality where priests commonly married foreign women. This in turn shows that Joshua and the other priests later in life chose not to adhere to strict YHWH-istic orthodoxy. In view of this later behaviour, the claim that these same men had, earlier in their lives, deviated from orthodox YHWH-ism gains credibility, although it can in no way be proven.

ii. מחלצות

After being stripped of his dirty clothes, Joshua is dressed in מחלצות (v. 4). The word is derived from the root חלץ = 'draw off, withdraw'[52] and is attested elsewhere only in Isa 3:22 in a list of luxury products worn by the ladies of Jerusalem. Accordingly, it is not part of any normal description of priestly vestments. Thomas points out that the Arabic cognate root of חלץ means 'to become pure, clear, genuine, white, unmingled'.[53] Similarly, the Akkadian *halaṣu* means 'to purify'.[54] In view of this, he argues that מחלצות, rather than indicating a particular dress, stresses the contrast between Joshua's old, ritually impure clothes (צאים) and his new, pure ones.[55] Radak's earlier understanding of the word מחלצות as an allegory of purity[56] points in the same direction. Such a sharp contrast between בגדים צאים and the מחלצות fits the present context, and is therefore adopted here.

In conclusion, I suggest that Joshua's old clothes were ritually filthy, providing a contrast to his new, pure clothes. The old ones symbolized Joshua's own impure state. Even though the evidence is not conclusive, I nevertheless suggest that this impure state stems from his unorthodox worship of YHWH.

3 The interpretation of 3:9

In the preceding section, I reached the conclusion that Joshua's change of clothes in vv. 3–5 describes his transformation from impure to pure. In this section, I shall investigate whether this occasion is a unique event or is part of an already existing ceremony. It is legislated in the Torah that the high priest had to change garments on two occasions: at the inauguration of the high priest and at the Day of Atonement. Hence, many scholars connect Joshua's change of clothes in Zech 3 with the one taking place at one of these two ceremonies.

The ceremony of inauguration

Beginning with an identification of Zech 3 with the ceremony of inauguration,[57] Exod 28–29 and Lev 9 describe the rites which were performed on that day. There are, however, few elements in common between these rituals and those described in Zech 3. Jeremias seeks to explain this discrepancy as mainly a difference in focus: the washing is of primary importance in the Pentateuchal texts, while in Zech 3 the changing of clothes from dirty to clean is emphasized because of Joshua's exilic experience.[58] His explanation, however, fails to convince if we believe that the exile plays no role in this vision (above). Hence, it is doubtful that Zech 3 tells of Joshua's inauguration as high priest.[59]

The Day of Atonement

There is more support for an identification of Zech 3 with the Day of Atonement. The rituals performed during that day are outlined in Lev 16. Similarly to the inauguration ceremony discussed above, there are significant differences between Lev 16 and Zech 3, causing many scholars to reject the notion that Zech 3 describes any part of the ritual of the Day of Atonement.[60] Because of the content of Zech 3:9, however, such an identification should not be totally dismissed. Two factors connect this verse with the Day of Atonement, the expression ומשתי את־עון הארץ־ההיא ביום אחד and the inscribed stone.

i. The removal of guilt in one day

The statement ומשתי את־עון הארץ־ההיא ביום אחד in Zech 3:9, meaning 'I (God) will remove[61] the guilt of the land in one day', is important for the understanding of the *Sitz-im-Leben* of Zech 3 as a whole. The expression ביום אחד = 'in one day'[62] points to a ceremony which takes place in one day. Based on this definition, the only day known in the OT when God removes the sins of His people is the annual Day of Atonement. Therefore, assuming that this feast was known to the people at the time of Zechariah,[63] it seems likely that the original audience of this material associated ביום אחד with this festival.

The עון in verse 9 is naturally connected with Joshua's עון in v. 4, pointing to a link between the removal of Joshua's guilt and of that of the land. I already determined that Joshua's impurity represents his own guilt, something which must have rendered him unable to carry the guilt of the people on the Day of Atonement. Thus, Joshua's cleansing prepares the way for the Day of Atonement and the cleansing of the land.

ii. An inscribed stone with seven facets

The function of the stone (אבן) placed before Joshua in 3:9 is not stated, a silence which has given rise to a multitude of different interpretations.[64] In this chapter, I will focus on the possibility of identifying the stone with the ציץ on the high priest's costume, thus connected with the high priestly task of carrying the guilt of the people (Exod 28). This interpretation, first suggested by Mitchell[65] and followed by several scholars,[66] is based on two main factors:

1 The stone is *engraved* (מפתח פתחה). Similarly, Exod 28:11–12 speaks about two stones on the ephod which are engraved with the names of the sons of Israel.
2 The stone is connected with *the removal of guilt*. Similarly, Exod 28:36–8 describes how a metallic plate (ציץ), inscribed with the words קדש לה', is fastened on the מצנפת and is instrumental in removing the guilt. This link is strengthened by the additional connection between the צניף in Zech 3:5 and the מצנפת in Exod 28:37. Further, based on the fact that both gems are described as engraved, Sellin suggests that each of the seven facets (עינים) of the stone in Zech 3 is engraved with one letter and together these form the words קדש ליהו (cf. Exod 28:36; 39:30 קדש לה').[67]

Mitchell's interpretation is not accepted by all. Chary and Rudolph point out several issues which are problematic:

1 According to Chary, the ציץ is not a stone but rather a decoration in the form of a flower (cf. 1 Kings 6:18, 32, 35).[68]
   - It is true that several exegetes translate ציץ as 'flower',[69] but both LXX (πέταλον) and Vulgate (*lamina*) understand ציץ as a thin metal plate. Further, the Talmudic scholars regard the high priestly ציץ to be a gold plate (*b. Sabb.* 63b).[70]
2 Chary claims that if the stone were placed on the priest's clothing, it would have been mentioned together with the garments in 3:5.[71]
   - The fact that the צניף is singled out in 3:5 points to its relevance as the one garment carrying the אבן. In other words, there is a veiled allusion to the stone in verse 5.
3 Rudolph argues that if the אבן were identical with the ציץ, it would have been placed *on* the *turban*, rather than *in front of* (לפני) Joshua, thus demanding the preposition ל or על.[72]
   - Rudolph's critique is justified. However, it is possible that the stone was given to Joshua separately, in order to emphasize his newly restored ability to perform the Day of Atonement.

To sum up, the identification of the stone in Zech 3:9 with the ציץ described in Exod 28:36 and 39:30 is convincing.

An additional potential problem with the identification of the אבן in Zech 3:9 with the ציץ concerns the interpretation of the two expressions הנני מפתח פתחה and על־אבן אחת שבעה עינים. Beginning with הנני מפתח פתחה, most scholars understand the root פתח to mean 'engrave',[73] following the Vulgate (*ecce ego cælabo sculpturam eius*), Symmachus (γλύψω γὰρ τὴν γλυφὴν αὐτοῦ) and Theodotion (τὴν γλυφὴν αὐτῆς).

The alternative is to read פתח as 'open', supported by the S (הא פתח אנא תרעיה = 'I am opening its gates'), by the TJ (paraphrasing האנא גלי הזיתה = 'I shall reveal its facets') and by Aquila (διαγλύφω ἀνοίγματα αὐτῆς).

The second expression שבעה עינים is understood by the majority of exegetes as 'seven facets'.[74] Lipiński challenges this reading: by understanding the root פתח as 'to open', he proposes the meaning 'sources' for עינים.[75] Together, both aspects create an image of seven sources bursting open. It is difficult, however, to see the relevance of such a picture in the present context, dealing as we are with a *stone*. To imagine fountains or springs flowing out of it forces the whole interpretation into symbolism which is not supported by the context. Hence, the traditional understanding of seven engraved facets seems superior.

A third understanding of עינים has also been suggested. As noted, according to the two previously mentioned interpretations, the עינים are on, i.e. are *features* of, the stone. Contrary to this, a few scholars argue that the עינים, given their normative translation 'eyes', are on, i.e. are *looking* upon, the stone. The seven eyes are accordingly understood as a metaphor of God's perfect watchfulness,[76] comparable with Zech 4:10.[77] In support for such an understanding of על, Keil quotes Gen 44:21 (ואשימה עיני עליו); Jer 39:12 (ועיניך שים עליו) and 40:4 (ואשים את־עיני עליו).[78] However, in all these examples, a possessive pronoun is attached to עינים, indicating that they belong to God. Similarly, Zech 4:10 has עיני ה'. Therefore, the occurrence here of עינים alone renders this interpretation unlikely. Furthermore, given that God is speaking in first person, עיני rather than עינים would have been expected.

In conclusion, I adhere to the traditional understanding of an 'engraved' stone with seven 'facets'.

Conclusion

The mention of עון in both vv. 3–5 and v. 9 points to a link between the removal of Joshua's guilt and that of the country as a whole. In view of this, I suggest that the symbolic change of Joshua's clothes in 3:3–5 is a *preparation* for his performance of the ritual taking place in 3:9. Further, I identify the day referred to in v. 9 with the Day of Atonement. This identification is based partly on the expression ומשתי את־עון הארץ־ההיא ביום אחד which speaks about 'one day' when God will remove the sin of the land, and partly on the occurrence of the engraved gem, equated with the ציץ on the high priestly turban, which signifies Joshua's ability to carry the guilt of the people.

JOSHUA'S RESPONSIBILITIES (ZECH 3:6–7)

Having suggested above that Zech 3:1–5 alludes to the reason why Joshua is guilty, i.e. the idolatry and the unorthodox worship of YHWH of the Jerusalem clergy, it is time to investigate whether the material in vv. 6–7 supports such an interpretation. In my view, the areas of Joshua's future tasks and responsibilities contain further hints at the origin of Joshua's guilt.

An admonition (3:6–7)

Zech 3:6 sets the tone for Joshua's obligations and responsibilities. I follow the understanding of most scholars who render the verb יעד 'to admonish'.[79] Thus, the tasks mentioned in v. 7 should not be understood exclusively as privileges but also as obligations. Further, it is possible that this verb indicates that Joshua, prior to this, did not adhere to these principles.[80]

Two or four conditions?

Verse 7 may contain two or four conditions, depending on the understanding of its syntax. The question is whether the repeated וגם is part of the protasis or the apodosis. From an exegetical point of view, two conditions give Joshua more ritual/political privileges and more authority and *vice versa*.

Most scholars regard only the first two statements as part of the protasis.[81] In support of this, Rudolph argues convincingly that the pronoun אתה forms the antithesis of the possessive pronouns attested in the first two clauses.[82] Keil further points out that since the second commandment already covers Joshua's official life, the third and the fourth statements are superfluous in the protasis.[83] In contrast to this, a smaller number of scholars argues in favour of four conditions.[84] Beuken's proposal is noteworthy in that he divides the protasis into two main parts, a general one to heed God's ways (בדרכי תלך) and a specific one (containing the following three clauses) which gives commandments in the areas of the cult, the temple and the temple courts respectively.[85]

Turning to the textual evidence, the Masoretic accents assign four conditions. In contrast, V[86] and S[87] both seem to place the main pause after the word תשמר, indicating only two. The LXX provides a slightly different text from the MT,[88] which may be regarded as supportive of four conditions, but in view of the many differences, it should be used cautiously. The TJ translates the initial words אם and גם literally, hence little can be surmised concerning its understanding of the division of the text.[89] Nevertheless, Cathcart and Gordon argue that the addition in TJ (ובאחיות מיתיא אחינך = 'and at the resurrection of the dead I shall raise you to life') following the second two statements reads more like the *continuation* of the preceding text than the beginning of something new. Therefore, since the clause about the resurrection must be part of the apodosis, the apodosis probably included also the two preceding statements. It follows that the translators understood the protasis to contain only the first two statements.[90]

In conclusion, Rudolph's insight concerning the contrast between the first and second person pronouns, together with the evidence from the versions, favours a protasis with only two conditions.

The first condition: בדרכי תלך

Rignell argues that the commandment בדרכי תלך indicates worship of YHWH alone, in contrast to idolatry.[91] In my view, his claim can be sustained: the expression הלך בדרך ה' sometimes indicates obedience to YHWH, in contrast to worship of other deities (e.g., 1 Kings 11:33). Also, the more frequent expression '*not* to walk in God's way' is often identical with idolatry (e.g., 2 Kings 21:21–22; Judg 2:17; 2 Chr 17:3–4). In view of the link between the expression 'not to walk in God's way' and idolatry, I suggest that בדרכי תלך in Zech 3:7 stresses sole obedience and devotion to God.[92]

The second condition: את־משמרתי תשמר

The majority of all attested examples of שמר משמרת concern priestly or Levitical duties (e.g., Lev 8:35; 18:30; 22:9; Ezek 44:8, 16; 48:11; 2 Chr 13:11; Neh 12:45), while a much smaller number express a more general aspect (e.g., 1 Kings 2:3). Taking into consideration that, in the present context, this command is spoken to the high priest rather than to a secular ruler, the more narrow priestly definition is probably the one meant here. Thus, I suggest that משמרת refers to Joshua's priestly role, as such forming a contrast to the preceding command which emphasized Joshua's personal piety.[93] The occurrence of the same expression in Ezek 44 and 48 is especially important for the present study as it portrays the contrast between those who keep God's משמרת and those who commit idolatry. It is possible that this aspect is present also in Zech 3:7, stressing that Joshua is admonished to keep his official life, similarly to his private one, untainted by idolatrous influence.

The first task: אתה תדין את־ביתי

The main concern in this section is the understanding of the verb דין. BDB lists the expression אתה תדין את־ביתי as a separate entry of the *Paal* דין, giving it the meaning 'to govern',[94] parallel with the following תשמר in ותשמר את־חצרי. Such a translation assigns to Joshua the task of governing/ruling/administering God's house.[95] This interpretation, however, has been contested. The Meyers argue correctly that the translation 'to govern' neglects the *legal* aspect of דין. Hence, they propose 'you will render judgement *in* my house', assuming haplography of one ב.[96] Nevertheless, it is impossible to adopt their interpretation as a whole since they seem to disregard completely the את preceding ביתי.[97] Therefore, I suggest that ביתי is the direct object: Joshua will judge *God's temple*.[98] It is true that normally the object of this verb is either animate (עם), or else the noun דין (Jer 5:28; 22:16; 30:13) or משפט (Jer 21:12), a word indicating judgement. Even so, 1 Sam 2:10 (ה' ידין אפסי־ארץ), despite its poetic language, is comparable with Zech 3:7 in that the verb דין has an inanimate object in both texts. I further propose that the verb דין carries a negative nuance in Zech 3:7, comparable especially with that in Gen 15:14 (cf. 1 Sam 2:10; Isa 3:13 etc.) where it indicates a negative judgement: Joshua is commanded to express a negative judgement of ביתי.

Concerning the practical meaning of תדין את־ביתי, the rendering in the Targum gives a hint: Joshua is commanded 'to judge those who serve in My sanctuary' (ואף את תדין לדמשמשן בבית מקדשי). This interpretation is supported by 1 Sam 2:10 where the expression אפסי־ארץ probably refers to the people of the earth. Hence, to judge a place may be taken to mean exercising judgement over the *people* in it. In the case of the temple, it would then relate to any aspect of the life and rule of its personnel. In view of the religious overtones of the two commandments to Joshua, combined with the conclusion above that Joshua's guilt represents that of the priesthood, I suggest that Joshua is called to chastise those whose religious practices deviate from the orthodoxy held by the author of Zech 1–8. This, however, must remain a conjecture.

The second task: תשמר את־חצרי

The verb שמר reappears in this task, forming a link to the second commandment in v. 7aa. The meaning most fitting in the present context is 'to keep, have charge of',[99] comparable with Gen 2:15; 30:31; Num 3:8. Joshua is given charge over 'God's courts', i.e. over His temple. While the first task gave Joshua authority to judge the temple, he is here assigned the responsibility to care for it.

The privilege: ונתתי לך מהלכים בין העמדים האלה

The phrase ונתתי לך מהלכים בין העמדים האלה poses several problems, the main one being the understanding of מהלכים. Assuming it to be a verbal form, it can be repointed as either a *Piel* or a *Hiphil* participle, giving the meaning 'the walking ones' or 'the leading ones' respectively. However, a participle, though grammatically a noun, is difficult since the preceding phrase ונתתי לך seems to demand a more concrete direct object. Hence, Calvin, followed by most scholars,[100] and by the lexica,[101] translated מהלכים as 'places to walk', i.e. as an actual noun where the structure מ־ + the root indicates a place.[102] The only recent exceptions, as far as I am aware, are Beuken,[103] VanderKam[104] and Rose,[105] who understand מהלכים as a *Piel* participle, but their interpretations are not without difficulties.[106]

The fact that the Masoretic pointing fits neither a *Piel* nor a *Hiphil* participle indicates that the Masoretes sought to convey a different word, possibly a plural form of מהלך attested in Ezek 42:4. Hence, the understanding of מהלכים as 'access' seems preferable. Even so, rather than receiving direct access to God, the preposition בין indicates that Joshua will have access *among* העמדים האלה, i.e. the angels at the heavenly court. Verse 7b is therefore a promise that Joshua, if he fulfils his obligations, is given access to God's angels.

To conclude, the first two statements in v. 7 are commandments concerning Joshua's own life, stressing his private obedience to God and his obligations as a priest of YHWH. On the condition that he keeps these two commands, the temple will become his responsibility where, with divine help, he will execute both judgement and care.

CONCLUSION

In this chapter, I have sought to show that Joshua is unclean both as an individual and as a member of the priesthood, possibly due to his idolatry and unorthodox worship of YHWH. Because of the high priest's state of guilt, he cannot fulfil his task to atone for the sins of the people on the Day of Atonement, thus leaving the people in the land without any means of becoming clean. The only solution in this situation is a divine intervention where the high priest is purified (vv. 3–5), followed by the celebration of the Day of Atonement when the guilt of the land is erased (v. 9).

This interpretation depends on several factors. Firstly, I maintain that Zech 3:8a, often regarded as an interpolation, is integral to the vision. Its content points to an understanding of Joshua as the representative of the Judahite priesthood. Furthermore, by regarding 8b as secondary, the priests are signs of the coming cleansing of the land in v. 9. Secondly, I regard v. 9 as the focal point of the vision, providing the framework for Joshua's cleansing in vv. 3–5. The removal of the iniquity of the land in one day, together with the occurrence of the inscribed stone, identified with the ציץ, an essential part of the costume of the high priest which signifies his ability to carry iniquity, point to the celebration of the Day of Atonement. Thirdly, I interpret 3:7aa as an admonition to Joshua to keep away from idolatry, both in his private life and in his office, while v. 7ab assigns to him the dual tasks of judging and caring for the temple and its clergy.

NOTES

1 This article is an abbreviated version of one chapter of my D.Phil. thesis, written under the supervision of Professor H.G.M. Williamson at the University of Oxford.

2 For example, Rignell, 1950, pp. 142–3; Petitjean, 1969, pp. 161ff.; Chary, 1969, p. 81.

3 Marti, 1904, p. 411; Mitchell, 1912, p. 156.

4 Compare Conrad, 1999, p. 95, who suggests that in the book of Haggai, Zerubbabel's 'was a political rather than physical presence among the remnant who returned'.

5 Compare Amsler, 1981, p. 84, who claims that Zech 3:8–10 was composed at the very beginning of Zechariah's ministry while Joshua could still be a sign of the coming of the branch (= Zerubbabel), and the hope of Zerubbabel becoming king was still alive. See also Rignell, 1950, p. 137; Mason, 1977, p. 52. This approach has been aptly criticised by Rose, 2000, pp. 144–5.

6 Compare Rudolph, 1976, p. 100.

7 *Contra* Coggins, 1987, pp. 44–6, who argues that Joshua, rather than Zerubbabel, is the particular subject of Zechariah, and to be identified with the branch in Zech 3:8.

8 Zech 6:13 speaks about two men. Concerning its interpretation, I follow Petersen, 1985, pp. 273 (translation), 276–8, who identifies the branch with Zerubbabel while Joshua is the second person. He understands the expression והיה כהן על־כסאו = 'beside his throne there will be a priest', to refer to Joshua. Furthermore, the following statement ועצת שלם תהיה בין שניהם indicates that two people rather than one are referred to.

For a contrary view, see Rose, 2000, pp. 248–9, who concludes that neither reference to the צמח in Zech 3 and 6 refers to Zerubbabel, but rather to a Messianic figure.

9 It should be mentioned that the issue of 3:8b is connected with the question of the originality of all of Zech 3, in that scholars in favour of an integral character of Zech 3 often argue that Zech 3 and 4, due to the references to Joshua and Zerubbabel found in both visions, together form the kernel of the vision cycle (see e.g. Mitchell, 1912, p. 147; Ackroyd, 1968, p. 183). Thus, by removing the allusion to Zerubbabel (the 'branch' in 8b) from Zech 3, only Zech 4 contains a reference to both leaders, and the symmetry is gone. For this reason, Redditt, 1992, proposes a two-step development of Zech 3: verses 1–7, 9 were first added to the cycle of visions, to be enlarged later by verses 8 and 10.

10 Rudolph, 1976, p. 102.

11 For example, Amsler, 1981, p. 83; Rudolph, 1976, p. 99.

12 Rose, 2000, p. 150.

13 Perowne, 1908, p. 82. Compare Meyers and Meyers, 1987, pp. 198–9.

14 Sellin, 1930, pp. 493–4.

15 Beuken, 1967, pp. 294–5, 297–8. Beuken gives additional reasons for a secondary origin of 3:6–7 on pp. 290–1, 295–6, 299–300.

16 Compare Beuken, 1967, pp. 291–3.

17 Jeremias, 1977, p. 224.

18 Compare Rothstein, 1910, p. 115.
19 No clear distinction between impurity and sin is made in the OT. Rather, as Toombs, 1962, p. 647, argues, moral and religious sin was seen as a form of inner uncleanness. For example, the case of suspected adultery, a clear case of *sin*, was treated as a problem of *uncleanness* (Num 5:28). Furthermore, Isa 30:22; Ezek 24:13; 36:25; 37:23, show that pagan idols and cult practices associated with them rendered Israel unclean, and the ritual of the Day of Atonement removed simultaneously the accumulation of guilt (עון) of both sin and uncleanness (Lev 16:16, 30). In view of this, in the following discussion guilt/sin and impurity are treated as two aspects of the same thing.
20 Mitchell, 1912, p. 151. Compare Sellin, 1930, p. 496.
21 Pointed out by Barthélemy, 1992, p. 945. LXX: ἀφέκετε [...] ἐνδύσατε [...].
22 Barthélemy, 1992, p. 945. Compare Smith, 1984, p. 198, note 4.b.
23 Petersen, 1985, p. 209.
24 For example, Mitchell, 1912, p. 156; Rudolph, 1976, p. 99.
25 For example, Radak, Wellhausen, 1898, p. 181; Marti, 1904, p. 410; Van Hoonacker, 1908, p. 610; Orelli, 1908, p. 188; Perowne, 1908, p. 82; Ehrlich, 1912, p. 333; Mitchell, 1912, p. 155; Nowack, 1922, p. 342; Sellin, 1930, p. 499; Rudolph, 1976, p. 99.
26 Scholars have suggested a variety of possible interpretations. For example Keil, 1888, p. 558, understanding מופת = 'wonder', sees the priests as a sign of God's mercy, having been brought out of the exile despite their guilt. Marti, 1904, p. 410, regards them as a guarantee for the completion of the building of the temple, while Petersen, 1985, pp. 209–10, considers their presence in Jerusalem as a sign of the end of the exile.
27 For example, Perowne, 1908, p. 82; Sellin, 1930, p. 499; Ackroyd, 1968, p. 189; Chary, 1969, p. 81; Mason, 1977, p. 52; Reventlow, 1993, p. 55, who all accept 8b as the originally intended result of 8a.
28 Sellin, 1930, p. 499.
29 Rudolph, 1976, p. 101.
30 In order to avoid the satanic connotations of the word 'satan', I have opted to translate the Hebrew השטן as 'the prosecutor', indicating his position as accuser in the heavenly court. The definite article used in Zech 3:1–2 indicates that השטן is a *function* rather than a personal name.
31 For example, Marti, 1904, p. 409; Meyers and Meyers, 1987, p. 185.
32 Mitchell, 1912, p. 151.
33 For example, Elliger, 1959, p. 121; Ackroyd, 1968, p. 184; Meyers and Meyers, 1987, p. 187.
34 Compare Keil, 1888, p. 553; Smith, 1984, p. 200.
35 Compare Orelli, 1908, p. 188; Jeremias, 1977, p. 208.
36 For example, Radak, Keil, 1888, p. 553; Orelli, 1908, p. 188; Perowne, 1908, p. 78; Sellin, 1930, p. 495; Elliger, 1959, p. 121; Chary, 1969, p. 75; Baldwin, 1972, pp. 113–14; Jeremias, 1977, p. 208; Amsler, 1981, p. 81; VanderKam, 1991, pp. 555–6; Redditt, 1995, p. 63; Rooke, 2000, p. 140.
37 See, e.g., Barstad's several monographs listed in the bibliography.
38 Jeremias, 1977, p. 208.
39 Compare Rothstein, 1910, pp. 112ff.
40 Mitchell, 1912, p. 150.
41 Rudolph, 1976, p. 96. See also Meyers and Meyers, 1987, p. 187; Orelli, 1908, p. 187; Ollenburger, 1996, p. 765.
42 Paul, 1991, p. 149.
43 Barstad, 1984, pp. 56–8.
44 The meaning of בער = 'burning' is not uncontested. BDB, p. 129a, *Piel* 3, understood it figuratively, translating 'be destroyed'. Alternatively, 1QIs[a] has סער. However, LXX

renders ברוח בער with πνεύματι καύσεως = 'spirit of burning'. In view of the latter translation, I see little reason to doubt the connotations of burning of the expression in question.

45 Compare Petersen, 1985, pp. 193–4.

46 Calvin, 1849, pp. 86–7, claims that Joshua's clothes were shabby and without adornment, in contrast to pagan priests who were dressed to impress.

47 See Horst, 1954, p. 221, followed by Amsler, 1981, p. 81, and Redditt, 1995, p. 64.

48 For example, Jepsen, 1945/48, p. 107; Sellin, 1930, p. 496; Reventlow, 1993, p. 53.

49 TJ curiously adds the clause ואסוהי איתתא דכשרא לכהונתא, equating Joshua's new clothes with him marrying a suitable wife, but there is no textual support for this interpretation. Cathcart and Gordon, 1989, p. 191, note 4, suggest that the custom of claiming a wife by casting a garment on her (cf. Deut 27:20; Ruth 3:9 and Ezek 16:8) may be an explicit link between clothes and marriage.

50 For example, Rashi and Radak to Zech 3:3.

51 For example, Orelli, 1908, p. 188; Mitchell, 1912, p. 152; Jepsen, 1945/48, p. 107.

52 BDB, p. 322.

53 Lane, 1863, vol. 1, p. 785.

54 *CAD*, H, pp. 40, 50–1.

55 Thomas, 1932, pp. 279–80, followed by VanderKam, 1991, p. 556.

56 רד"ק - זכריה ג:3 - הם חליפות בגדים נקיים <u>וזה משל על הזכיות</u>
כלומר כיון שיוסר העין יראו בך הזכיות וכן ת"י ואלבש יתך זכוון

57 Radak, Beuken, 1967, pp. 284, 302; Mason, 1977, p. 50; Jeremias, 1977, pp. 209–11, 218; Redditt, 1995, p. 64.

58 Jeremias, 1977, pp. 209–11, 218. Jeremias gives additional reasons for his interpretation, focusing on the use of the words מחלצות and צניף.

59 Compare Petersen, 1985, pp. 198–9.

60 For example, Petersen, 1985, pp. 199–201.

61 The *Paal* ומשתי is here understood transitively.

62 The temporal expression ביום אחד can be understood in two ways, either 'in one day' or 'in the same day', the latter in accordance with Gen 40:5 (בלילה אחד = 'the same night'). Scholars are divided over the issue. For lack of clear indications as to which understanding is preferable here, I adopt the former since it is the more commonly attested meaning.

63 Several scholars, e.g.Vaux, 1961, pp. 509–10, and Rylaarsdam, 1962, p. 314, date Lev 16 to a time later than Zech 1–8, mostly due to the absence of the Day of Atonement from the narrative in Neh 8:14–15. However, Williamson, 1985, pp. 293–4, argues that for the narrow perspective of Neh 8 which focuses exclusively on the reading, teaching and application of the Law, the Day of Atonement had no relevance, and hence is not mentioned. Thus, he hesitates to draw conclusions concerning the dating of the Day of Atonement from the silence in Neh 8. Milgrom, 1991, pp. 1070–1, even argues actively for a pre-exilic date of the Day of Atonement.

64 For example, Keil, 1888, p. 600 (a symbol of the kingdom of God); Wellhausen, 1898, p. 181 (a precious stone in the royal diadem), VanderKam, 1991, pp. 568–70 (a symbolic act, 'restoring the damaged relations between God and his people'), to name but a few.

65 Mitchell, 1912, pp. 157–8.

66 For example, Thomas, 1956, p. 1071; Ackroyd, 1968, pp. 190–1; Amsler, 1981, pp. 85–6; Redditt, 1995, p. 65; Rooke, 2000, p. 140. Of special interest is Sellin, 1930, pp. 500–1, who maintains that Joshua remains the focal point throughout the vision, he identifies the stone in Zech 3:9 with the ציץ. The difference between the אבן here and the ציץ in Exod 28:36–8 is, according to him, that the tradition of the Day of Atonement in the Torah is a later development of the ceremony described here in Zech 3 (cf. note 62). Hence, he

argues that Zech 3 foreshadows the Day of Atonement, and that the ציץ in Exodus is a later priestly development of the אבן here in Zechariah.

67 Sellin, 1930, p. 500, followed by Elliger, 1959, p. 124, and Rignell, 1950, pp. 131–4. In support of the assumed shorter form of the tetragrammaton, Sellin cites the spelling attested in the Elephantine papyri. For references, see Porten, 1968, pp. 105–6, note 5, who attests that the normal spelling in the papyri is יהו while it is written יהה in the ostraca.

68 Chary, 1969, p. 79.

69 For example, Noth, 1962, pp. 225–6.

70 This understanding is followed by several modern scholars, e.g. Childs, 1974, p. 527; Milgrom, 1991, pp. 511–13. The latter provides a helpful guide to the different translations.

71 Chary, 1969, p. 79.

72 Rudolph, 1976, p. 100.

73 For example, Wellhausen, 1898, p. 181; Van Hoonacker, 1908, p. 612; Sellin, 1930, p. 500.

74 Ibid.

75 Lipiński, 1970, pp. 25–9, followed by Smith, 1984, pp. 198, notes 9.b–c, 201–2, and Baldwin, 1972, p. 115. The latter further develops the idea of water, and suggests that the water might trigger the branch to shoot up (v. 8), washing away the guilt (v. 9) and ensuring prosperity (v. 10) (pp. 117–18).

76 Marti, 1904, p. 411; Perowne, 1908, p. 83. See also Petitjean, 1969, p. 181.

77 Beuken, 1967, pp. 287–8. He argues that the link between Zech 3:9 and 4:10 is stressed by the fact that only in these two instances in the Bible is the word עין treated as a *masculine* noun.

78 Keil, 1888, p. 600.

79 For example, VanderKam, 1991, p. 558.

80 *Contra* Mitchell, 1912, p. 154; Reventlow, 1993, p. 54.

81 For example, Calvin, 1849, p. 94; Keil, 1888, p. 556; Marti, 1904, p. 410; Mitchell, 1912, p. 154; Nowack, 1922, p. 340; Sellin, 1930, p. 493 (translation); Thomas, 1956, pp. 1069–70; Elliger, 1959, p. 120; Ackroyd, 1968, pp. 186–7; Chary, 1969, p. 78 (see translation); Baldwin, 1972, p. 115; Rudolph, 1976, p. 93, note 7; Amsler, 1981, p. 78 (see translation); Smith, 1984, p. 198, note 7a; Meyers and Meyers, 1987, p. 194; Ollenburger, 1996, p. 764 (see translation).

82 Rudolph, 1976, p. 93, note 7.

83 Keil, 1888, p. 557.

84 For example, Orelli, 1908, p. 188, who regards the first two statements as general commandments, while the following two address the high priest's obligations. See also Ehrlich, 1912, p. 333; Bič, 1962, p. 48; Petersen, 1985, p. 206; Jeremias, 1977, p. 212; Redditt, 1995, pp. 64–5.

85 Beuken, 1967, pp. 291–3.

86 V: *Haec dicit Dominus exercituum: Si in viis meis ambulaveris et custodiam meam custodieris, tu quoque judicabis domum meam, et custodies atria mea, et dabo tibi ambulantes de his, qui nunc hic assistunt.*

87 הפשיטא: הכנא אמר מריא חילתנא אן באורחי תאזל ופוקדני תטר אנת תדונוהי
לביתי ותטר דרתי ואתל לך דמולכין בינת הלין דקימין

88 LXX: Τάδε λέγει κύριος παντοκράτωρ Ἐὰν ἐν ταῖς ὁδοῖς μου πορεύῃ καὶ ἐὰν τὰ προστάγματά μου φυλάξῃς καὶ σὺ Διακρινεῖς τὸν οἶκόν μου καὶ ἐὰν διαφυλάξῃς καί γε τὴν αὐλήν μου καὶ δώσω σοι ἀναστρεφομένους ἐν μέσῳ τῶν ἑστηκότων τούτων.

89 ת: כדנן אמר יוי צבאות אם באורחן דתקנן קדמי תהך ואם ית מטרת מימרי תיטר
ואף את תדין לדמשמשין בבית מקדשי ואף תיטר ית עזרתי
ובאחיות מיתיא אחינך ואתין לך רגלין מהלכן בין סרפיא האלין

90 Cathcart and Gordon, 1989, p. 192, note 14.
91 Rignell, 1950, p. 119.
92 *Contra* Chary, 1969, p. 75, who argues that idolatry on the part of the clergy had been eliminated by the time of Zech 3. Hence, it is in his view more likely that דרך refers to irregularities in the cultic practices in the rebuilt temple. However, there is no support for this assumption.
93 Compare Thomas, 1956, p. 1069; Baldwin, 1972, p. 115; Reventlow, 1993, p. 54.
94 BDB, p. 192, 5.
95 For example, Wellhausen, 1898, p. 181; Van Hoonacker, 1908, p. 609; Nowack, 1922, p. 341; Sellin, 1930, p. 498; Elliger, 1959, p. 120 (translation); Beuken, 1967, p. 293; Chary, 1969, p. 76.
96 Meyers and Meyers, 1987, p. 195. See also Baldwin, 1972, p. 115. Jeremias, 1977, p. 215, opposes such an interpretation, but does not substantiate his critique.
97 See Rose, 2000, p. 71. He himself understands חדין as 'govern' (pp. 72–3).
98 Due to the parallelism between ביתי and חצרי, I interpret ביתי as 'my temple'.
99 BDB, p. 1036, 1a.
100 Keil, 1888, p. 557; Wellhausen, 1898, p. 181; Marti, 1904, p. 410; Van Hoonacker, 1908, p. 609; Orelli, 1908, p. 188; Perowne, 1908, p. 81; Nowack, 1922, p. 341; Sellin, 1930, p. 498; Chary, 1969, p. 76; Jeremias, 1977, p. 217.
101 GK §53o, although viewing מהלכים as a *Hiphil* participle, nevertheless suggests revocalizing it as a plural noun of מהלך 'goings', comparable to מהלך in Ezek 42:4. Similarly, BDB, p. 237b, 3, suggests the translation 'free access'.
102 Calvin, 1849, p. 94.
103 Beuken, 1967, pp. 293–6.
104 VanderKam, 1991, p. 560.
105 Rose, 2000, pp. 74–82.
106 See, e.g., Jeremias, 1977, pp. 217–18.

Chapter 2

Why is Second Zechariah so Full of Quotations?

Rex Mason

I am sure there must be an English proverb which runs, 'Choose a title in haste and repent at leisure'. When Christopher Tuckett kindly invited me to stir myself from retirement, brush the camphor dust from my suit and come here to read a paper, he needed a title before I had really thought through what I wanted to say. And now I see the title I chose staring me accusingly in the face I realize there are at least two things wrong with it. It is based on the old joke about the lady who said she loved Shakespeare because he was so full of quotations. The point of that joke, however, was that Shakespeare has been quoted so often by others in the course of the 'reception history' of his work. But while the title of our seminar calls for it, I am not competent to talk about the reception history of Second Zechariah and anyway, fortunately, there are many others here who are. I meant, of course, Second Zechariah's 'quotation' of other sources.

But, more seriously, it is the term 'quotation' when applied to chapters 9–14 of the book of Zechariah which begs so many questions its name must be 'Legion'. The establishing of just when, and how, one author may be said to be 'quoting' another is a problem, not only for Biblical studies but for all literary studies, as Schultz (1999) demonstrated. In 1973 I submitted a thesis to the University of London entitled 'The Use of Earlier Biblical Material in Zechariah IX–XIV: A Study in Inner Biblical Exegesis' (Mason, 1973). This, while available to scholars, was never published. Its conclusions have been available only in an article published in 1982 (Mason, 1982a), in some allusions I have made in other work on these chapters, and in those made by others which have appeared in their publications. I was, of course, following in the steps of others, notably Stade (1881/2) and Delcor (1952). However, that thesis has now been published along with a number of papers by scholars who have also been working in this area (Boda & Floyd, 2003). Many of these papers, while all agreeing that there is strong dependence on earlier Biblical material in Zech 9–14, discuss the criteria which need to be established in order to be able to claim 'quotation', and the terminology which should be used to describe it when it is thought to have been found. Terms like 'quotation', 'allusion', 'echo', 'inter-textuality', 'verbal parallels' and others are all discussed, and some contributors, in particular, call for the application of strict methodological and terminological procedures. This is to be welcomed, although I feel that the ways in which one writer is influenced by another are extremely complex. Obviously, to say that Second Zechariah uses in any way earlier Biblical material means that some of that literature must have been available in some written form to at least some people and must have established itself as of value and significance, even if it is far too early to talk of its achieving 'canonical' status. But how easily it was accessed we cannot know. Even in these days of ready indexes and concordances written texts can be influencing even the nuances of our speech and thought, sometimes when we are hardly aware of it. So I remain sceptical about the possibility of absolute precision in determining always where a relationship (of whatever kind) exists and of defining it with a systematic clarity and thoroughness which will command unanimity of assent. This is particularly true about the Old Testament where we normally lack clear 'quotation markers' such as are to be found in the New Testament, like 'It has been said', or 'To fulfil the scripture which said ...'.

Re-reading my thesis recently after many years I was somewhat comforted to find that, at the outset, I had anticipated many of the difficulties and objections which have later been raised about the method of Biblical study known as 'Inner Biblical Exegesis'. Of course to say that one had 'anticipated' them is in no way to say that one has 'countered' them. But in the Introduction I said that the method suffers from the danger of subjectivity and of circularity of argument whereby, because an investigator finds a method of allusion in one place, he or she can then more easily find it elsewhere. There is the difficulty of determining the relative dates of the books being compared, or those sections within those books which are being seen as examples of the exegesis of one by another, and so of being sure in which way dependence is operating. Further, even where there is striking similarity of vocabulary or even ideology between two passages, it is always possible that both are dependent upon another source unknown to us. In the case of such literature as Zech 9–14 (as opposed, say, to the Qumran literature or the New Testament) we do not know just what stage of fixation in writing and general acceptance the alleged 'earlier' works had achieved. When, for example, we find examples of so-called 'exegesis' in the work of the Chronicler by the changes he makes to the parallel material in the Deuteronomistic History, it is always possible that he had a different form of the text before him and so made no changes whatever.

I mentioned all these in pp. iii–v of the Introduction of the thesis and reiterated them in an article on 'Inner Biblical Exegesis' (Mason, 1990b). I said at the time, however, that these dangers did not mean that the method should not be used, but that it should be used with caution and with humility, realizing that it is just *one* tool available to the scholar among many, and certainly does not provide in itself the one master key to unlock every interpretative mystery. I would have been greatly strengthened and encouraged in that view had I then, by some prophetic insight, been able to have read John Barton's later book in which he says that this applies to a greater or lesser degree to *all* methods of Biblical study (Barton, 1984). I have discussed my reactions to the papers and work of other scholars more fully in my response in the forthcoming volume and will not, therefore, pursue it here. In the thesis I have indicated in full where I find dependence on earlier material in Zech 9–14 and what use I think is being made of it. I do not propose, therefore, to defend the argument that there is use of such material in these chapters here, simply resting on the general unanimity of scholarly opinion that they do exhibit considerable dependence, however much we may all differ in detail about where we find it and how we should describe it.

If, then, I am a little worried about the possible ambiguity of the title and the unqualified use of the word 'quotation', that leaves me happy only with the interrogative pronoun 'Why?'! And that is, indeed, the point of this paper. In all the discussions about the existence of dependence on earlier Biblical literature and what it should be called, the question of just *why* writers did refer to it has been somewhat pushed to the margins. I was interested in considering what the methods of 'Inner Biblical Exegesis' employed in these chapters might have to tell us about the circles from which they emanated. But that still leaves the question of why they used it in the first place. This paper is merely an exercise in expressing a few first thoughts which have occurred to me on the matter. They would need to be developed much further to offer any systematic treatment of the theme, if, indeed, they are not found to be wide of the mark altogether. Even so, it is impossible not to be heavily indebted to the work of others and, in particular, John Barton's book *Oracles of God: Perceptions of Ancient Prophecy in Israel after the Exile* (Barton, 1986), which I gave myself the pleasure of re-reading in preparation for this paper, and Fishbane's invaluable work, *Biblical Interpretation in Ancient Israel* (Fishbane, 1985).

Barton maintains that ancient documents were seen as important simply because they were old (Barton, 1986, p. 62). They carried for later generations the authority of antiquity, just as for us, all the great scholars, and for our laity, all the great preachers, had died by the end of the nineteenth century! There is nothing new about this in Zech 9–14. It is generally acknowledged that Hosea influenced at least the present form of the book of Jeremiah (see, for example, Carroll, 1986, p. 119; Holladay, 1989, pp. 45–7) and that Ezekiel was influenced by Jeremiah (Miller, 1955). It is interesting that proto-Zechariah, so soon after the exile, begins with an exhortation to his hearers to avoid the mistakes of their ancestors and heed the words which God spoke through the 'former prophets' (1:2–6). Fascinating for our purpose here is his statement that not only had their ancestors disappeared, caught up in the judgement the prophets had threatened, but those very prophets who had spoken to them had also passed on (1:5). But, if the messengers had gone, 'my words and statutes' do, by implication, live on (1:6). Their power and living effect had not been exhausted by one historical context. It is a claim (whether by Zechariah or his editors) that the message he now brings comes with the same force, and continues the same authentic divine 'words and statutes' which pose the same life and death call for obedience now in this new situation. Already a prophet, however new and different his message, is feeling the need to justify himself by appeal to the authority of those who had gone before him. That is hardly surprising when one thinks that Yahwism, which had been the official religion of the monarchic state of Judah before the exile, now had to be re-defined in the entirely new situation of the Persian Empire and the destruction or removal of all the old religion's institutions, the temple and its liturgy and even the monarchy itself. The encouragement of the prophets Haggai and Zechariah for the rebuilding of the temple is one sign of the need for that continuity. Zechariah's appeal to the authority of the 'former prophets' must be seen as part of the same process. The authority of those prophets was seen in that their prediction of the coming national disaster had proved correct. Carroll said that one energizing motive in later prophecy was the need to explain why the predictions of the earlier prophets had not materialized (Carroll, 1979a). There is a great deal in his demonstrations of the methods used to 'explain away' such failed predictions which is valuable, and to which we must yet allude. Yet

I also have made the point that the words of the earlier prophets were regarded as valuable, authoritative and at least worthy of such 'reinterpretation' because of their 'success' (Mason, 1984, pp. 226–7). Zechariah can point to the disaster of the exile as vindication of the conditional threats those prophets uttered, just as encouraging signs of renewal can also be traced to promises with which these prophets could at least be credited. Such an appeal, of course, also served the purposes of theodicy. It helped to explain why the disaster had happened in a way which kept safe belief in God's wisdom and power.

Evidence of the appeal to earlier prophecy in Zech 9–14 is far more diffuse. One has to look everywhere, just as one is told to do to find Christopher Wren's memorial in St Paul's Cathedral. But a similar kind of *Mahnspruch* is to be found at 10:1–2, calling on the people to turn to the LORD for rain rather than to seek the superstitious help offered by *teraphim* and the dreams of soothsayers. Yet the appeal 'authenticates' itself by its obvious reliance on Jeremiah 14, a collection of oracles headed 'Concerning the drought'. This also includes one of the many attacks in Jeremiah on the false prophets, a point implicit in Zech 10:2, and made explicit by the editorial junction of the passage with 10:3ff. with its attacks on false shepherds. Even here, it is worth noting, the authority of Ezekiel is called in as well, with the paralleling to 'shepherds' of his word *'ttûdîm* for 'he-goats' (Ezek 34:17) used in the same context of an attack on Israel's false leaders.

This brings us to another important point when we ask the question 'Why?' of the use of earlier material. Not only does its use testify to the belief that the ancients had spoken authentically in the name of God, but it establishes a real sense of continuity between the present speaker and his community and the prophets and their circles of old. And once the note of genuine continuity has been established, then surely the *authority* and *genuineness* of the later speakers are also validated. We have already seen how proto-Zechariah's appeal to the earlier prophets was couched in terms which established his claim to be the channel of the same authentic divine word now. For him, no doubt, it was important to give validity to the community of post-exilic Jerusalem for the plans to rebuild the temple, and to authenticate the roles of Zerubbabel and Joshua in that post-exilic era.

How would we expect this to be expressed in the use of earlier Biblical material in chapters 9–14, which we must assume are later, at least in their present form, than chapters 1–8? Naturally one thinks of the attitude to leadership, about which varied, some have said conflicting, signals are given. Since proto-Zechariah assigns an apparently messianic term 'Branch' to Zerubbabel, who was a Davidide, attention naturally focuses on the picture of the coming king in Zech 9:9f. I have discussed this more fully elsewhere (Mason, 1973, pp. 36–63; 1997, pp. 138–41). Here, therefore, only the briefest summary is possible. The three adjectives used to describe him and his role, *saddîq*, *nôsa'* and *'anî'*, while all, in one form or another, descriptive of the king in the Psalms are all also used of the Servant in Second Isaiah (e.g. Isa 50:8; 49:6; 53:4). As Eisenbeis pointed out long ago, the quotation in v. 10 from the royal Psalm 72 (v. 8) has a very different setting from that in the Psalm which envisages his foes bowing down before him and licking the dust. Zech 9:10, on the contrary, says that he will speak 'peace' (*shalom*) to the nations (Eisenbeis, 1969, pp. 215–21). The 'riding on a donkey' may, as Fishbane among others has suggested (Fishbane, 1985, pp. 501–2), refer to the promise in the 'Blessing of Jacob' in Gen 49:10. As the Genesis passage stands it is clearly a piece of pro-Judean and pro-Davidic propaganda. The point is, however, that there is no suggestion of any Davidic link in Zech 9:9f. It might be said to take further the cautionary note which appears in Zech 4:6 where the prophet (or a later contributor) brings God's admonition to Zerubbabel that his mission will be achieved not by human and military strength but by God's spirit alone. The Davidic line *is* mentioned in Zech 9–14, but in no 'messianic' or 'triumphalist' way. That line, together with various branches of the priestly line and others, will need to join in the general mourning of repentance and will need to experience the divine cleansing before the time of salvation is ushered in (12:10–13:1). Indeed, it is expressly said that God will deliver Judah first in order to keep the house of David and the citizens of Jerusalem from getting too 'uppity' (12:7).

I have argued elsewhere that there is some evidence to suggest that Zech 1–8, as we have it now, has been edited in such a way as to 'downplay' earlier hopes centred on Zerubbabel, and so the Davidic line, in favour of a greater emphasis on the role of the priesthood in post-exilic Judah (Mason, 1982b, pp. 147–8). That is not to say that the role of Governor disappeared. It clearly did not. But some accommodation had to be made to the fact that any exalted 'messianic' hopes centred on a restored Davidic monarchy were not realized. Not only does this process appear to have gone farther in chapters 9–14 but, what is also apparent, there has been extreme disappointment at those who have become the official leaders of the community in the days when these chapters achieved their present form. For, interspersed throughout are bitter attacks on those seen as 'false shepherds' in a number of what I have called 'controversy passages', notably 10:1–3; 11:4–17; 13:7–9. But, as has already been stated, these passages are couched very much in the language and employ substantially the imagery of earlier prophets, especially of Jeremiah and Ezekiel. Again, there is no space or time here to demonstrate and develop this which is argued at length in the thesis, but, if it contains any substance, it is further demonstration that a group, in this case the prophet and his circle, are appealing to the authority of earlier prophecy in order to justify their claims to be its true heirs and authentic practitioners in their stand over against those who claim to be God's official representatives in the community.

Whenever and by whatever process Zech 9–14 assumed their present shape, similar problems must have been posed for the prophet/s and the circle he/they were addressing to those faced by the immediate post-exilic prophets, Haggai and Zechariah. How could prophecies whose fulfilment had either been delayed or observably falsified by events be shown to be still relevant? This aspect of post-exilic prophecy and its later reception has been well documented by Barton, Fishbane, Carroll and others. Fishbane speaks of a process whereby there could be 'a transcendence of the terrors of irrationality of history through an assertion and expectation of divine control over it' (Fishbane, 1985, p. 510). But this process must itself raise similar questions in time: '… while the very transformation of the older exoteric oracles into esoteric codes initially solves the problem of their unrealized nature by protecting them from disconfirmation … the risk inevitably taken by disclosing the secret intent of these oracles is far more than their simple empirical failure. What is ultimately put at stake is the very rational order which gives cognitive coherence to time and its terrors.' (Fishbane, 1985, p. 511). The community of faith must therefore be given grounds of hope which both reassure and at the same time call to faithfulness in the light of that hope. The Chronicler was faced with exactly the same problem of cognitive dissonance. He solved it by assuring his readers that the present theocratic state, though for a time subject to the Persian powers, *was* itself a valid, although interim, fulfilment of the ancient divine purposes, a first instalment of a greater fulfilment yet to come, a fulfilment which depended in large measure on the present faith and obedience of the community.

No such belief informs the outlook of Zech 9–14. Here the older prophetic promises are restated, but with some significant differences which guide the principles of exegesis. It has always been an interesting matter for speculation, ever since Eichorn as early as the eighteenth century proposed that these chapters were entirely post-exilic (Eichorn, 1783, p. 415), a view given much wider currency by the work of Stade already alluded to, as to just why these chapters were added to Zech 1–8. One can only speculate. I have tried elsewhere to suggest that, for all the differences, there are certain broad and general themes of common interest between the two sections which someone thought fit to join by the same editorial heading *massa'* (Mason, 1976). The interest in divinely appointed leadership, the need for a cleansing of the community, an appeal to the authority of the earlier prophets, a marked universalism and a strongly Zion-centred theology, characterize both sections. That may help to explain why there is no mention of an interpreting angel revealing secrets and explaining visions as in chapters 1–8. Perhaps, the author(s)/editor(s) felt that by joining 9–14 to 1–8 the same divine authority was being claimed for all which was said here.

But in general, as I have said, several things mark the exegesis of chapters 9–14. Traditional eschatological hopes are strongly affirmed, particularly in 9–10, and again the Zion tradition is given new hope in 12–14. Yet, if I read them aright, very little is said of the *imminence* of these hopes, which indeed are culled in a somewhat anthological fashion from large sections of Old Testament prophecy, without being worked into the kind of neat scheme which could be predicted accurately and attached to specific historical events, as now, Barton maintains is the case with Joel 2:28–3:21 (Barton, 2001, pp. 92–3). This, indeed, is another characteristic of the exegesis here. It is notoriously difficult to 'date' these chapters by supposed historical allusions. The 'three shepherds' of 11:8 are so vague as to have given rise to no fewer than thirty suggestions even by the time of Kremer writing in 1930! And even the 'sons of *yawan*' of 9:13 might be symbolic or refer to Greek traders before the rise of the Greek empire. But all this helps enormously. Vagueness serves the reputations of prophets extremely well as Cassandra well knew, a point made by John Barton who also says that it is the very vagueness of Zech 9–14 which makes them such a favoured quarry for Christian interpreters in the New Testament (Barton, 1986, p. 193).

The third feature of the exegesis in these chapters is the introduction of a predicted time of suffering before the new age can come. This is shown to be of increasing severity. In chapters 12–13, in true Zion theology tradition, nations assemble threateningly against Jerusalem, but are defeated by Yahweh who will then cleanse the whole community and usher in the new age, an age when prophecy will be no more because all to which it has pointed has been fulfilled (13:2–6). In chapter 14, however, a much severer picture is painted. Here the nations not only gather to threaten Jerusalem but actually take it and subject its population to all kinds of privation and suffering before, then, the decisive intervention of God and his 'holy ones' takes place. Not only does this kind of exegesis of earlier prophecy push the looked-for fulfilment of hopes into an indefinite future, but it explains to the faithful why, far from experiencing the golden future, they are suffering so much present distress.

That leads into a fourth principle of the exegesis in these chapters. The reason given for the delay in the fulfilment of these earlier prophecies, one of the features Carroll highlighted in his treatment of 'prophecy which failed', is in this case not the responsibility of the community as a whole, but of the leadership, who are denounced in vocabulary and with the exact imagery used in the books of Jeremiah and Ezekiel to explain a principal reason for the disaster of the exile. To be sure, as there, the sin of this leadership does infect the whole flock, but 10:1–3, 11:4–17 and 13:7–9 leave no doubt as to where the true responsibility lies, just as 12:10–13:1, and 13:2–6 show the need for a divine act of cleansing of the whole leadership and community before the new age can dawn. The reason for this exegesis is not only to rationalize the 'failure' of past prophecy, but to give the prophet and his community a sense of identity, of the elect 'us' over against 'them', destined to be preserved by God and delivered as a saved, refined remnant (e.g. 13:8–9). A 'sect' theology is emerging, seeing itself as separate from, and destined for a different fate from, the main apparatus of the theocracy.

It is time to draw these rambling comments to a close. I have been speculating as to just *why* these chapters practise the form of exegesis of earlier Biblical exegesis that I believe they do, and the answers are probably neither new nor profound. Yet, amidst the plethora of conflicting terms offered and criticized in the literature I cited at the beginning, I do want to hang on to the term 'exegesis' for what is going on, providing we define it fairly broadly. In the article on 'Inner Biblical Exegesis' to which I alluded, I suggested that so-called 'glosses', the order and arrangement of material, often of diverse origin, the re-use of earlier general Biblical themes, as well as quotation, or allusion, may all serve as forms of exegesis. I would define exegesis as 'means by which we make an older written text contemporaneous'. As has been well documented, the means by which such a process is carried out are many and various. The older word may simply be restated: 'Listen to this, it is still true'. It may be reinterpreted: 'It appeared to mean that, but actually it means this and applies to our present situation today', or, 'The prophet's hearers thought he meant this to refer to their time, but actually, of course, it is really addressed to us'. It may be corrected quite openly, like the reinterpretation of Jeremiah's 70 years of exile prediction in Dan 9. It may be reversed: 'God said that then, but now He's going to do exactly the opposite', with all kinds of reasons advanced for the apparent divine *volte face*. One is reminded of James Barr's description of fundamentalist exegesis of the Bible. All kinds of exegetical methods are employed in order to succeed in the one overriding aim of establishing the infallibility of the divine word (Barr, 1977).

I have, therefore, suggested various reasons for which more and more extensive use is being made of earlier Biblical material in these chapters. There is the need to convince contemporaries that the word of God spoken so authentically and authoritatively long ago, is still a living and relevant factor for them. There is the need to present the credentials of those who now address them, and assure them that they also are in the line of the 'true' prophets who bear the genuine word of God. Especially where something of a 'sect' type is emerging, at odds with much of the official leadership and establishment of their day, there is the need to show that they and their circle are the 'true Israel'. There are the requirements of theodicy, to show that however much appearances may be to the contrary, neither God nor his word have failed. And where the pressure of those events and that present situation grows too intense, one can always fall back on a greater generality about the fulfilment of the ancient promises and throw that fulfilment into an, as yet, unspecified and more distant future. By all such methods of exegesis the relevance and authority of the ancient word and the reliability of its contemporary exponents can be maintained. These are some of the reasons which, I believe, help to explain *why* the use of earlier Biblical material is so important a factor in Zech 9–14.

Chapter 3

The Literary Contexts of Zechariah 9:9

Terry Collins

Zechariah 9:9 has already been the subject of much scholarly analysis. There was, for example, the detailed study by Adrian Leske,[1] who demonstrated clearly the importance of the tradition stemming from Deutero-Isaiah when considering the context of this verse. I do not wish to question this well-established observation,[2] but I would like to extend the discussion in three directions. First, I want to emphasize the literary nature of the material, rather than its usefulness in reconstructing the historical circumstances of the Second Temple period. Secondly, I want to show that the literary contexts of Zech 9:9 are plural rather than singular and that the so-called Enthronement Psalms must be included in the list of literary influences. Thirdly, I want to demonstrate that Zech 9:9 is in fact modelled on a particular literary form, which it exploits by deliberately varying the expected contents.

I am inclined to question the ease with which some commentators move from the literary to the historical, bolstered by a questionable use of sociological models. Even in purely literary terms, Zech 9–14 is, in the words of Robert Carroll, 'one of the most obscure collections of oracles in the Hebrew Bible'.[3] The historical context is even more obscure, and could lie anywhere within a range of two centuries, concerning which Blenkinsopp asserts that the years 515–445 BCE represent 'a period about which we know practically nothing as far as Judah is concerned'.[4] And of the period after Nehemiah we know even less, so that even J. Bright, who was never one to draw back from producing 'history' from the thinnest of evidence, had to concede that 'to attempt a history of the Jews in this period is a frustrating task indeed, … no period in Israel's history since Moses is more poorly documented'.[5] It seems to me that to use Zech 9–14 (or any similar passages of unknown provenance) in order to throw light on the historical circumstances of Judah in the late Persian and early Greek periods is an exercise in the use of obscurity to throw light on total darkness. The procedure does not produce very good history or particularly safe sociology, and the determination to persevere with it is even more unfortunate, if it implies a disguised continuation of the historicist prejudice which thinks that the main use of a literary text is to allow us to reconstruct history. While not denying the role of historical considerations, I believe that there is value in a piece of literature quite apart from its historical context.

Any discussion of the literary contexts of Zech 9:9, must, in my opinion, take account of at least five main strands:

1 The passages in Zech 9–14 relating to the theme of the Advent of the Lord.
2 The Biblical descriptions of theophanies, especially in relation to Divine Warrior imagery.

3 The Enthronement Psalms.
4 'Proclamations of a Divine Arrival' as a distinct literary form.
5 The Royal Psalms, especially Ps 72.

THE ADVENT OF THE LORD IN ZECH 9–14

Predictions of a dramatic arrival of the Lord make up one of the more prominent elements in Zech 9–10. It is mentioned in 9:14, for example: 'Then the Lord will appear over them, and his arrow will go forth as lightning; The Lord will sound the trumpet and march forth in the whirlwinds of Teman.'[6] The text goes on to say that God's coming will be an occasion of salvation, and that it will inaugurate an age of peace, prosperity and happiness for his people.

The very opening lines of Zech 9 speak of a visitation by the Lord, which will bring judgement and fire upon the neighbouring nations, especially Tyre and the Philistines. The language used here is quite traditional and somewhat reminiscent of the first chapter of Amos, except that Zechariah gives greater attention to Jerusalem and the temple[7] as the location for the divine intervention: 'Then I will encamp at my house as a guard, so that none shall march to and fro. For now I have seen with my own eyes' (9:8). The Lord is cast in a military role, as a warrior who will fight against the enemy. We find a similar image in Isa 31:4–5. 'So the Lord of hosts will come down to fight on Mount Zion and upon its hill. He will protect and deliver it, he will spare and rescue it.'

We will return to the image of the Divine Warrior later. For the moment, I want to draw attention to the way this description of the Lord's arrival in Zech 9 is matched by another one in chapter 14: 'Then the Lord will go forth and fight against those nations, as when he fights on a day of battle' (14:3). The positioning of divine advents at the beginning and at the end of the material in Zech 9–14 is unlikely to have been accidental. The interesting thing is that these twin advents at the start and finish of Zech 9–14 are matched by another pair in Zech 1–8, where references to God's imminent coming are also found near the beginning and the end. One occurs in Zech 2:10 (MT 14), 'Sing and rejoice O daughter Zion! For behold, I come and I will dwell in your midst', and another in 8:3, 'Thus says the Lord: I will return to Zion and dwell in the midst of Jerusalem'. So the book of Zechariah offers us no less than four announcements of the coming of the Lord,[8] in chapters 2, 8, 9 and 14. This feature of the literature is worth underlining, because it forms a major part of the literary context for the arrival of the king riding on an ass in Zech 9:9.

THEOPHANIES

Awesome theophanies form an ancient element in the religious language of Israel, as is evident from the poetry in Deut 33: 'The Lord came from Sinai and dawned from Seir upon us; He shone forth from Mount Paran, He came from the ten thousands of holy ones, With flaming fire at his right hand' (33:2). Significantly, this is also one of the oldest texts that refer to the Lord as King: 'Thus he became king in Jeshurun' (33:5).

The mention of Sinai and fire reminds us of the pyrotechnic displays associated with the appearance of the Lord in Exod 19:16–19, or the threatening picture in Isa 30:2: 'Behold, the Name of the Lord comes from afar, burning with his anger and in thick rising smoke; his lips are full of indignation, and his tongue is like a devouring fire; to sift the nations with the sieve of destruction.' Further, the idea of a theophany from the south is taken up in Hab 3: 'God came from Teman and the Holy One from Mount Paran. His glory covered the heavens, and the earth was full of his praise. His brightness was like the light, rays flashed from his hand' (3:3–4). The image in the last line is echoed in Zech 9:14: 'his arrow will go forth as lightning ... and march forth in the whirlwinds of Teman'.

There are many prophetical texts which describe the appearance of God as something awesome, and harmful to those who are classed as his enemies. There are, for example, the threatening theophanies in Amos: 'Prepare to meet your God, O Israel. He who forms the mountains and creates the wind. The Lord God of Hosts, he who touches the earth and it melts, and all who dwell in it mourn' (Am 4:13 and 9:5). It is a small step from the idea of God as a dangerous force to the image of God as a warrior, and the reference in Zech 9:14 to God's 'arrow' evokes that picture. The well-known theophany in Isa 63:1 continues the tradition of an appearance of God, coming from the south, and joins it to the image of the Divine Warrior: 'Who is this that comes from Edom, in crimsoned garments from Bozrah, he that is glorious in his apparel, marching in the greatness of his strength?'

The theophanies regularly employ the image of the Divine Warrior, and this is the case in Zech 9:14: 'The Lord will sound the trumpet and march forth'. It is also the case in Zech 14:3–5: 'Then the Lord will go forth and fight against those nations as when he fights in the day of battle'. In this latter instance, the Lord appears as a giant figure, standing alone, astride the valley made when the Mount of Olives is split in two by an eschatological earthquake. This is close to the scene in Hab 3:12: 'You bestrode the earth in fury, you trampled the nations in anger. You went forth for the salvation of your people, for the salvation of your anointed.' The Lord's 'enemies' are most frequently the nations, but the label may also be applied to Israel or to some particular group within Israel.

Usually the Divine Warrior is portrayed as acting alone, as in Isa 63:3: 'I have trodden the winepress alone, and from the peoples no one was with me', and this seems to be the case in Zech 14. However, the theophany in Zech 9 shows an interesting difference, because it allows for a significant role to be played by the human armies of Judah and Ephraim in the fight against God's enemies: 'For I have bent Judah as my bow; I have made Ephraim its arrow' (9:13); 'Together they shall be like mighty men in battle, trampling the foe in the mud of the streets. They shall fight because the Lord is with them, and they shall confound the riders on horses' (10:5). In other texts, especially in the Isaian corpus, prominence is given to God acting alone with no need for any human help: 'And the Assyrian shall fall by a sword not of man, and a sword not of man shall devour him' (Isa 31:8). Nevertheless, the idea that God fights alongside the armies of Israel persisted right up to the exilic period, as is evident from Ps 44:9, for example, which laments that 'you have not gone out with our armies'. The author of Zech 9–14 retains the idea in chapters 9–10 but not in chapter 14. Does this mean that he sees a place for Israel's participation in earlier phases of the eschatological conflict, but excludes it from the final stage?

The image of God the Warrior is closely related to the image of God as a King, because one of the main functions of kings in the ancient world was precisely to lead the nation in battle, to fight against the enemy and destroy or at least subdue them. The enforcement of justice was another part of the king's role, as we see in Ps 45:4: 'In your majesty ride forth victoriously for the cause of truth and to defend the right'. Consequently we find that justice and judgement are regularly cited as the motive for the intervention of the Lord, the Warrior King. An example of this can be seen in Isa 66:15: 'By fire and by his sword will the Lord execute judgment upon all flesh'. Further, the vivid portrayal of a theophany of the Divine Warrior and Judge in Isa 59 is preceded by a lengthy description of a world without justice, which provides the motive for the Divine Warrior's intervention: 'The Lord saw it, and it displeased him that there was no justice, ... then his own arm brought him victory ... He put on righteousness as a breastplate, and a helmet of salvation upon his head ... For he will come like a rushing stream which the wind of the Lord drives. And he will come to Zion as Redeemer' (Isa 59:15–20).

THE 'ENTHRONEMENT PSALMS'

The idea that God will come to exercise judgement and impose justice is given great prominence in those psalms which talk about the kingship of God. We can take Ps 98:9 as an example: 'For he comes to judge the earth. He will judge the world with righteousness and the peoples with equity'. Psalm 98 is, of course, one of that special set of psalms, sometimes referred to as the Enthronement Psalms, because of the particular way in which they refer to the coming of God the King.[9] I believe that these psalms deserve to be given more attention in any study of the literary background of Zech 9–14. In particular, they help to throw light on the use of the word צַדִּיק in Zech 9:9, as we shall see below.

There is no agreement on the dating of the Enthronement Psalms, or even on their existence as a distinct group. The answers given are linked to people's views about the cultic feasts of the pre-exilic Jerusalem temple, and how far the book of Psalms can be used as evidence to reconstruct the liturgy of that period. Some say that the psalms about divine kingship and the rule of justice are pre-exilic compositions, which look to the present world rather than to some eschatological event. Others say that, while they may have been influenced by pre-exilic traditions, these psalms are essentially post-exilic productions with a strong eschatological intention.[10]

The debate centres around the key figure of Deutero-Isaiah, and whether he influenced the language of the Enthronement Psalms or was influenced by them. Gunkel considered these psalms to be post-exilic compositions of an eschatological nature, influenced by Deutero-Isaiah. Mowinckel reversed the order of dependence and argued that these Psalms were pre-exilic compositions, originating in an annual festival of Yahweh's kingship which centred on a procession of the ark. My own inclination is to agree with Gunkel, and see the present form of these psalms as post-exilic expressions of traditional themes.[11] These and other psalms with pre-exilic roots, whether in their original form or revamped, no doubt had a liturgical usage after the return to Judah, but they were also brought more into the personal realm of an intellectual and spiritual meditation on the problem of theodicy – the justice of God's actions and the rightness of his governance. This was an important part of the editing of Psalms as a book to be read and valued outside of the liturgy of the temple.

Whatever position we adopt regarding the origins of the Enthronement Psalms, they were certainly in existence before Zech 9–14, and so it is quite reasonable to accept that they would have had some influence on its composition. In fact, it can be shown that there are a number of points of contact between Zech 9–14 and the Enthronement Psalms at the level of vocabulary and imagery. However, I believe the relationship goes much deeper. They are both concerned with the same underlying theological problems, which presented traditional Israelite faith with a new challenge in the post-exilic world, and which can be generally summed up in the word 'theodicy'. The psalms of God's kingship are based on faith in God's power to save and to maintain order in a potentially dangerous world. Similarly, the basic schema underlying Zech 9–14 is a vision of the future salvation of God's holy people: distressed here and now but sooner or later to be delivered and ultimately to be exalted on a universal scale. In both cases, there is the same belief in the triumph of the good, and it is easy to discern in this problematic part of the explanation for the transition to apocalyptic thinking and writing.

One important difference between Zech 9–14 and the Enthronement Psalms lies in their respective views on the timing of the ultimate triumph.[12] For the psalms of God's kingship, the salvific event has already taken place, or is at least in process of realization. The Lord is already enthroned above the cherubim and is about to exercise his beneficial rule on earth. Hence the general tone of rejoicing which characterizes these psalms: 'The Lord is King, let earth rejoice' (97:1). For Zech 9–14, on the other hand, the salvific event is still some way off in the future. One day there will be a divine act of intervention with great power, and a show of force by the Divine Warrior. Only after that will the rule of God commence: 'And the Lord will become king over all the earth; on that day the Lord will be one and his name one' (14:9).

There are four main areas where the language of Zech 9–14 overlaps with that of the Enthronement Psalms. In every case, we see the same change in the time scale with a shift from the present/proximate future to the remote future.

1 The Enthronement Psalms and Zech 9–14 both use the traditional language of theophanies. For example, we can note Ps 97:3–7: 'Fire goes before him. His lightnings light up the world, the earth sees and trembles. The mountains melt like wax before the Lord of all the earth.'[13] Here the English versions correctly employ a dramatic present tense in the translation. We can contrast this with the tenses used to translate Zech 9:14: 'Then the Lord will appear over them and his arrow go forth like lightning. The Lord God will sound the trumpet and march forth in the whirlwinds of the south.'
2 The intervention of the Divine Warrior is found in both Zech 9–14 and in the Enthronement Psalms. In the latter, the Lord is here and now a glorious king, mighty in battle (Ps 24:8), who consumes his foes on every side (97:3), so that it can be said that the shields of the earth belong to him (47:9). In Zech 14:1–3, this intervention is transposed to a vague, future 'day of the Lord'. First Jerusalem will be besieged and pillaged, and only after that will the Lord go forth and fight against those nations.

3 For the psalmist the glorious vision of a universal submission to the Lord is already under way. The Lord is great in Zion; he is exalted over all the peoples (99:2–3). All the families of peoples are invited to bring an offering, enter his courts and worship the Lord (95:7–9). The author of Zech 9–14 shares this hope for universal peace and harmony based on an acceptance of the rule of God in Zion, but for him it is all still a long way off. And even when it comes it will be on a less ambitious scale. Only after the Lord's visitation will what is left of Philistia become a remnant for our God, like a clan in Judah (9:7). Only after the great showdown battle will 'every one that survives of all the nations ... go up year after year to worship the King, the Lord of Hosts' (14:16).

4 In the Enthronement Psalms, salvation is a present reality, or at least just around the corner: 'his right hand and his holy arm have gotten him victory' (98:1). In Zech 9–14, on the other hand, salvation is seen as something still to come in an undefined future: 'On that day the Lord their God will save them, for they are the flock of his people' (9:16). The Enthronement Psalms also use the image of the flock of sheep, so at least the two sets of writings share that much in their vision of the present reality. But whereas for the psalms this is a reason for the sheep to rejoice: 'Serve the Lord with gladness! Come into his presence with singing! Know that the Lord is God. We are his people, and the sheep of his pasture' (100:3), for the author of Zech 9–14 they are the flock doomed to die (11:4). He is really quite pessimistic about the times in which he lives. His description of what is happening to the flock doomed to die is a very gloomy one: 'Those who buy them slay them and go unpunished; and those who sell them say, "Blessed be the Lord, I have become rich". And their own shepherds have no pity on them' (11:5). This pessimism[14] certainly contrasts with the great optimism and enthusiasm of the Enthronement Psalms: 'Make a joyful noise to the Lord all the earth, break forth into joyous song. Let the hills sing for joy together before the Lord, for he comes to judge the earth. He will judge the world with righteousness and the peoples with equity' (98:4–9).

It is difficult to avoid the conclusion that the author of Zech 9–14 was aware of the Enthronement Psalms and made use of their language and imagery, but that he also consciously changed the focus of the eschatological event and the general mood of the writing.[15]

PROCLAMATIONS OF THE COMING OF THE LORD

So far we have, I hope, established four main points. The idea of a future coming of the Lord is one of the key motifs in Zech 9–14. It is linked to the tradition of theophanies of the Divine Warrior, and it reaches a climax with the inauguration of the universal kingship of the Lord in 14:9. The literary contexts of Zech 9–14 include Zech 1–8, the book of Isaiah, parts of the book of The Twelve, the book of Psalms, especially the Enthronement Psalms.

These observations put us in a better position to approach the much debated passage in Zech 9:9–10, which describes yet another arrival of one referred to as 'your king'. We shall now examine this text more closely, starting with the first half of

v. 9: 'Rejoice greatly, O daughter Zion. Shout aloud, O daughter Jerusalem. Behold, your king comes to you'. The words have a familiar ring to them, and there are in fact a number of texts that contain very similar language. The main examples are in Isa 35:4; 30:27; 40:9–11; 62:11; Zeph 3:14–17; Zech 2:10.[16] They make up a small but significant group of oracles in the prophetical literature, and a careful study of them shows that they share a sufficient number of structural features to justify our classifying them as a 'Literary Form' in their own right.[17] (The principal texts involved are set out schematically in Table 3.1.)

Structurally, we can distinguish two main parts to the literary form: an optional introductory part plus the body of the proclamation, which has seven elements.

The introduction

The introduction lies outside the actual words of the proclamation and gives some hint of the implied scene in which someone is delegated to take the message or make the proclamation.[18] It is an optional element and may vary in length. Extended examples of this feature can be seen in Isa 40:9 and Isa 52:7–10.

The proclamation

The text of the message to be proclaimed, in its abstract form, includes seven elements:

1 An imperative, indicating the response expected: 'rejoice', 'do not fear' etc. (May be quite complex, as in Zeph 3:14–17.)
2 A vocative proper noun, revealing the identity of the recipients. (May be omitted if they are already identified in the introduction.)
3 The interjection particle הנה – 'behold'.
4 The identity of the one who is coming (namely God by various titles).
5 The verb יבוא, comes/is coming/will come.
6 The mode of his coming.
7 The effects of his coming (good for some, bad for others), frequently involving the nations in one capacity or another.

ZECHARIAH 9:9

When we superimpose this schema onto the text of Zech 9:9, we see immediately that the first five elements are all present and correct in the first half of verse 9.

1	imperative	'Rejoice greatly, Shout aloud'
2	identity of recipient	'daughter Zion, daughter Jerusalem'
3	interjection הנה	'behold'
4	identity of the one coming	'your king'
5	the verb יבוא	'comes to you'

Table 3.1 Proclamation of arrivals

	Zech 2:10 (MT 2:14)	Isa 35:4	Isa 40:9–11	Isa 62:11	Isa 30:27	Zeph 3:14–15	Zeph 3:16–17
1	(oracle of the Lord)	say to those who are fearful of heart	go up on a high mountain, etc: say to the cities of Judah	say to daughter Zion			on that day it shall be said in Jerusalem
2	sing and rejoice	be strong do not fear				sing aloud shout rejoice and exult with all your heart	do not fear
3	Daughter Zion					daughter Zion Israel daughter Jerusalem	Zion
4	for behold	behold	behold	behold	behold		
5	I (the Lord)	your God	your God	your Salvation	the name of the Lord	the King of Israel the Lord	The Lord your God
6	will come and dwell	comes	comes	comes	comes	is	is
7	in your midst	with vengeance	with might		from afar burning with anger	in your midst	in your midst a warrior
8	many nations will join themselves to the Lord	he will save	his arm rules he will feed gather … carry … lead his flock	his reward is with him (= Isa 40:10)	to sift the nations	you shall fear no more	he gives victory

Up to this point, therefore, Zech 9:9 has the typical form of a prophetic proclamation of the coming of the Lord. Consequently, the form points the reader familiar with the convention towards the conclusion that the one who is coming is none other than God himself. This expectation is reinforced by the immediate context of the oracle which contains a reference to the Divine Warrior in 9:8.

The second half of Zech 9:9, however, steers us in a completely different direction by telling us that the king will be meek and humble and will come riding on an ass. The introduction of a human king does not fulfill the expectation set up in the opening line. At the same time, verses 9b–10 do continue the form of the proclamation. They give us elements 6–7 of the schema, since they describe the manner of the king's coming and the effects this will have, and hence they are an integral part of the structure of the oracle and not something just tacked on. But while there is continuity in the form, there is discontinuity in the ideas. We appear to be dealing with a sophisticated stylistic feature, consciously used, in which expectation is fulfilled in the form but is foiled in the contents.[19]

It is against this background that we should approach the task of analysing the implications of what we are told about the king who is to come, the manner of his coming and the effects it will have. The first thing we are told about the king is that he will be צַדִּיק. This means 'right and good', in various senses of the term: legal, religious, moral, social or just plain pragmatic. The צַדִּיק is someone who demonstrates צֶדֶק or צְדָקָה, goodness and uprightness in his actions. Besides their general meaning, both these terms often have a technical meaning related to judgement and the administration of justice for the good ordering of society. In this sense, the term צַדִּיק is frequently applied to God and takes on a special significance. It becomes part of the 'word-field' associated with the concept of God as ruler of the world and the supreme judge, who is just and upright but also kind and merciful to the weak. This is reflected in the Enthronement Psalms, e.g. Ps 98:9, but is found in a number of other places: Ps 7:12; 119:137; 116:5. It becomes very important to the theodicy at the heart of apocalyptic writings.

PSALM 72

There is a significant example of the application of the root צדק in various forms to a human king in Ps 72:1. This contains a prayer to God that he will give the king the quality of צְדָקָה as a gift, so that he can judge God's people with צֶדֶק. Rather as Solomon received the gift of wisdom in answer to a prayer at the start of his reign, the king of Ps 72 receives the divine quality of צְדָקָה so that he can act for God in caring for the people. There is here a certain blurring of the human and the divine realms, which has its origins in the view of the ideal king as one chosen, even adopted, by God and endowed with quasi divine attributes.[20] The classic list of such attributes is the one in Isa 9:6, where the future king is called, among other things, 'Wonderful Counselor, Mighty God and Prince of Peace'.

When it comes to the dispensing of justice, the meek and humble are said to be God's special concern. Hence it is highly significant that the meek and humble are singled out as the potential recipients of justice at the hands of the king in Ps 72:2, 'That he may judge thy people with צֶדֶק and thy meek ones with מִשְׁפָּט'. The word used for the meek is עֲנִיִּים and they are referred to as 'the meek of the people' and 'your meek' (i.e. the Lord's own).[21] The idea that the anointed one will give just judgement to the meek is also found in Isa 11:3–4, which is another text extolling the virtues of the ideal king: 'He shall not judge by what his eyes see, but with צֶדֶק he shall judge the poor ... and the meek of the earth.'

The prominence given to the עֲנִיִּים in Ps 72 and Isa 11:3–4 goes a long way to explaining the use of the word עָנִי to describe the king in Zech 9:9. In Ps 72, the messianic figure receives the gift of צְדָקָה, right judgement, so that he can show צֶדֶק to the עֲנִיִּים. In Zech 9:9, the king himself is said to be both צַדִּיק and עָנִי. He shares the quality of justice with the Lord, and he shares the quality of humbleness with the people. In this way, the vocabulary of the oracle in Zech 9:9–10 combines with its structural features noted above to bring out the intermediary role of the messianic king, standing between the divine realm and the human realm.

Portraying the king as meek and humble is not such a radical departure from the traditional view of kingship in Israel. According Deut 17:15–20, the king must be an ordinary Israelite, whose heart must not be lifted up above his brethren. Throughout the Deuteronomist history, those who are chosen by the Lord to bring salvation to Israel are regularly portrayed as of lowly origin and as people who, at first glance, appear unlikely candidates for the task. The list includes Gideon and Jephthah, Saul and David. Then there are the prophets, who regularly express their sense of unworthiness for their call. Finally, there is the supreme example of Moses, the servant of the Lord and the meekest of men עָנָו (Num 12:3). In Zech 9:9, the new king's meekness is symbolized by his action of entering Jerusalem riding on an ass, like 'ordinary folk'. In this he stands in marked contrast to the last known kings of Judah who, in the days of Jeremiah, used to ride in and out of Jerusalem in horse-drawn chariots (Jer 17:19–25).

Besides being meek, the king in Zech 9 is said to be נוֹשָׁע 'saved', and the implication is that he is saved by the Lord, just as the king is said to be saved נוֹשָׁע by God rather than by horses or armies in Ps 33:16–17. The use of this word in Zech 9:9 has been a cause of trouble for some commentators and translators, starting with the LXX which has σῴζων, 'bringing salvation', and continuing right up to the RSV and NRSV which translate it as 'victorious'. There is, however, nothing strange about the idea of the Lord's anointed being both saved and a bringer of salvation at the same time. Just because the victory comes from God, it does not mean that the king has been somehow demilitarized and 'spiritualized'. In Ps 2, the Lord's anointed is surrounded by hostile nations, and he is assured of victory by God. At the same time he still has to do his own fighting: 'you shall break them with a rod of iron' (Ps 2:9). Psalm 118 gives us another example of a king who is surrounded by his foes 'like bees', and trusts in the Lord. He is saved by the Lord, who fights for him: 'The right hand of the Lord does valiantly'. But he too fights and defeats the foe: 'In the name of the Lord I cut them off' (118:10–16). This psalm is particularly interesting in our discussion for a number of reasons. Besides emphasizing the theme of salvation, it also contains a memorable statement of the idea that the Lord's anointed is of humble and obscure origins: 'The stone that the builders rejected has become the head of the corner' (v. 22), which is of course cited in Acts and applied to Jesus as the messiah.[22]

The result of justice is peace, שלום. This is the message of Ps 72:7, which affirms that the king's justice will produce peace until the moon fails. It is also the message of

Zech 9:10, which says that the messianic figure will speak peace to the nations (RSV 'command peace'). The arrival of the ideal king will have the effect of putting an end to fighting. The bows of war, the chariots and the war-horses will be abolished (Zech 9:10). That does not mean that there will not be an initial period of fighting during which the enemy will be defeated and disarmed, before finally there will be שלום, and the weapons can be put away and swords beaten into ploughshares etc. In Zech 9:10 (unless we change the MT), it is the Lord who will do the cutting off of the bows of war and the chariots and the horses. This is in line with the picture in Ps 46, where it is God who breaks the bow and makes wars cease – to the ends of the earth. It is also very reminiscent of Isa 9:2–7 where the paraphernalia of battle will be burned, and although this action is directly linked to the arrival of a new Davidic king, ultimately the victory belongs to the Lord: 'the zeal of the Lord of hosts will do this' (9:7).

Zechariah 9:10 brings us back to the model form of proclamation analysed above, since it gives us the mode of the king's coming (element 6), the effects of his coming (element 7), including the involvement of the nations. Moreover, it is important to remember how often the nations figure in the Enthronement Psalms.[23] The nations are also present in Ps 72:11, which predicts that the kings of the nations will all come to bow down before the Davidic king and serve him. This element is only implicitly hinted at in Zech 9:10, but it reappears in a new form in Zech 14:16, where we are told that the remnants of the nations will all come to worship the Lord as King in Jerusalem.[24] The universal rule of the messianic king as the representative of the Divine King is underlined in the closing phrase of Zech 9:10: 'his dominion shall be from sea to sea, and from the river to the ends of the earth'. This is in fact a close imitation, if not a citation, of Ps 72:8, just as the opening words of Zech 9:9 are a close imitation of the proclamations in texts like Zech 2:10 (MT14) or Zeph 3:14–15.

The literary dependence of Zech 9:9–10 on written antecedents is incontrovertible. It is more than probable that the dependence was conscious and deliberate on the part of the author. Moreover, imitation and variation as literary techniques depend for their impact and effectiveness on a reciprocal awareness and connivance on the part of the reader. As readers we are involved in the game not only of spotting the allusions and citations, but also of recognizing the departures from the models and the ways in which the material is being recycled and given new shades of meaning. When we approach Zech 9:9–10 in this way, we can see how a new lease of life is being given to some old language about the kingship of the messiah and the kingship of God. The language of the proclamation of the arrival of a king had a long history. Originally, it was used in relation to the arrivals of human kings. Then it was transferred to the divine realm of God as king. In Zech 9:9 it is returning to the sphere of human kingship. However, the baggage it has acquired in the form of its associations with divine kingship cannot simply be dropped.

NOTES

1 Leske, 2000.

2 Rex Mason, for example, pointed out twenty-five years ago that the picture of the Davidic Messiah in Zechariah was influenced by the figure of the servant in Isa 53 (Mason, 1977).

3 Carroll, 1979b, p. 14.

4 Blenkinsopp, 1984, p. 240.

5 Bright, 1960, p. 389.

6 The translations in this article are, for the most part, taken from the RSV.

7 Although even in Amos, 'The Lord roars from Zion' (Am 1:2).

8 Gerhard von Rad asserts that 'the principal element in the message of Zech 1–8 is the proclamation of the imminent advent of Jahweh': von Rad, 1975, p. 285.

9 The principal psalms concerned are 24, 47, 93 and 95–100.

10 The best analysis of the debate concerning the Enthronement Psalms is still the study by Lipinski, 1962.

11 Even if there was a pre-exilic festival of Yahweh's Kingship, the Enthronement Psalms, in their post-exilic setting, ceased to be part of a cultic procession with the ark, since there was no ark in the Second Temple: 'It shall not be made again' (Jer 3:16).

12 This distinction becomes a problem when these texts have to be translated into a language like English, in which the verb forms are rigidly fixed into 'tenses', according to the time of an event. This was not the case in Biblical Hebrew.

13 Compare Am 9:5.

14 It ranks alongside the bitterness of Qohelet at his most cynical, or the anger of Job at its height. And perhaps the origins of Zech 9–14 are to be sought in the same thought-world as those writings.

15 A similar shift in perspective would explain why, in the editing of Psalms, it was decided to include Ps 94 among the Enthronement Psalms.

16 Related examples can also be seen in Isa 30:2; 52:7–10; 60:1–3.

17 This literary form had its roots in an oral form related to a *Sitz im Leben*, in keeping with classical form criticism theory. In fact it seems to represent a double strand, combining the role of messengers sent in advance to say someone is coming (as in Gen 32:3–6 or Num 20:14–17), and the role of the watchman on the walls of the city, as in 2 Sam 18:24–25.

18 There are some similarities with the commissioning scenes in the prophetic literature, which describe the sending forth of a messenger from the divine presence.

19 The technique of the 'surprise ending' is known elsewhere in prophetical literature. The best examples are seen in Amos: 'Come to Bethel and sin' (4:4), and 'You only have I known, of all the families of the earth; therefore I will punish you' (3:2).

20 This may be behind the difficult reference to 'your throne, O God' in Ps 45:6.

21 For a full discussion of this term, see Van den Berghe, 1962.

22 It is interesting to note that Ps 118 is cited by all four evangelists as they comment on Jesus' entry into Jerusalem, whereas Zech 9:9 is only used by two of them.

23 In Ps 96:7–9, the families of the earth come into the temple to worship the Lord. In Ps 47:9, the princes of the people gather as the people of the God of Abraham.

24 Actually, the text says 'King YHWH of Hosts' – מֶלֶךְ יהוה צְבָאוֹת.

Chapter 4

Bad Divination in Zechariah 10:1–2

Johannes Tromp

In this contribution I hope to suggest a plausible interpretation of Zech 10:1–2, a passage which has received relatively little attention in the history of research. Crucial to my interpretation is that these few lines are *not* to be read in their immediate context. This approach stands in contrast with the nowadays dominant trend which assumes that Deutero-Zechariah must form a carefully edited whole, almost as a matter of principle, even if its meaning largely escapes the interpreters.

ON THE COHERENCE OF DEUTERO-ZECHARIAH

The appearance of the monograph on Deutero-Zechariah by Magne Sæbø, in 1969, marked the apotheosis of what might be called the 'atomistic' approach to these chapters.[1] Sæbø's careful analysis of Zechariah 9–14 led him to conclude that this part of the book consisted of several collections of independent prophetic oracles, transmitted, interpreted, and edited in many stages. Sæbø has been criticized because of the overly detailed character of his procedure, and not entirely without justification. However, his basic contention, that the text of Deutero-Zechariah has had a long and intricate pre-history, is undoubtedly correct, even if this fact is occasionally ignored, or, perhaps worse, turned into a pretext for ignoring the historical dimensions of this literature.

It seems that, after Sæbø's study, most researchers have attempted a different approach. Already in 1961, P. Lamarche had argued for viewing Zechariah 9–14 as a literary unity, and offered a corresponding literary analysis, based on formal criteria.[2] Some years later, in 1964, B. Otzen suggested an alternative literary analysis, based on the criterion of cohering content.[3] From these attempts, it mainly appears that Deutero-Zechariah tends to evade comprehension, and invite speculation.[4]

A second important trend in the research on Deutero-Zechariah has been to view these chapters as derivative.[5] From an early stage of modern study on, scholars have recognized allusions to earlier 'Biblical' books, either to the older literature in general,[6] or to Proto-Zechariah in particular.[7] It is now usually taken for granted that the authors of Deutero-Zechariah were characterized by 'a learned preoccupation with older prophetic language', characteristic, according to Michael Fishbane, of late Biblical prophecy as a whole.[8] I shall return to this assumption and its consequences for the interpretation of Zech 10:1–2 presently.

For now, it suffices to say that if Deutero-Zechariah were the result of intense study of earlier prophecy, it may at least be unified to an extent because the circles in which it was made shared the same intentions.[9] Carol and Eric Meyers in their commentary of 1993, however, go considerably further by suggesting that Zechariah 9–11 are not 'random collections of eschatological prophecies, but, rather, coherent reflections of the prophetic struggle to make sense of a troubling world in light of the Israelite heritage.'[10] Specifically commenting on Zechariah 10, they continue: 'If Zechariah 10 seems diverse, in other words, it is because of the various and complex materials upon which it can draw.'[11] It is doubtful, however, whether the effort to save the literary unity of that chapter justifies turning the author of Zechariah 10 into a muddleheaded figure.

The approach of Michael Floyd seems subtler. He regards Zechariah 9–11 as a *maśśā'*, which he understands as a 'reinterpretation of a previous revelation', in particular of Zechariah 1–8.[12] Zechariah 12–14 would be another *maśśā'*, a restatement of the prophecies of Zechariah 1–11 in the context of new circumstances. The entire book, according to Floyd, is unified by the integrative programme as stated in the introduction in Zech 1:1–6.[13] His analysis of Zechariah 9–11 leads him to conclude that this unit 'is generically diverse,' but 'this diversity does not make for incoherence, but rather serves to develop a coherent line of thought.'[14] However, as we shall see, the coherence Floyd reconstructs is based on abstract meanings gleaned from formal considerations, and appears to necessitate distortions when the text itself is read in detail.

In brief, the problem which interpreters of Deutero-Zechariah are continually facing is that of demarcation: it is unclear where to begin and where to end.[15] In his 1908 commentary on the Twelve Prophets Van Hoonacker replaced 10:1 before 9:17, followed by 9:16b and 10:2–3; after that, no more was needed than to delete a few words to make perfect sense of the text. This procedure is now generally rejected as arbitrary, and rightly so. However, there seems to be little less arbitrariness in adopting the chapter-division in our printed Bibles to try to make sense of it, as if those responsible for it were in a better position to understand Zechariah.[16] A glance at the ancient versions reveals that by the time the present chapter-division was made, the text as well as its interpreters must already have been hopelessly confused.

This observation may justify the return to an approach of the text of Zechariah in its smallest meaningful parts.[17] In the next section, I shall argue that Zech 10:1–2 is one of those smallest meaningful parts. As observed by many scholars, the relationship of this passage to the ones preceding and following it is a matter of catchword-association. I shall take this one step further, and suggest that it is no more than that.[18]

THE DEMARCATION OF ZECH 10:1–2

Chapters 9 and 10 of the book of Zechariah are connected to each other by the recurrent mention of shepherds. In chapter 9 several kings of foreign nations are threatened and Yahweh is praised as the king of Judah and Ephraim who will defeat their oppressors; in this connection, allusion is made to the traditional metaphor for a king as a shepherd leading his flock (9:16). In chapter 10 the same metaphor occurs. In v. 3, the text mentions the anger of Yahweh against 'the shepherds', and it continues by describing how Judah and Joseph will subdue even Assyria and Egypt. There are more similarities between both passages, for instance the comparison of the joy of massacring one's enemies with that of a drinking party (9:15; 10:7).

A shepherd occurs in 10:1–2 as well. Here, people who have apparently received misleading weather forecasts are compared to a flock without a shepherd. It seems to me that the subject matter of these two verses differs immensely from that of chapters 9 and 10:3–12, and I am not convinced by attempts to understand 10:1–2 as an integral part of 10:1–12.[19]

Hanson considers chapters 9 and 10 as a coherent composition, although in his view chapter 10 was written later than chapter 9, as a response to chapter 9. In chapter 9 salvation is promised for Yahweh's people as a result of his victorious combat; chapter 10, including vv. 1–2, resumes this theme, reapplying the earlier promises to new circumstances, and introducing it with an indictment of the leaders who by their neglect of the people have allowed them to practise a defiled cult (10:1–3a). The 'degenerate cult' leading to the delay of the fulfilment of the promises in chapter 9, consists of 'fertility practices directed at teraphim and diviners'.[20]

Because of the close connection laid between 10:1–3a and the rest of that chapter, Hanson is forced to read much into Zech 10:1–3a which is not there. The shepherd mentioned in 10:2 is identified with the shepherds (plural) in 10:3a. However, the point in 10:2 is that the flock is straying because they have *no* shepherd, not because they have *bad* shepherds. Moreover, Hanson turns the lies of the teraphim and the diviners into a 'degenerate cult'; the corollary idea that fertility practices could be directed at diviners is absurd.[21] Most importantly, however, the theme of Zechariah 9 and of Zech 10:3–12 is war, not rain; and if a defiled cult would have been the reason behind the composition of chapter 10, one would have expected the authors to say something about its purification or removal.

Meyers and Meyers, treating chapter 10 as a separate unit, see the prophet's concern for the Israelites from the North, who have gone into exile in Assyria but have never returned, as one of the main issues in Deutero-Zechariah. The reason for their assumedly pitiful situation is found in their failure to let themselves be guided by true prophets. Meyers and Meyers suggest that the shepherds in Zech 10:2, 3 and 11:3–7 are to be interpreted as false prophets.

This interpretation is unusual, but that in itself is no reason to reject it. More problematic is the way in which they have to allegorize the rain in 10:1: 'we are presented with the simple sad fact that the Israelites' reliance on false prophetic intermediaries, rather than on Yahweh directly, led them to a situation of hopelessness and a sense of emptiness'.[22] It is unclear to me how asking the teraphim for rain bears on the supposedly sorry situation of the Israelite exiles in Assyria. Moreover, whereas Meyers and Meyers allegorize the concrete situation, in which rain is the issue, they turn what is explicitly presented as an image (כמו צאן) into a metaphor for the people's failure to let themselves be guided by true prophets.

Floyd regards 10:1–2 as a part of 10:1–12, a section in which the people are exhorted to respond to what has been said in 9:12b–17. There it is stated that Yahweh is making a double restoration: both of the people's territorial integrity and of their productivity.[23] So God is bringing a new situation, and the prophet tells them to react properly. In this context, Zech 10:1–2 means: 'If they seek such blessings from Yahweh on the basis of the prophet's true revelation, they will come to see that their local leaders are both the main cause of their present problems and the main impediment to Yahweh's plan for changing the situation'.[24]

Again, much is read into the text which is not there, and the meaning of several phrases has to be distorted in order to be smoothed into the desired coherence. The 'rain' in 10:1 is made into 'such blessings' (apparently as mentioned in the preceding passage, but there no mention is made of rain), and the emphasis of 10:2 is entirely shifted from the teraphim and the soothsayers to the image of the flock without a shepherd. Floyd claims that 'in 10:2b the problem of bad leadership is introduced'. Obviously, he recognizes the theme of leadership in the 'shepherd' of 10:2b. Then he continues that it is because the *leaders* failed to ask Yahweh, that the people 'founder aimlessly like wandering sheep without a shepherd'. Thus, the comparison in 10:2b is forced to provide both the cause and the result of the people's problems. The question of why the author of Zech 10:1–2 would suddenly turn his attention to rain instead of war, is hardly discussed.[25]

This brief survey of attempts to read Zech 10:1–2 as part of a larger coherent section shows in my opinion that the meaning of these two verses is anything but clarified by reading them in combination with the rest of chapter 10 or within the context of chapters 9–11. Therefore, it is justifiable to investigate whether their meaning is clearer when they are *not* read within a wider context.

Finally, I must set out my reasons to limit my attention to Zech 10:1–2 (as opposed to, for instance, 9:17–10:2, or 10:1–3a). These reasons are mainly pragmatic:

1 Zech 9:17, although admittedly obscure, has the appearance of forming the conclusion to the preceding section.[26]
2 Zech 10:1 begins with a new imperative and subject matter.[27]
3 The new sentence starting in Zech 10:1 is continued by conjunctions in 10:2 (כי and על כן).[28]
4 In Zech 10:3 a new sentence begins, set in the first person.

It could be argued, on the basis of the change in perspective from v. 3a (first person) to 3b (third person), that there is reason to see v. 3a as separate from v. 3b and the rest of chapter 10, and should therefore be attached to the unit 10:1–2.[29] However, the link between v. 3a and v. 3b (bad shepherds versus God taking matters into his own hand) seems strong enough. Moreover, the shepherds and he-goats of v. 3a most likely refer metaphorically to leaders in a political sense, whereas the shepherd in v. 2 is part of a comparison illustrating the situation of certain people.

THE TEXT AND MEANING OF ZECH 10:1–2

Whereas in earlier commentaries the text of Zech 10:1–2 was often conjecturally changed, most translators and commentators today retain the text as given in the editions of the Masoretic Bible:

1 שַׁאֲלוּ מֵיְהוָה מָטָר בְּעֵת מַלְקוֹשׁ
יְהוָה עֹשֶׂה חֲזִיזִים וּמְטַר־גֶּשֶׁם
יִתֵּן לָהֶם לְאִישׁ עֵשֶׂב בַּשָּׂדֶה׃

2 כִּי הַתְּרָפִים דִּבְּרוּ־אָוֶן וְהַקּוֹסְמִים חָזוּ שֶׁקֶר
וַחֲלֹמוֹת הַשָּׁוְא יְדַבֵּרוּ הֶבֶל יְנַחֵמוּן
עַל־כֵּן נָסְעוּ כְמוֹ־צֹאן יַעֲנוּ כִּי־אֵין רֹעֶה׃

The only real text-critical doubts[30] concern the switch from the second person imperative שַׁאֲלוּ in v. 1a to the third personal pronoun לָהֶם in v. 1c. This tension is sometimes solved by pointing the imperative as a third person perfect form, שָׁאֲלוּ,[31] or by reading either a second personal pronoun instead of the third,[32] or לֶחֶם, 'bread' instead of לָהֶם, 'to them'.[33] Usually, however, the text is left as it stands.

In the translations, the Masoretic layout of the text is usually also closely followed. This, however, is a less felicitous decision. The sentences as constructed by the Masoretes have a strained syntax, and are difficult to translate:

> Ask from Yahweh rain in the spring,
> Yahweh is the maker of thunderbolts and of downpour of rain,
> He will give to them, to everybody, vegetation in the field.

However, nothing appears to be wrong with the text or the syntax if גשם is connected with the following clause, and not with מטר;[34] this reading also solves the peculiar apposition of לאיש to להם:[35]

שאלו מיהוה מטר בעת מלקוש
יהוה עשה חזיזים ומטר
גשם יתן להם לאיש עשב בשדה

Thus, without any changes to the text, the following smooth translation can be made:

> Ask from Yahweh showers in the spring.
> Yahweh, the maker of thunderbolts and showers,
> will give rain to them, to everybody vegetation in the field.

The second verse is not entirely without its problems, but the following rendering will give little cause for dispute:

> Surely,[36] the teraphim tell lies,
> the soothsayers have idle visions,
> and relate nonsensical dreams;[37]
> the comfort they bring is false.
> Therefore they are wandering on[38] like sheep,
> they are being oppressed because they have no shepherd.

Until recently, the common interpretation of this verse was that the teraphim here represent false deities, idols, and the gist of vv. 1 and 2 together would be that one should not ask idols for rain, but Yahweh, because he is the maker of rain, and the idols and soothsayers are not.

This interpretation, however, does not do justice to what is said in the text. The teraphim are not accused of being unable to bring rain, but of telling lies. What, then, are the teraphim saying?

The teraphim are saying they will bring rain

Such a message comes close to absurdity. It would presuppose a situation in which the teraphim have said: 'We will bring rain, but Yahweh will not'; while Yahweh is contrasted as saying: 'I will bring rain, but the teraphim will not'. The hearers of such a message can go home with a feeling of great relief, because either of them, Yahweh or the teraphim, will make it rain; surely, farmers who need the rain could not have cared less who brought it.

The teraphim are saying they will not bring rain

If the teraphim would have predicted a drought, that would suit the oracle in v. 1: 'The teraphim may have said that there will be a drought, but Yahweh, who is in fact the one responsible for the weather, will bring rain.' Such a message would be in perfect agreement with the other prophecies in chapters 9 and 10, which are also oracles of salvation. However, the characterization of the teraphim's lies as 'false comfort' in v. 2b excludes this possibility. The teraphim's words must have contained good news, not bad news.

In more recent studies, more attention has been paid to the exact function and nature of the teraphim. K. van der Toorn, for instance, has argued that the way in which the Old Testament literature speaks about the teraphim shows that they are objects representing human forms, probably those of deceased ancestors, which could be used to consult the divinity.[39] The next lines of course also contain references to divination: קוסמים and dreams. In the recent commentaries, this suggestion has rightfully been adopted.[40]

However, one important aspect of this insight is that the teraphim may be *idola*,[41] meaning 'statuettes', but that they are not idols in the sense of 'false gods', divine beings of such a nature and stature that they would be in a position of competing with Yahweh. Although the identification of the teraphim with ancestors in particular has not remained undisputed,[42] it seems clear that they represent superhuman beings of a low rank, let us say: spirits of some kind.[43] These spirits are certainly not responsible for the climate, but they are capable of informing mankind, no doubt by use of a medium, of what goes on in the other world.[44] This implies that the issue at stake is not idolatry: teraphim are divinatory instruments, representing ancestors or some other kind of spirits; they are objects which could be used to consult superhuman beings about the plans of the gods.[45] Moreover, it is not at all excluded that they, just like soothsayers and dreamers, were used to consult Yahweh himself, as I shall now argue.

In Judges 17, a man named Micah is depicted as making for himself a household shrine, including images of Yahweh, as well as an ephod and teraphim. The man is consistently designated as a Yahwist (17:2, 3, 13); if the ephod and the teraphim were instruments for divination, it is likely that they were used to consult Yahweh; at least, when the priest is asked for an oracle, he answers in the name of Yahweh (18:6).

That spirits could be consulted to find out God's will is also confirmed by the story of Saul and the witch of Endor in 1 Samuel 28. After Saul had seen the mighty Philistine forces, he consulted (שאל) Yahweh, but Yahweh did not answer, 'either by dreams, or by *urim*, or by prophets' (1 Sam 28:6; cf. v. 15).[46] In despair, he visited a medium, who summoned for him the spirit (the word used is אלהים, 1 Sam 28:13) of the deceased Samuel, who answered Saul's questions concerning Yahweh's future actions.

This passage also shows that dreams were thought to reveal Yahweh's will. In the Old Testament dreaming is never condemned. Quite the contrary, it appears to be a dominant means of receiving revelations: even if the root חלם is not used, it is striking to see how often prophets are presented as receiving Yahweh's information at night.[47] To be sure, some dreams can be interpreted erroneously, or those who claim to have had a prophetic dream may be liars, but that is an entirely different problem, namely that of false prophecy, which is not defined by the use or non-use of certain techniques, but by truthfulness (see esp. Jer 23:28–32[48]). I shall return to the problem of false prophecy in the next section.

To complete this survey, the קוסמים could be expected to be able to inform those who consulted them about the will of Yahweh. When Saul arrives at the woman of Endor, he tells her to 'consult', קסם, a spirit (1 Sam 28:8). False prophets are called קוסמים in Mic 3:6, 9, 11 and on numerous occasions in Ezek 13. Nonetheless they all claim to be prophets of Yahweh.

This leads us to a third possibility concerning the question of the teraphim's and soothsayer's alleged lies.

The teraphim are saying Yahweh will bring rain

As noted above, v. 2b implies that the teraphim, together with the קוסמים and the dreams, must have given a comforting message, in other words, they must have given the reassuring answer that the rains would come in their season. Since the prophet denounces their words as lies, he must have been of the opposite opinion. The dispute between him and the teraphim and the others is not whether one should consult either Yahweh or the teraphim. It is possible, even likely, that people used teraphim precisely to consult Yahweh. The dispute between the prophet speaking here and the other diviners is about the correct answer to the question: will there be rain?[49] The teraphim said 'yes', so we may conclude that the prophet said 'no'.[50]

If this is correct, the only possible conclusion is that v. 1b–c, where rain is promised, contains the positive answer of the prophet's opponents, which the prophet consequently characterizes as nonsense. In other words, those lines are a quotation of Yahweh's answer according to the teraphim and קוסמים, as follows:

> Ask from Yahweh showers in the spring!
> 'Yahweh, the maker of thunderbolts and showers,
> will give rain to them, to everybody vegetation in the field!'
> Surely, the teraphim tell lies etc.

A subsidiary advantage of this interpretation is that the change from second to third person in the quotation is less harsh. One could paraphrase the entire passage vv. 1–2:

> Go ahead, ask rain from Yahweh, and the soothsayers may well tell you that he will give it; but they are liars, and you are being misled.

BAD DIVINATION

Why does the prophet denounce the divinators as liars? The easy answer to that question is that such divinatory techniques were illegal according to Deut 18:9–14 (a list of illegal forms of mantic, not including, by the way, dreaming).[51] The author of this piece was aware of that, and therefore he protested against it.[52]

However, the dispute in Zech 10:1–2 does not seem to be about the proper divinatory technique. Maybe the prophet speaking here used other techniques, or maybe none, and found his own method of divining Yahweh's will more trustworthy. It might also be that he believed that the diviners came to wrong conclusions *because* they used particular methods. But his objection is that they are giving the wrong answer, not that they are forbidden.[53] In other words: the issue in Zech 10:1–2 does not seem to be that divination *per se* is a bad thing; the issue is that the prophet disagrees with his colleagues, whom he accuses of bad divination.

It has often been noted that Zech 10:1–2 bears striking resemblance to Jeremiah 14. A brief comparison between both passages may serve to illustrate my point.

After a description of a drought in Jer 14:1–6, the prophet prays to Yahweh on behalf of the people (14:7–9). However, Yahweh answers that the people have been sinful (the exact nature of their sin is not mentioned) and that the current situation is his punishment (14:10–12). The prophet objects that his colleagues had told the people that no harm would come to them (14:13). God answers that those prophets have prophesied lies (שקר) in his name, and that he has not sent them to deliver that message (in his answer the terms חזון and קסם also occur), and that the opposite of what they predict will happen (14:14–17a). The passage is concluded with a lament, a confession of (unidentified) sins, and the praise of Yahweh as the only maker of rain, as opposed to the vanities of the nations (הבלי הגוים; 14:17b–22).

The similarity of this passage with Zech 10:1–2 seems so strong that it has often been thought that the passage in Zechariah is dependent on that in Jeremiah.[54] This assumption is consistent with the view on Deutero-Zechariah as derivative literature. The dependence of Zech 10:1–2 on Jeremiah 14 appears, according to R. A. Mason, from the following observations: in both passages, the words נשם, בשדה, עשב and הבל are used; moreover, there is great similarity between Jeremiah's expression חזון שקר וקסם (Jer 14:14) and הקוסמים חזו שקר in Zech 10:2; finally, Jer 14:22 concludes with a contrast of Yahweh with the vanities of the nations which are incapable of giving rain.[55] R. Nurmela subscribes to Mason's view, but adds that Zech 10:1–2 is *also* dependent on Jer 10:13–15 (= 51:16–18). The latter passage contains the nouns מטר, שקר and הבל, and more clearly than Jer 14:22, contrasts Yahweh as the bringer of rain with idols.[56] Further influence from Deut 11:13–17 is suspected by K. J. A. Larkin, because in that passage, the train of thoughts, though differently worded, is identical to that in Zech 10:1–2: the command to obey God is followed by a promise of rain and fertility, and concluded by a warning not to serve other gods.[57]

I shall restrict myself to the relationship between Jeremiah 14 and Zechariah 10, because the case for dependency is certainly the strongest here. However, not too much should be made of the presence of נשם in both texts, which is a very common term for rain. The idea that God gives it is also very common (see, apart from the texts already mentioned, Job 5:10; 36:26–33; 37:1–13; 38:25–8; Ps 135:7; 147:8). Even the idea that God will give it on condition that he is faithfully obeyed, occurs quite often (e.g., Deut 28:1–14; 1 Sam 12:16–19; 1 Kgs 8:33–6; 18; Isa 30:18–26). I shall not dwell on the coincidence of עשב and שדה: 'vegetation in the field', that is where it belongs (e.g., Gen 3:18; Exod 9:22, 25; 10:12, 15; Jer 12:4).

Rain is an important theme in the Old Testament, because its absence is catastrophic.[58] Equally important, and a constant cause of concern, is the trustworthiness of God's prophets: if the prophets give the wrong advice, so that people act contrary to God's intentions, the consequences can also be disastrous.[59] Therefore, wrong information from the prophets is often described in strong terms: שקר is one of those terms, particularly in the book of Jeremiah (Isa 9:15; Jer 5:31; 7:4, 8; 14:14; 20:6; 23:32; 27:15; 29:9; Mic 2:11; Zech 13:3), as is שוא, especially in the book of Ezekiel who prefers the pair חזה שוא and קסם כזב (Ezek 12:24; 13:6, 7, 9, 23; 21:34; 22:28; Lam 2:14). Although I have not come across an instance in which און and הבל are used to designate prophetic words, these terms do occur, with the required meaning, as parallel terms for שקר and שוא (Jer 16:19; Hos 12:12).

The agreement between Zech 10:1–2 and Jeremiah 14 lies in the coincidence of two issues of great importance for daily life in Judah: rain and trustworthy prophets. The verbal agreements can be sufficiently explained by this thematic agreement; the thematic agreement alone is insufficient to prove literary dependence.

Jeremiah 14 shows that it is not prophecy *per se* that is criticized. The prophets (נבאים) who have predicted peace and prosperity are called liars whose predictions have proved false. Both they and the figure of Jeremiah are described as speaking in the name of Yahweh, but their words point in opposite directions. Prophecy as such is a good thing, but there are trustworthy prophets on the one hand and not so trustworthy prophets on the other. Characteristic of the latter category is that their predictions fail to come true, even if they are made in the name of Yahweh (cf. Deut 18:22).

A final remark concerns the referents of the 'shepherd' in v. 2. There, the prophet says that the people are in trouble, comparing them to a flock without a shepherd. In chapter 9 and in 10:3–12 the word 'shepherd' is used as the well-known metaphor for kings. Here, however, the context is not a political one, so that it seems unlikely that kings or other kinds of leaders are intended.[60] The image of the shepherdless flock is especially intended to symbolize the plight of the people who are receiving wrong information about God's intentions with regard to this year's late rain. They are being misled, like sheep which have no guidance or protection at all. The prophet may not have thought about any particular dignitary when he used the word 'shepherd'; his main intention was to point out that the people had no one to lead them into the proper direction, and were therefore on the track to destruction (cf. Num 27:17; Isa 63:11).

CONCLUSIONS

Zechariah 10:1–2 is best explained if it is *not* read within the context of chapters 9 and 10:3–12. It is a fragment without context, but its gist is quite clear: whereas the people are being told by some prophets (designated by referring to their various mantical techniques) that Yahweh will bring the rain normally due by the end of winter, this prophet is convinced that the rain will not come. The people's apparent failure to give credence to his warning, causes him to compare them with a flock of sheep, roaming around without a shepherd, that is, without guidance and protection.

The position of this fragment within Deutero-Zechariah is not entirely fortuitous: chapter 9 ends with an admittedly mysterious reference to agriculture, and 10:3–12 begins with mentioning shepherds. In this sense, Zech 10:1–2 might be considered transitional: the correspondences mentioned may have given the editor of these prophecies reason to arrange them in this way.

It can no longer be taken for granted that the editor responsible for the present arrangement believed them to cohere in any other way, or even whether he ascribed them to Zechariah. It is a well-known fact that the last book of the twelve prophets, Malachi, is in fact a collection of anonymous prophecies, formally divided from the preceding book only by the heading משא. The same heading occurs in Zech 9:1 and 12:1, and it has been suggested that from Zech 9:1 on, the volume of the minor prophets was supplemented by three collections of unascribed prophecies.[61]

Notwithstanding the fragmented character of Deutero-Zechariah and the obscure history of its compilation, it must be recognized that there is the distinct possibility that, as soon as the compilation was made, readers did regard them as a more or less coherent unity. The alternative possibility, however, should not be ruled out: there is precious little evidence from the ancient sources that anyone has ever tried to read the book of Zechariah as a coherent literary unity.[62] What people looked for in this obscure document, were prophecies which they deemed useful (the obscurer the better), and it does not seem that they even expected coherence.[63] Even in the ancient translations no apparent attempt is made to connect the various prophecies in a meaningful way.[64] Both the way in which Deutero-Zechariah was formed, and the way in which it used to be used gives cause to reconsider the usefulness of modern literary analyses of larger portions of this text rather than its brief constituent parts.

NOTES

1 Sæbø, 1969; cf. Tigchelaar, 1996, p. 91.
2 Lamarche, 1961.
3 Otzen, 1964; criticized by Butterworth, 1992, pp. 190–1.
4 Compare Floyd, 2000, pp. 305, 441.
5 Stade, 1881, pp. 41–96.
6 For example, Delcor, 1952.
7 For example, Nurmela, 1996.
8 Fishbane, 1985, p. 498.
9 Compare Sæbø, 1969, p. 214. Editorial unity is stressed by Chary, 1969, p. 139, but has little consequences for his interpretation of 10:1–2, on the function of which he merely comments: 'Cette petite section … est un appel à la fidélité, puis un regard en arrière, justifiant l'exil qui dure encore, enfin une transition vers la nouvelle annonce du salut' (p. 178).
10 Meyers and Meyers, 1993, p. 230.
11 Meyers and Meyers, 1993, p. 231.
12 Referring to Weis, 1986 (*non vidi*); for a description of Weis's understanding of *maśśā'*, see Floyd, 2000, pp. 306, 450–1, 631–2.
13 Floyd, 2000, pp. 308–9.

14 Floyd, 2000, p. 450; cf. his (theoretically perfectly sound) remark on the 'somewhat different generic components' of the *maśśā'* Zech 9:1–11:17: 'Such diversity in the component parts of a work does not necessarily mean that the work as a whole has no genre of its own, or that its pieces form only an anthology or collection' (p. 308).

15 Compare Tigchelaar, 1996, p. 89.

16 Against Meyers and Meyers, 1993, p. 230.

17 So also Tigchelaar, 1996, p. 92.

18 So also Marti, 1904, p. 433; Horst, 1964, p. 249; Rudolph, 1976, p. 191, and other mainly German language commentaries, most recently Reventlow, 1993, p. 100.

19 I shall now pass over proposals to see different connections, such as those which connect 10:1–2 to the preceding passages (Stade, 1881, pp. 19–20: 9:17–10:2; Lamarche, 1961, pp. 47–55: 9:11–10:1; 10:2–3a; Otzen, 1964, pp. 216–18: 9:16–10:3a; Van der Woude, 1984, pp. 162, 185: 9:1–10:2).

20 Hanson, 1975, pp. 325–34; similarly Gaide, 1968, pp. 23, 79–83.

21 Compare Nurmela, 1996, p. 114: 'Yahweh is referred to as the contrast to the idols (in Zc mainly practitioners of divination, etc.).'

22 Meyers and Meyers, 1993, p. 232.

23 Floyd, 2000, pp. 440–1.

24 Floyd, 2000, p. 443.

25 Floyd, 2000, p. 472: 'the unit takes a somewhat different turn at 10:1. Up to this point the emphasis has been on the people's joining Yahweh in his struggle against their external foes, but now the emphasis shifts to their joining his struggle against the internal threat of corrupt leadership.'

26 Chary, 1969, p. 177; Butterworth, 1992, p. 74.

27 Butterworth, 1992, p. 74.

28 Butterworth, 1992, p. 75.

29 Butterworth, 1992, pp. 74–5, referring to Mason, 1973, p. 96; Petersen, 1995, p. 70; cf. Lacocque, 1981, p. 163.

30 The Septuagint differs quite strongly from the Masoretic text in some instances: for 'the late rains' (מלקוש) it reads 'the early and late rains' (καθ' ὥραν πρόιμον καὶ ὄψιμον), a harmonization with Deut 11:14; חזיזים is rendered by φαντασίας, which may reflect a misunderstanding of the Hebrew as deriving from the root חזה, 'to see' (Jansma, 1950, p. 80); the phrase מטר גשם is rendered by 'winter rain'; the last word, רעה, is rendered by ἴασις, 'remedy', which may go back to a reading with the root רפא (Jansma, 1950, p. 83); in the other ancient Greek translations and the Syrohexapla, the reading ποιμήν is 'restored'. The word תרפים is rendered by ἀποφθεγγόμενοι, which may well be a correct interpretation (see below).

31 Jansma, 1950, p. 81; so also Otzen, 1964, p. 247; Van der Woude, 1984, p. 185; and Petersen, 1995, p. 69.

32 Marti, 1904, p. 433.

33 Duhm, 1911, p. 191.

34 Meyers and Meyers, 1993, p. 183, acknowledge that the expression מטר־גשם is 'unusual'; the reference to Job 37:6 is not helpful, however, because that passage is incomprehensible. To this proposal one may compare LXX, where ומטר גשם is connected to the last phrase (καὶ ὑετὸν χειμερινὸν δώσει αὐτοῖς).

35 Hanson, 1975, p. 324, translates לאיש עשב as 'to each of the plants'; however, the attributive use of pronominal איש is, to my knowledge, unattested (cf. Cowley, 1910, § 139b–c; Joüon, 1923, § 147d).

36 On כי, see Sæbø, 1969, pp. 209–10.

37 Or: 'and the dreams tell nonsense', but taking חלמות as the object, not as the subject, of ידברו is grammatically preferable; see Mitchell, 1912, p. 298. The alternatives make

little difference for the interpretation of these lines. On the switch from *qatal*-forms to *yiqtol*-forms (here, as in the next verse), see Joüon, 1923, § 113o.

38 This translation of נסעו is generally accepted. The conjectures proposed include נסו, 'they flee'; נעו, 'they are unstable, without home'; נתעו, 'they are broken' (see Kittel's edition). The root נסע means 'to break up camp', 'depart,' 'to move on' (so also LXX and Syr). The image seems to be that of sheep that are left on their own, each of them individually leaving the flock and wandering in stray directions.

39 Lacocque, 1981, p. 164; Van der Woude, 1984, p. 186; Van der Toorn, 1990; cf. *idem*, 1997.

40 Meyers and Meyers, 1993, pp. 184–7; Petersen, 1995, p. 72; and Floyd, 2000, pp. 472–3.

41 So often the Vulgate's rendering; here the Vulgate reads *simulacra*.

42 Schmidt, 1996, pp. 122–31.

43 For the designation *ilānu*, 'gods' for minor deities in Mesopotamian texts, see Van der Toorn, 1997, pp. 116–17, and cf. Porter, 2000, pp. 243–8.

44 Van der Toorn, 1997, pp. 114–18.

45 The Septuagint's ἀποφθεγγόμενοι, if it means 'prophets' (as in Mic 5:12 LXX; Ezek 13:9), might reflect this understanding of חרפים.

46 Petersen, 1995, p. 71, and Floyd, 2000, p. 472, suggest that שאלו in Zech 10:1 means 'to ask (namely, for rain)', but is also used to connote 'the making of an oracular inquiry'. This technical use of שאל indeed exists, but the construction with מן shows that this technical meaning is not intended in this instance.

47 For brevity's sake, I retain the crude term 'dream', although I am well aware of the much more refined categories developed by Husser, 1994.

48 Compare Husser, 1994, pp. 162–6.

49 Floyd, 2000, p. 472, understands the people's question to have been at what time the spring rains would come. However, that is unlikely to have been the question: everybody knew at what time the spring rains were supposed to come.

50 More exactly speaking, one could say that the prophet did not say 'yes', which in practice boils down to saying 'no'. Compare Huffmon, 1983, p. 356.

51 Husser, 1994, p. 159.

52 See especially Person, 1993, pp. 119–21; cf. Rudolph, 1976, p. 191.

53 So rightly Meyers and Meyers, 1993, p. 188.

54 Remarkably, Jeremiah 14 is absent from the 'liste quasi exhaustif' of allusions to other Biblical literature in Delcor, 1952, p. 387.

55 Mason, 1982a, p. 345; cf. *idem*, 1976, p. 235; Larkin, 1994, pp. 87–8.

56 Nurmela, 1996, pp. 114–19.

57 Larkin, 1994, pp. 88–9; cf. Ho Fai Tai, 1996, pp. 73–83.

58 Meyers and Meyers, 1993, p. 181.

59 Meyers and Meyers, 1993, p. 188; but cf. my comments above.

60 So Petersen, 1995, p. 72.

61 Stade, 1882, pp. 307–9; cf. Horst, 1964, p. 212; Hanson, 1975, pp. 292–3.

62 Barton, 1986, pp. 149–51.

63 Barton, 1986, p. 193.

64 Note that the connection of רעה in v. 2 and the same word in v. 3 was lost on the translator of the Septuagint or his *Vorlage*, enabling him to misread the first instance (see n. 30 above).

Chapter 5

The Septuagint of Zechariah as Witness to an Early Interpretation of the Book

Arie van der Kooij

This contribution concerns the issue of 'exegesis' in the Old Greek version of the book of Zechariah (LXX–Zechariah). To what extent or in which respect does LXX–Zechariah testify to early exegesis, and to which type of exegesis? A crucial question is, of course, *how* to find traces of exegesis. The method of analysis of the Greek version will be the subject matter of the first part of this paper. The second part will contain an application of the method described to a certain passage in LXX–Zechariah (9:9–10). Since the Greek version of this book is part of LXX–Minor Prophets (LXX–MP), which is to be regarded as the work of one translator,[1] LXX–Zechariah will be dealt with as part of LXX–MP.

METHOD OF ANALYSIS

In order to determine the characteristics of a version such as LXX–MP, it is useful, first of all, to analyse the style of translation (the translation technique).[2] On the basis of formal comparisons between MT and LXX, the Old Greek of MP turns out to be a literal translation, albeit not one of the books that have been rendered in a most literal or slavish way.[3] However, analyses of LXX books, such as the matter of word-order variations, are of limited value. Closer analysis is needed because the statement that a translation is literal in the sense of word order does not necessarily mean that the same version is also literal as far the aspect of lexical equivalence is concerned. A translation can be 'at the same time quite literal regarding word order and quite free regarding lexical equivalence'.[4] Or to mention another aspect, a translation can be literal regarding word order, but this does not say anything about the equivalence on the level of syntax. It may well be that on closer analysis the same word order appears to reflect an interpretation of the Hebrew text which differs syntactically from its Masoretic form. Although LXX–MP can be classified as a literal translation, at the same time it is one of the books in the LXX that is characterized by lexical variety.[5] To give two examples:

- Hebrew מצבה has been rendered as θυσιαστήριον in Hos 3:4, and as στήλη in Hos 10:1,2; Mic 5:13
- Hebrew תרפים has been rendered as δήλοι in Hos 3:4, and as ἀποφθεγγόμενοι in Zech 10:2.

The approach which provides a closer analysis of LXX in comparison with MT (and Qumran) might be termed philological. Examples of this are the articles by T. Muraoka on LXX–Hosea and the volumes of *La Bible d'Alexandrie*, the annotated French translation of LXX books.[6] Its great advantage is that matters of grammar and of lexical equivalences are studied in more detail, including the issue of the underlying Hebrew text.[7] This approach can help us find an answer to the question of what the LXX text might mean (in comparison to MT) on the level of words, sentences, and even pericopes,[8] and, secondly, what might have been the reason for a different reading (another *Vorlage*, or harmonization with another passage).

However, in order to reach a broader understanding of a version such as LXX–MP in its historical and cultural context there are two basic questions:

1 Who were the translators, that is to say, to which groups in society did they belong in ancient Judaism?
2 Which mode of reading regarding prophecies was prevalent in their time?

It is true, as J. Joosten states: 'Not every prima facie divergence of the Septuagint with regard to the MT is to be interpreted as a pointer to the culture, the opinions or the beliefs of the translators',[9] but in order to prevent prima facie judgements it is important to express our views on the translators, because our picture of them has a bearing on the weighing of the evidence. The same applies to the issue of the genre of the text. In the case of prophecies, the question arises of how they were read and interpreted at that time and this too has a bearing on the evaluation of the evidence.

The translator as scholar-scribe

Although the translators of Biblical books have much in common with professional dragomans (e.g., dragomans at court), the available evidence points to the milieu where the Biblical books were read and studied, that is, the milieu of scribes and scholars in ancient Judaism.[10] In my view, the translators belonged to a literate and learned group of people, just like scholars such as Jesus ben Sira[11] and his grandson, translator of the work of his grandfather. Like professional dragomans of the time, the scribe-translator was a learned person who mastered two (or more) languages, thus being able to produce a translation, either orally or in writing. (The first chapter of Daniel offers a good example of learned, bilingual Jews, namely, Daniel and his friends at the court of Babylon: see vv. 4, 17.) Moreover, as a scribe he was familiar with matters of content and of interpretation of the Biblical book involved. It means, in principle, that he did not produce his translation on an ad hoc basis, nor intuitively (Helsinki school), but as one acquainted with the Biblical text he was going to translate.

In being a Jewish scribe of that time he had recourse to a set of devices by which he was able to interpret words and phrases in a way which, in some respects, is incompatible with our modern philological approach.[12] Furthermore, as a scribe he was trained in the reading of Biblical texts, and as a result he was familiar with a reading tradition. I am not stating 'the' reading tradition because, given the pluriformity within ancient Judaism, in particular cases the same Hebrew text could be, and actually was, read and interpreted in various ways. Be that as it may, from the perspective of the model of the scribe-translator it is more plausible to regard specific renderings which differ from MT (e.g., regarding vocalization, or syntactical interpretation of the text) as part of the reading and interpretation of the text that was current in the milieu of the translator rather than to regard them as misunderstandings, or errors. It all means that a text like LXX–MP actually marks a moment in the reception history of the (or, a) Hebrew text of the Minor Prophets.

The mode of reading of prophecies

My second question concerns the way the prophecies in the Biblical books were read and understood in scribal circles in Early Judaism, in the second and first centuries BCE. Presumably because of the dramatic events in the first part of the second century BCE, a growing interest in both the Law and the Prophets is apparent among Jewish priests and scribes of that time. In one way or another the ancient prophecies were considered to be a source of hope, which was based on a reading and interpretation of these prophecies as referring to events of the age in which the reader/interpreter was living.[13]

One of the earliest passages that reflects this attitude and interest is found in Ben Sira 36:13–20:

> Gather all the tribes of Jacob
> that they may inherit the land as in days of old.
> Show mercy to the people called by your name:
> Israel, whom you named your firstborn.
> Take pity on your holy city,
> Jerusalem, the foundation for your throne.
> Fill Zion with your majesty,
> your temple with your glory.
> Give evidence of your deeds of old;
> fulfil the prophecies spoken in your name,
> reward those who have hoped in you,
> and let your prophets be proved true.

This part of the prayer in ch. 36 contains motifs well known from the prophetic literature: the return of the tribes of Jacob to the land, and the restoration of Jerusalem and its temple. The author urgently pleads with God to rescue his people by fulfilling the prophecies, or visions. It is clear from the passage cited that the ancient prophecies in question were seen as predictions which had not yet been fulfilled, although the hope is given expression that the time of their fulfilment may be close at hand. This implies that the prophecies were envisaged as being still to be trusted as predictive revelations.

Another passage that offers a clear illustration of the interest in the words of the prophets is found in Tobit 14:3–5. It reads in translation as follows (according to the longer version[14]):

> (3) When he [Tobit] was dying, he sent for his son Tobias and gave him these instructions:
> 'My son, you must take your children
> (4) and be off to Media with all haste,
> for I believe God's word spoken against Nineveh by Nahum.
> It will all come true; everything will happen to Asshur and Nineveh that was spoken by the prophets of Israel who were sent by God. Not a word of it will fall short; all will take place in due time.
> It will be safer in Media than in Assyria and Babylon.
> I know, I am convinced, that all God's words will be fulfilled. It will be so; not one of them will fail.
> Our countrymen who live in Israel will all be scattered and carried off into captivity out of that good land. The whole of Israel's territory with Samaria and Jerusalem will lie waste; and for a time the house of God will be in mourning, burnt to the ground.
> (5) But God will have mercy on them again and will bring them back to the land of Israel.
> They will rebuild the house of God, yet not as it was at first,
> not until the time of fulfilment comes.
> Then they will all return from their captivity and rebuild Jerusalem in splendour; then indeed God's house will be built in her as the prophets of Israel foretold.'

It strikes one how strongly the reliability of the words of the prophets is emphasized in this passage by Tobit in his last words. It betrays a strong interest in the issue of the prophecies and their fulfilment on the part of the author of this passage in the book.[15] The passage discerns three stages in history:

- the time of the destruction of Nineveh (fulfilment of the prophecy of Nahum), and the time of the exile and of destruction in the land of Israel, including Jerusalem
- the (first) return and the rebuilding of the temple
- the time of the fulfilment of the prophecies (of salvation).

It is interesting to see that the rebuilding of the temple in v. 5a, presumably under Zerubbabel and Joshua, is not regarded as the fulfilment of prophecies: the temple was rebuilt at that time, but 'not as it was at first' (οὐχ ὡς τὸν πρῶτον).[16] Instead, 'afterwards, then' (μετὰ ταῦτα) the city of Jerusalem will be rebuilt gloriously, and the temple in her, 'as the prophets of Israel foretold about her' (καθὼς ἐλάλησαν περὶ αὐτῆς οἱ προφῆται τοῦ Ισραηλ). Also it is clear that the oracles of salvation were seen as predictions of events long after the period of the exile. It seems likely that the fulfilment passage refers to events in the present and the near future of the author.[17]

Another passage that testifies clearly to the interest in the question of how to apply ancient prophecies to the time of the second century BCE is of course Daniel 9. Daniel, the wise, is 'inquiring into the books' (v. 2) 'in the hope of discerning the correct application of Jeremiah's seventy-year oracle concerning the period of Jerusalem's desolation'.[18] From the answer given by the *angelus interpres* in vv. 24–27 it is evident that the underlying concern is the question of how to relate the seventy-year oracle in the book of Jeremiah to particular events in the second century BCE.

As is well known regarding the reading of the ancient prophecies as predictions of events in the second and first centuries BCE, the findings in the caves of Qumran have yielded impressive evidence of this type of exegesis. In 1QpHab, one of the major examples of the *pesher*-literature, it is made explicit that the prophecy of

Habakkuk was looked upon as not yet fulfilled, because its author, the prophet Habakkuk himself, did not know when the end of the age would be, in which the predicted events were supposed to happen. It was 'the Teacher of Righteousness, to whom God has disclosed all the mysteries of the words of his servants, the prophets' (7:4–5). He is seen as the one who was able and authorized to apply the prophecies of Habakkuk to events in his time.

Thus, in the Hellenistic period the mode of reading prophecies as predictions about the past, the present and the near future of the reader/interpreter was the prevailing one in early Judaism. As far as the Minor Prophets are concerned, we have also clear evidence from Qumran: the surviving fragments of the *pesher*-literature show that the Minor Prophets were of major interest to the Qumran community. The evidence concerns Hosea, Micha, Nahum, and Habakkuk.

Before turning to LXX–MP, and more in particular to LXX–Zechariah, I would like to point out that, in the literature referred to above, two different models of fulfilment-interpretation are to be distinguished. Both have in common that ancient prophecies in the sense of predictions were understood as referring to the present and near future of its reader/interpreter. Yet there is a clear difference between the *pesher*-method of Qumran and the way words of the prophets are interpreted in a text such as Tobit 14. The latter reflects the idea that prophecies of doom, such as regarding Nineveh (Nahum) and the exile of Israel, have come true in the past, whereas the prophecies of salvation concerning Jerusalem will be fulfilled much later, in any case later than the time of Zerubbabel and Joshua (cf. Daniel 9). The *pesher*-method testifies to a different model: here *all* the words of the prophets, words of doom and words of salvation as well, are being applied to the *recent* past, present, and near future of its interpreter. In Tobit 14 Nahum's prophecy about Nineveh is understood as prediction of the destruction of this famous city by the Medes, long ago, whereas in 4QpNahum this city is taken as a cipher for Jerusalem as the city of 'the seekers of smooth things', a group of people in the time of the interpreter.

LXX–ZECHARIAH

Since this conference concerns both OT and NT, it seemed appropriate to focus on a passage in LXX–Zechariah that has been quoted in the NT. I had been thinking of Zech 12:10, the passage about 'the one whom they have pierced', which is cited in John 19:37, but this did not work out well because of the fact that 'the pierced one' is not found in LXX. Surprisingly, the Greek text is about 'dancing' (ἀνθ' ὧν κατωρχήσαντο) instead of being pierced. Another text one would have liked to consider, because it has been quoted in Matt 26:36 and Mark 14:27, is Zech 13:7 where it is said, 'Strike the shepherd', but here again the LXX presents a different text ('shepherds', plural, and not singular). Let us therefore discuss the passage about the king riding on an ass, Zech 9:9–10, a passage quoted in Matt 21:5 and John 12:15. In line with the above I will approach this text, beside issues of a text-critical and philological nature, from the perspective of the model of scribe-translator and from that of the mode of reading prophecies at the time of the translator (second century BCE).

Zechariah 9:9–10

MT	LXX
גילי מאד בת ציון	χαῖρε σφόδρα θύγατερ Σιων
הריעי בת ירושלם	κήρυσσε θύγατερ Ιερουσαλημ
הנה מלכך יבוא לך	ἰδοὺ ὁ βασιλεύς σου ἔρχεταί σοι
צדיק ונושע הוא	δίκαιος καὶ σῴζων αὐτός
עני ורכב על חמור	πραῢς καὶ ἐπιβεβηκὼς ἐπὶ ὑποζύγιον
ועל עיר בן אתנות	καὶ πῶλον νέον
והכרתי רכב מאפרים	καὶ ἐξολεθρεύσει ἅρματα ἐξ Εφραιμ
וסוס מירושלם	καὶ ἵππον ἐξ Ιερουσαλημ
ונכרתה קשת מלחמה	καὶ ἐξολεθρευθήσεται τόξον πολεμικόν
ודבר שלום לגוים	καὶ πλῆθος καὶ εἰρήνη ἐξ ἐθνῶν
ומשלו מים עד ים	καὶ κατάρξει ὑδάτων ἕως θαλάσσης
ומנהר עד אפסי ארץ	καὶ ποταμῶν διεκβολὰς γῆς

MT: Rejoice greatly, O daughter of Zion! Shout aloud, O daughter of Jerusalem! Behold, your king comes to you, righteous and saved he is, humble and riding on an donkey, on a colt, the foal of a donkey. I will cut off the chariot from Ephraim and the war horse from Jerusalem; and the battle bow shall be cut off, and he shall proclaim peace to the nations; his dominion shall be from sea to sea, and from the River to the ends of the earth.

LXX: Rejoice greatly, O daughter of Zion! Proclaim it aloud, O daughter of Jerusalem! Behold, your king comes to you, just and saving he is, modest and mounted on a ass, and a young foal. He shall destroy the chariots from Ephraim and the horse out of Jerusalem; and the bow of war shall be utterly destroyed, and there shall be a large crowd and peace from the nations; and he shall rule the waters as far as the sea, and the rivers to the ends of the earth.

As a whole, the Greek version of both verses is fairly close to the MT, but on closer inspection there are renderings which invite comment. The Greek κηρύσσω as equivalent of the Hiphil of Hebrew רוע is not a common one in LXX; it is only attested in LXX–MP (Hos 5:8; Joel 2:1; Zeph 3:14). Regarding the reading נושע in MT, which is best understood as 'saved'[19] (cf. Deut 33:29 LXX σωζόμενος; see also Ps 33:16), LXX offers the participle active σῴζων, which might reflect Hebrew מושע. This difference creates a different picture: while the MT is about a humble king being saved by God, LXX reflects the idea of a king who will be saving.[20] The rendering πῶλον νέον may well be considered a free translation of Hebrew עיר בן אתנות as far as the second part of the expression is concerned ('young' as interpretation of בן אתנות). For πῶλος as equivalent of עיר, see, e.g., Gen 49:11. The notion of 'young' may well carry the idea of a foal which no one has yet ridden, as Mark 11:2 puts it. (Compare also passages such as 1 Sam 6:7 and 2 Sam 6:3.)

The first verb in MT v. 10 is first person sing. ('I will cut off'), but LXX has third person singular, 'he (the king) shall destroy'. Contextually speaking, the first person fits in with the Niphal form נושע, in the sense of being saved by God: He will save by cutting off the chariots and the war horses (cf. Mic 5:9). The third person in LXX, however, is in line with the idea that the king is the one who saves; he will destroy the chariots from Ephraim and the war horse from Jerusalem.

In the last part of v. 10 the Hebrew expression 'from … to …' has not been rendered literally,[21] but the Greek text conveys the same meaning as the Hebrew; it refers to the worldwide rule of the king. For the expression κατάρχω ὑδάτων, see LXX–Nahum 1:12 where it is said of God κατάρχων ὑδάτων πολλῶν (MT is different here).

A more intriguing difference concerns the clause which in MT reads 'and he shall proclaim peace to the nations'; LXX: 'and (there shall be) a large crowd and peace from (the) nations'. How to interpret this part of the LXX text? Does the word πλῆθος carry the meaning 'large crowd' here as T. Muraoka assumes, or should it be taken in the sense of large quantity of goods (cf. LXX–Micha 2:13; Zech 14:14)?[22] And how to explain the differences between MT and LXX? One could argue that LXX testifies to a divergent Hebrew text, namely, ורב ושלום מגוים. However, this does not help us any further because the question remains what this text might mean, apart from the fact that the resulting collocation has no parallel in the Hebrew Bible.

As to the meaning of the LXX phrase as it stands, one wonders whether there are other related passages in LXX–MP which may shed light on it. In my view, two passages are of interest here: LXX–Zech 8:22 and 14:16.

> 8:22
> καὶ ἥξουσι λαοὶ πολλοὶ καὶ ἔθνη πολλὰ
> ἐκζητῆσαι τὸ πρόσωπον κυρίου παντοκράτορος ἐν Ιερουσαλημ
> καὶ τοῦ ἐξιλάσκεσθαι τὸ πρόσωπον κυρίου
> (cf. MT)
>
> 14:16
> καὶ ἔσται ὅσοι ἐὰν καταλειφθῶσιν
> ἐκ πάντων τῶν ἐθνῶν τῶν ἐλθόντων ἐπὶ Ιερουσαλημ
> καὶ ἀναβήσονται κατ' ἐνιαυτὸν
> τοῦ προσκυνῆσαι τῷ βασιλεῖ κυρίῳ παντοκράτορι
> καὶ τοῦ ἑορτάζειν τὴν ἑορτὴν τῆς σκηνοπηγίας
> (cf. MT)

Both texts have a particular motif in common, namely, that many nations (8:22), or 'all who will be left from the nations' (14:16), shall go to Jerusalem to seek or to worship the Lord. The latter passage in particular sheds light on our text as far as the πλῆθος from the nations is concerned; it therefore is likely to take the Greek πλῆθος here in the sense of 'large crowd' of people.[23]

But what about the 'peace from the nations'? This element of the LXX clause also makes good sense if read in the light of one of the texts just mentioned, Zech 14:16, and its immediate context (vv. 12–15). Verse 16 is about all those who will be left from the nations that have come against Jerusalem. The latter part of the verse refers to what is stated in v. 12: the Lord will smite all the nations that have waged war against Jerusalem. There is a contrast between v. 12 and v. 16: unlike the nations in v. 12, those from them that will seek the Lord in Jerusalem will do so in peace, not in war.

Although, admittedly, the LXX clause is a rather cryptic phrase, if read in the light of both passages elsewhere in the book of Zechariah, it makes good sense: at the time when the king has come to Zion and has saved Ephraim and the city of Jerusalem by destroying the chariots and the war horses, a large number of people from the nations will come to Jerusalem to seek and to worship the Lord, and they will do so in peace.

There is another passage in LXX–MP which I would like to mention in this connection, LXX–Amos 9:11–12:

MT	LXX
ביום ההוא	ἐν τῃ ἡμέρᾳ ἐκείνῃ
אקים את סכת דויד	ἀναστήσω τὴν σκηνὴν Δαυιδ
הנפלת	τὴν πεπτωκυῖαν
וגדרתי את פרציהן	καὶ ἀνοικοδομήσω τὰ πεπτωκότα αὐτῆς
והרסתיו אקים	καὶ τὰ κατεσκαμμένα αὐτῆς ἀναστήσω
ובניתתיה	καὶ ἀνοικοδομήσω αὐτὴν
כימי עולם	καθὼς αἱ ἡμέραι τοῦ αἰῶνος
למען יירשו	ὅπως ἐκζητήσωσιν
את שארית אדום	οἱ κατάλοιποι τῶν ἀνθρώπων
וכל הגוים	καὶ πάντα τὰ ἔθνη
אשר נקרא שמי עליהם	ἐφ' οὓς ἐπικέκληται τὸ ὄνομά μου ἐπ' αὐτούς
נאם יהוה עשה זאת	λέγει κύριος ὁ ποιῶν ταῦτα

Instead of MT v. 12, 'that they may possess the remnant of Edom …' the LXX reads 'that the remnant of men may seek (me), …'. B.A. Jones holds the view that the underlying Hebrew, reconstructed by him as למען ידרשו שארית אדם, attests a text which is primary to MT.[24] For the use of דרש he points to Amos 5:4ff., for the use of שארית to Amos 1:8 and 5:15, whereas the universal perspective is in line with Amos 9:7. '… Unlike the MT text of Amos 9:12, the LXX reading is literally well integrated into its immediate context' (p. 189). Beside the fact that the occurrences of the terms mentioned elsewhere in the book of Amos do not say so much, the main difficulty with his view is that the collocation שארית אדם is unusual and strange; in the book of Amos, and elsewhere, the first word occurs in combination with a particular people (1:8: Philistines, and 5:15: Joseph), and never with the notion of mankind. As I have argued elsewhere, the rendering in LXX is best understood as an interpretation in line with Zech 14:16 ('all who will be left from the nations').[25] The expression 'the tent of David' in the LXX seems to refer to the city of David, Jerusalem (compare Isa 1:8; 16:5; 54:2).[26] The idea is that when this city, including the temple, will be rebuilt, the remnant of men, and the nations, will come in order to seek the Lord. Just as in the case of LXX–Zech 9:10, this text attests the motif of nations that will seek the Lord in Jerusalem.

So far the discussion is of the intriguing clause in LXX–Zech 9:9–10. The interpretative relationship between this passage and other texts in LXX–Zechariah (8:22; 14:16) and in the rest of LXX–MP (Amos 9:11–12) as well, testifies to a translator who, as a scribe, was well acquainted with the book of the Minor Prophets as a whole.

Let us now turn to the second aspect of the method of analysis as outlined above, the mode of reading prophecies at the time of the translator. In view of the great interest of scribes and scholars in ancient prophecies as a source of hope at that time, it is my contention that the scribe-translator of MP considered our passage to be a prediction of events in the end time, a period of history which he believed to live in. Admittedly, one cannot prove this, but I venture this reading of our text on the basis of some related passages, both inside and outside LXX–MP. One of these passages is LXX–Hosea 3:4–5:

MT	LXX
כי ימים רבים	διότι ἡμέρας πολλὰς
ישבו בני ישראל	καθήσονται οἱ υἱοὶ Ισραηλ
אין מלך ואין שר	οὐκ ὄντος βασιλέως οὐδὲ ὄντος ἄρχοντος
ואין זבח	οὐδὲ οὔσης θυσίας
ואין מצבה	οὐδὲ ὄντος θυσιαστηρίου
ואין אפוד ותרפים	οὐδὲ ἱερατείας οὐδὲ δήλων
אחר	καὶ μετὰ ταῦτα
ישבו בני ישראל	ἐπιστρέψουσιν οἱ υἱοὶ Ισραηλ
ובקשו את יהוה	καὶ ἐπιζητήσουσι κύριον
אלהיהם	τὸν θεὸν αὐτῶν
ואת דוד מלכם	καὶ Δαυιδ τὸν βασιλέα αὐτῶν
ופחדו אל יהוה	καὶ ἐκστήσονται ἐπὶ τῷ κυρίῳ
ואל טובו	καὶ ἐπὶ τοῖς ἀγαθοῖς αὐτοῦ
באחרית הימים	ἐπ' ἐσχάτων τῶν ἡμερῶν

Verse 5 has an important element in common with Zech 9:9, namely, the figure of a king, in Hosea called 'David their king'. According to v. 5, the Israelites will return 'afterwards' (μετὰ ταῦτα) and they will seek the Lord and David their king, etc. The question is how this verse was understood by our scribe-translator. The expression 'afterwards' marks the end of a period described in v. 4, a long period in which the Israelites will live without king, without sacrifice, altar, priesthood, and manifestations (so LXX). The remarkable thing is that LXX offers here a number of quite unusual equivalents.[27] For instance, LXX has 'manifestations' for Hebrew '*terafim*'. This rendering refers to the Urim (see MT/LXX–Num 27:21) or the Thummim (cf. MT/LXX Deut 33:8), used by priests as a device for divination. Whatever the meaning and connotations of terms like '*massebah*' and '*terafim*' in MT may have been in its original setting (concerning Northern Israel), our translator clearly preferred renderings carrying a positive connotation. In the Greek text as it stands, the cultic terms used are best understood as pertaining to the temple cult in Jerusalem.

The question is whether v. 4 was taken to refer to the period of the Babylonian exile (including possibly the earlier Assyrian exile) in which Israel lived without king and temple, or whether it was understood by the translator and his colleagues as referring to a much longer period of life in exile, or diaspora, even extending to the first half of the second century BCE, in line with the underlying idea in Tobit 14:3–5. There is reason to believe that the latter was the case. An interesting parallel is to be found in LXX–Daniel 3:37–38:

ὅτι δέσποτα ἐσμικρύνθημεν παρὰ πάντα τὰ ἔθνη
καί ἐσμεν ταπεινοὶ ἐν πάσῃ τῇ γῇ σήμερον
διὰ τὰς ἁμαρτίας ἡμῶν
καὶ οὐκ ἔστιν ἐν τῷ καιρῷ τούτῳ
ἄρχων καὶ προφήτης οὐδὲ ἡγούμενος
οὐδὲ ὁλοκαύτωσις οὐδὲ θυσία
οὐδὲ προσφορὰ οὐδὲ θυμίαμα
οὐδὲ τόπος τοῦ καρπῶσαι ἐνωπίον σου
καὶ εὑρεῖν ἔλεος

This passage is part of the prayer of Azariah in the furnace, not attested in MT. Strictly speaking within the setting of the Daniel story, this passage refers to the situation of the Babylonian exile, but having been produced in the second century BCE it is plausible to assume that it was also meant to refer to events in that time, in particular to the profanation of the temple under Antiochus IV.[28]

There is another element which points in the same direction. The beginning of v. 5 in LXX–Hosea 3 reads 'and afterwards the Israelites will return' (καὶ μετὰ ταῦτα ἐπιστρέψουσιν οἱ υἱοὶ Ισραηλ). It is to be noted that the same phrase is found in Tobit 14:5b: 'Afterwards they will all return from their captivitiy' (καὶ μετὰ ταῦτα ἐπιστρέψουσιν ἐκ τῆς αἰχμαλωσίας πάντες), including the expression μετὰ ταῦτα which belongs to eschatological idiom.[29] Although some had returned at the time of Zerubbabel (cf. Tobit 14:5a), many 'Israelites' were still outside the land, living spread all over the world. As Tobit 14:5b attests, there was a strong belief in Jewish circles that *all* Israelites would return at some time in the near future, 'as the prophets had foretold'. (For the idea of the 'near' future, see 2 Macc 2:18, a passage which constitutes the end of a letter about the purification of the temple after the crisis under Antiochus IV: 'We have confidence that God will *soon* (ταχέως) show us compassion and gather us from everywhere under heaven to the holy place'. See also Ben Sira 36:10.)

Thus, there is reason to believe that the passages such as Hos 3:5, Amos 9:11–12 and Zech 9:9–10 have been read and interpreted by the LXX translator as predictions about events in his time, as well as events hoped for in the near future. The passage in Tobit 14 turns out to be of particular interest. Several motifs, the restoration of the city (LXX–Amos 9), and of the temple cult (LXX–Hosea 3 and LXX–Amos 9, in both instances implicitly), the return of the Israelites (LXX–Hosea 3), and the coming of the nations in order to seek the Lord in Jerusalem (LXX–Amos 9; cf. LXX–Zech 9:10), are also found in Tobit 14:5–6 (for the notion of the nations, see v. 6: 'All the nations in the whole world will be converted in the true worship of God'; see also Tobit 13:13).

The motif of a royal figure (LXX–Zech 9:9–10; see also LXX–Hosea 3:5), however, is not found in Tobit 14, but regarding this element, another contemporaneous writing, 1 Maccabees, is of great interest, the more so because of specific points of textual agreements between this writing and LXX–MP (see below). The royal figure of LXX–Zech 9, who will save Israel and Jerusalem from enemies (v. 9: 'He shall destroy the chariots from Ephraim and the horse out of Jerusalem'), fits the picture of Maccabean leaders as presented in 1 Maccabees. This applies in particular to Simon, because he is depicted as the leader who saved Israel from the enemies in the land, including the occupants of the citadel at Jerusalem (1 Macc 13–14; see, e.g., 14:36: 'In his time and under his leadership the nations were successfully evicted from the land; so too were those who had occupied the City of David in Jerusalem').

One might raise the objection that, in 1 Maccabees, Simon is not designated as 'king' (the term used in Zech 9), but as 'leader and high priest' (ἡγούμενος καὶ ἀρχιερεύς, 1 Macc 14:41). However, this does not constitute a real problem. The ideology involved in 1 Maccabees is that of the 'priestly monarchy', with an emphasis on the aspect of monarchy.[30] Simon, the high priest, although not being referred to as 'king', also had royal authority as 'leader' of the Jewish nation. The Maccabean leaders, Simon in particular, are portrayed, in the words of D.W. Rooke, 'in terms of the Davidic monarchy'.[31] (It is to be noted that these leaders were not considered as royal figures in the sense of descendants of David, but in the sense of leaders *like* David and Solomon.[32])

The reign of Simon is described in 1 Maccabees as a time of peace, a time of recognition by the nations, and most importantly, it is presented as a time in which prophecies of salvation for Israel came true (1 Macc 14:4–15). Interestingly, some of the verses in this passage correspond to the wording, or to clauses, in LXX–MP. As to v. 9 (πρεσβύτεροι ἐν ταῖς πλατείαις ἐκάθηντο), see LXX–Zech 8:4 (ἔτι καθήσονται πρεσβύτεροι καὶ πρεσβύτεραι ἐν ταῖς πλατείαις Ιερουσαλημ), and as to v. 12 (καὶ ἐκάθισεν ἕκαστος ὑπὸ τὴν ἄμπελον καὶ τὴν συχῆν αὐτοῦ καὶ οὐκ ἦν ὁ ἐκφοβῶν αὐτούς), see LXX–Micha 4:4 (καὶ ἀναπαύσεται ἕκαστος ὑποκάτω ἀμπέλου αὐτοῦ καὶ ἕκαστος ὑποκάτω συχῆς αὐτοῦ, καὶ οὐκ ἔσται ὁ ἐκφοβῶν). (For another case of close correspondence, see 1 Macc 5:15 [… καὶ Τύρου καὶ Σιδῶνος καὶ πᾶσαν Γαλιλαίαν ἀλλοφύλων] and LXX–Joel 4:4 [Τύρος καὶ Σιδὼν καὶ πᾶσα Γαλιλαία ἀλλοφύλων].)

CONCLUSION

In the above, the passage of LXX–Zech 9:9–10 has been interpreted by weighing the evidence from two perspectives: first, that of the model of scribe-translator, and second, that of the prevailing mode of reading prophecies in scribal circles at that time. As it turned out, related passages in LXX–MP were important for a better understanding of the passage in LXX–Zechariah, as well as passages such as Tobit 14:3–6. The latter reflects a mode of reading prophecies that, in my view, also applies to LXX–MP, whereas the fulfilment interpretation as attested in 4QpNahum is of a different type.

The Old Greek of Zech 9:9–10 represents a version which is fairly literal. Yet the scribe-translator made a version of this passage which differs from the MT in some respects. He did so in order to create not only a stronger coherence within LXX–MP, but also to produce a text that served the interests of the prophecy as prediction.

In the light of interesting points of contact between LXX–MP and 1 Maccabees, there is reason to believe that the passage in Zech 9 was understood by the translator, and his milieu, as a prediction of Simon, the Maccabean leader of whom it is said 'In his time and under his leadership the nations were succesfully evicted from the land; so too were those who had occupied the City of David in Jerusalem' (1 Macc 14:36).

As may be noted finally, a parallel of the type of translation and interpretation, as outlined above, is to be found in the Vulgate of Zech 9:9–10. This version too is fairly literal, but the choice of 'salvator' (as rendering of the Hebrew נושע) is part of a particular (Christian) reading of this prophecy. In this case too the translator was a scholar, and prophecies like this one were considered by him as predictions which asked for a fulfilment interpretation.

NOTES

1 See Ziegler, 1971; Muraoka, 1989, 2002, pp. ix–x.
2 For older studies on LXX–MP, see Jansma, 1950, pp. 35–7.

3 See, e.g., Sollamo, 1979, pp. 280ff.; Wright, 1989, pp. 46–50.
4 Wright, 1989, p. 28. On the issue of how to evaluate lexical consistency, see Wade, 2000.
5 See Ziegler, 1971, pp. 8–11; *La Bible d'Alexandrie 23.4–9: Les Douze Prophètes: Joël, Abdiou, Jonas, Naoum, Ambakoum, Sophonie*, Paris: Du Cerf, 1999, pp. 184–5.
6 Muraoka, 1983, 1995; *La Bible d'Alexandrie: Osée*, and *La Bible d'Alexandrie: Joël* etc.
7 An interesting aspect in this regard concerns the cases in which a Greek equivalent seems to reflect the influence of late Biblical Hebrew, or Aramaic. See Joosten, 2001.
8 See Dogniez, 1998.
9 Joosten, 1998, p. 64.
10 See Van der Kooij, 1998a, 1998b.
11 See, e.g., Blenkinsopp, 1995, pp. 15–20.
12 For an example of this, see Weissert, 1973.
13 Compare Barton, 1986, pp. 179–213; Van der Kooij, 1998a, pp. 88–94.
14 Compare the evidence from Qumran: see, e.g., 4Q198 (4QTobit^{c} ar), a fragment containing a few words of Tobit 14:2–6. See DJD XIX, Oxford: Clarendon Press, 1995, pp. 57–9.
15 M. Rabenau has argued, on good grounds, that a passage such as 14:3b–7 is to be regarded as an addition, dating to the second half of the second century BC (Rabenau, 1994, pp. 188–9). Usually, the book as a whole is dated c. 200 BCE; see, e.g., Ego, 1999, p. 900.
16 Compare Ezra 3:12.
17 Compare Rabenau, 1994, pp. 188–9.
18 Fishbane, 1985, p. 482.
19 On this issue, see Van der Woude, 1984, p. 174, and Larkin, 1994, p. 68.
20 For a recent discussion of Zech 9:9 (MT), see Leske, 2000 (with lit.), and Sweeney, 2000, p. 664.
21 For a literal rendering, see LXX–Ps 71:8 (ἀπὸ … ἕως).
22 See Muraoka, 1993, p. 193.
23 For the expression πλῆθος ἐκ, see LXX–Exod 19:21 and 1 Macc 5:12.
24 Jones, 1985, pp. 186–9.
25 Van der Kooij, 1989.
26 Van der Kooij, 1989, p. 55.
27 See Muraoka, 1995, pp. 247–8. See also *La Bible d'Alexandrie: Osée*, pp. 81–2.
28 Compare Collins, 1993, p. 201.
29 Compare Van der Kooij, 2002, p. 139.
30 On this concept, see Goodblatt, 1994, pp. 30–56.
31 Rooke, 2000, p. 299.
32 It is to be noted that Simon as depicted in 1 Maccabees resembles Solomon in many respects; see Schenker, 2000, pp. 159–61.

Chapter 6

The Use of Zechariah in Matthew's Gospel

Paul Foster

The fourth appendix to the 27th edition of the Nestlé-Aland Greek New Testament (NA27) lists the scriptural allusions and citations from the Old Testament and Apocrypha that are contained in the various NT books.[1] Under the Zechariah subheading there are fifteen references to Matthew's gospel.[2] Twelve of these references are classed as allusions and the other three are listed as direct citations (distinguished by giving the Matthean reference in italicized typeface for the latter category).[3] On the whole the distinction is fairly self-explanatory when one looks at the level of correspondence between such OT texts and their use in the gospel of Matthew. Only at one point will the NA27 classification be called into question, that is in regard to the use of Zech 11:12 in Matt 26:15, which it will be argued is better taken as a citation rather than an allusion to the OT passage in question. However, what will be questioned is the value of the allusions category as a whole.

Obviously, the distinction between citations and allusions is problematic, as is the definition of these two terms. Stanley notes that part of this confusion arises at a methodological level and even in regard to the category of citations alone he states, 'Even the fundamental question of what constitutes a "citation" (as over against, say, a paraphrase or an allusion) receives almost no theoretical examination in the standard studies on the subject.'[4] Yet, it needs to be stated from the outset the use of the OT by the writers of the NT does not fall into an easy dichotomy of citation and allusion. Perhaps the formula quotations are the closest thing we have to a modern citation given in quotation marks and fully referenced, but it would be an unnecessary stricture to say that this is the only legitimate form of the category of citations. The distinctions are of course blurred at a number of points, the way the OT is used is better seen as being on a continuum ranging from exact verbal affinity to very free rendering. However, some limits must be drawn.

It seems not without justification to require some level of verbal affinity in order to claim that a NT text is dependent upon some passage in the OT. Thompson understandably bemoans the lack of precision on the part of scholars in their quest for NT allusions. While his definition of a 'quotation' may be too narrow, requiring the presence of an explicit citation formula, nonetheless he does make the important point that allusions should be taken as 'statements which are *intended* to remind an audience of a tradition they are presumed to know'.[5] This cannot be done simply in terms of a set number of words in common, but depends on the distinctiveness of the vocabulary being borrowed as well as the number of shared terms. In this sense, a distinctive phrase shared by two authors has a higher level of probability of being an example of dependence than a longer phrase that is a commonplace in the literary environment of the later author.[6] Moreover, drawing on the work of the literary critic Perri,[7] Thompson discusses the requirements for an allusion to function successfully in a literary work. He notes that:

> in order for the allusion to be successful, the audience must *recognize* the sign, *realize* that the echo is deliberate, *remember* aspects of the original text, and *connect* one or more of these aspects with the alluding text in order to get the author's point. Despite their differences literary critics concur that allusion involves (1) the use of a sign or marker that (2) calls to the reader's mind another known text (3) for a specific purpose.[8]

These factors will be borne in mind when discussing the Nestlé-Aland list of allusions. Once these so-called Zecharian allusions have been analysed, this paper will focus more attention on the small group of four citations taken from the prophetic text which do display some level of dependence on the text of Zechariah itself. It will be argued that Matthew has drawn upon these passages because they fit his overall theological outlook, in particular that the events surrounding Jesus' entry into Jerusalem and his suffering were foreseen and, moreover, were in full accord with the divine plan.

THE SO-CALLED ALLUSIONS TO ZECHARIAH

Here it is argued that, of the eleven allusions to the text of Zechariah as listed in NA27, ten of them are so tenuous that either no link can be established, or the possible link is so weak that it is impossible to argue for dependence on the text of Zechariah. The one remaining allusion, Matt 24:30, is seen as being dependent on the text of Zechariah only in a secondary sense, since this text was not taken directly from the OT, but shows signs of already being combined with other OT material in the pre-synoptic tradition before being incorporated by Matthew. For convenience, these eleven references will be treated in the order in which they occur in the text of Zechariah. A useful distinction is made by Stanley in relation to what he classifies as a 'reader centred' approach as opposed to an 'author centred' approach. The former is limited to only those passages that a reader might be able to identify as a quotation or allusion; however, the latter approach generates a wider group of texts that reflects the author's knowledge of scripture. Yet even in relation to this larger category produced by an author centred approach, Stanley insists upon 'substantial verbal agreement with a known passage of Scripture'.[9]

Zech 1:1//Matt 23:35

בַּחֹדֶשׁ הַשְּׁמִינִי בִּשְׁנַת שְׁתַּיִם לְדָרְיָוֶשׁ הָיָה דְבַר־יְהוָה אֶל־זְכַרְיָה
בֶּן־בֶּרֶכְיָה בֶּן־עִדּוֹ הַנָּבִיא לֵאמֹר׃

ὅπως ἔλθῃ ἐφ' ὑμᾶς πᾶν αἷμα δίκαιον ἐκχυννόμενον ἐπὶ τῆς γῆς ἀπὸ τοῦ αἵματος Ἅβελ τοῦ δικαίου ἕως τοῦ αἵματος Ζαχαρίου υἱοῦ Βαραχίου, ὃν ἐφονεύσατε μεταξὺ τοῦ ναοῦ καὶ τοῦ θυσιαστηρίου.

The obvious point of contact here is in terms of the name 'Zechariah, son of Berechiah (so MT) /Barachiah' (so LXX Zech 1:1; Matt 23:35). That any correspondence between Zechariah the OT prophet and the shadowy figure in Matt 23:35 is intended is to be doubted. Obviously the major problem is that there is no tradition of martyrdom surrounding the OT prophet. As Davies and Allison observe, 'there is, however, no biblical evidence of his death as a martyr; and as Jerome observed, the temple was in ruins in his time.'[10] Yet, perhaps even more significantly, there is neither any post-Biblical account of a martyrdom of Zechariah,[11] as is the case with the traditions that developed around Isaiah.[12] Hence, it is not appropriate to find a reference to the text of Zechariah in Matt 23:35. Despite this sensible conclusion, the problem remains that only the Matthean version of this synoptic saying contains the genealogical element υἱοῦ Βαραχίου.[13] It must be admitted that this does make the name Zechariah, and that of his father, correspond to the appellative given to the OT prophet especially in the LXX version of Zech 1:1 (i.e., Ζαχαριαν τὸν τοῦ Βαραχιου υἱὸν Αδδω). However, the OT, in both LXX and MT forms, traces the ancestry back as far as Zechariah's paternal grandfather. The identity of Zechariah son of Barachiah still remains problematic. Harrington offers the following summarized discussion:[14]

> The three possibilities are (1) the OT prophet Zechariah son of Barachiah, (2) Zechariah son of Jehoida in 2 Chr 24:20–22, and (3) Zechariah son of Bareis (Josephus, *War* 4:334–44). For the author of Q it was option 2. For Matthew and his community it was probably option 3, though all three seem to have gotten mixed together.

Although Harrington does not give reasons, it appears that the first possibility is rejected because there is no tradition of a violent death surrounding the OT prophet. The second is seen as appropriate to Q because it incorporates the first and final cases of violent death in the OT (in the arrangement of books in the Hebrew Bible[15]) and also because Q is seen as predating the destruction of the Temple.[16] The third possibility is supported for Matthew since that gospel is seen as being written post-70 CE and the intention is to contemporize the narrative by laying the blood guilt of all innocent victims on the Matthean opponents.

In terms of the Matthean sense, the identification with the Zechariah mentioned in Josephus can be strengthened when it is recognized that some mss of *Bell.* read the name of the father as Bariscaeus or Baruch. The former could easily be taken as interchangeable with the form Matthew preserves. This Zechariah was a wealthy individual who was killed in the temple by the Zealots in 69 CE. Josephus reports the actions and motivation of the Zealots in the following terms:

> and as they intended to have Zacharias the son of Bareis, one of the most eminent of the citizens, slain, so what provoked them against him was that hatred of wickedness and love of liberty which were so eminent in him: he was also a rich man, so that by taking him off, they did not only hope to seize his effects, but also to get rid of a man that had great power to destroy them ... So two of the boldest of them fell upon Zacharias in the middle of the temple, and slew him (Josephus, *Bell.* 4.334–44).

The close correspondence between the location and violent nature of his death means that he is most likely the person referred to by Matt 23:35. Hence this Matthean text is unlikely to be alluding to the prophetic figure, or the introduction to his recorded oracles.

Zech 2:10//Matt 24:31

The allusion contained in Matt 24:31 to the text of Zech 2:10 (MT Zech 2:6) is closer in form to the more expansive LXX form of the second chapter of Zechariah.[17] The relevant part of 2:10 in the version reads:

> LXX Zech 2:10 ἐκ τῶν τεσσάρων ἀνέμων τοῦ οὐρανοῦ συνάξω ὑμᾶς

The corresponding phrase in Matt 24:31 mentions the four winds and a gathering of the elect:

> καὶ ἐπισυνάξουσιν τοὺς ἐκλεκτοὺς αὐτοῦ ἐκ τῶν τεσσάρων ἀνέμων

The correspondence of the phrase 'from the four winds' and the reference to 'gathering' (although the Matthean text uses a slightly different compound verb) must be held in tension with the dissimilarities between these two texts. The syntax of the two quotations is substantially different in terms of the location of the verb. Further, the Zechariah text makes reference to τοῦ οὐρανοῦ while the Matthean text makes the objects of the gathering explicit, τοὺς ἐκλεκτούς. Finally, the subject of the gathering is different in each case. In the LXX of Zechariah it is the Lord who declares in the first person that he will do the gathering. By comparison, in Matthew the gathering is done by the angels, who are admittedly sent as the agents of God.

Although the ideas that are contained in Matt 24:31 may in origin partially stem from the LXX form of Zechariah, there is little doubt that Mark has served as the primary source for Matthew.[18] While the depiction of angels in Matt 24:31 does not draw on the Markan parallel, neither does it appear to be dependent on the text of Zech 2, despite the mention of two angels in 2:7, since their function in the prophetic book is not the ingathering of the elect. Angels, it must be noted, are not an uncommon element in eschatological visions, nor is the mention of a trumpet an unfamiliar motif, used here in Matthew but no parallel in Zech 2 (cf. Isa 27:13; Joel 2:1; Zeph 1:16; *Apoc. Abr.* 31:1; 1 Cor 15:52; 1 Thess 4:16). Thus it appears that Matthew has drawn this text from his Markan source, and although the ideas of LXX Zech 2:10 may lie behind the Markan text in some way (although the shared language is common enough to be accounted for in other ways), Matthew's additions and redactional alterations move 24:31 even further away from any possible connection with the Zecharian text.

Zech 7:9//Matt 23:23

The 'woe' of Matt 23:23 and the imperative contained in the LXX of Zech 7:9 do have the term ἔλεος in common as well as employing terms that share the κρίνω semantic domain.

τάδε λέγει κύριος παντοκράτωρ κρίμα δίκαιον κρίνατε καὶ ἔλεος καὶ οἰκτιρμὸν ποιεῖτε ἕκαστος πρὸς τὸν ἀδελφὸν αὐτοῦ (LXX Zech 7:9).

However, the triad of virtues extolled in Matthean text (τὴν κρίσιν καὶ τὸ ἔλεος καὶ τὴν πίστιν) cannot be said to be directly dependent on Zech 7:9, but rather reflects a widespread OT call, especially in the prophetic literature, for the practice of real justice. As Hagner notes in relation to the background of the Matthean triad of ethical behaviours: 'The call to these virtues is clear in the OT (for examples, cf. *justice:* Isa 1:17; Jer 22:3; *mercy:* Hos 6:6; Zech 7:9–10; and the combination of them in Mic 6:8; *faithfulness:* Hab 2:4).'[19] Thus it is best to understand both Matt 23:23 and Zech 7:9 as sharing a common ethical perspective, rather than to see the Matthean text alluding to the material in Zechariah as one of its primary sources for formulating this specific critique of the scribes and the Pharisees.

Zech 8:6//Matt 19:26

Jesus' hard word about the difficulty the rich have in entering the Kingdom of Heaven evokes shock in his disciples (Matt 19:25). They protest that salvation is, therefore, an impossibility, but Jesus replies that 'this is impossible with men, but all things are possible with God' (Matt 19:26). The text in Zechariah that NA27 classifies as an allusion, describes the Lord of Hosts declaring that the remnant will again repopulate the streets of Jerusalem. The word of consolation is that, if the remnant consider this wonderful, it shall not be too wonderful for God.

The niphal of the Hebrew verb פלא has a range of meanings such as 'to be wonderful, marvellous' or 'to be too difficult, beyond one's power'. Again, however, the correspondence appears to depend more on the LXX text than the MT. The double use of ἀδυνατήσει in the Greek form of Zech 8:6 may perhaps be seen as being echoed in Matthew's description that things ἀδύνατον with men are δυνατά with God. Thus, both passages, apart from sharing one term in common, also share a similar theological outlook on the omnipotence of the deity in comparison to limited human power. Such a contrast is obviously not unique to Zechariah, nor is the term ἀδύνατον so unusual that the Matthean material must be dependent on the passage in Zech 8:6.[20] In fact there is a much closer Philonic parallel, πάντα γὰρ θεῷ δυνατά (*De virt.* 26). This same idea is also found in LXX Job 10:13; 42:2; Mk 9:23 and Lk 1:37. Therefore the alleged allusion to Zech 8:6 is seen as having no stronger basis than any other of the texts listed. At best one can say that the ideas present in Zechariah reflect the all-surpassing power of God in comparison with humanity, and that Matthew shares this theological understanding, but is not dependent upon Zechariah for this shared belief.

Zech 8:17//Matt 5:33

Any link between these verses is extremely tenuous. Although both passages are concerned with oaths their respective prescriptions are vastly different. The MT form of Zech 8:17, וּשְׁבֻעַת שֶׁקֶר אַל־תֶּאֱהָבוּ warns against perjury. This is perhaps a little more explicitly described as a false oath in the LXX καὶ ὅρκον ψευδῆ μὴ ἀγαπᾶτε. By comparison Matt 5:33–7 proscribes the use of oaths, but while arguing against Torah legislation[21] depicts the practice of giving oaths to God, ἀποδώσεις δὲ τῷ κυρίῳ τοὺς ὅρκους σου (5:33b). Thus the two passages contained in Zechariah and Matthew exhibit a totally different attitude to the misuse of vows. The former sees the corrective as coming from their proper usage, the latter, however, sees their use as so flawed that only abolition can be appropriate. Once again the only point of contact between these two verses is that they illustrate the importance of oaths in the religious milieu of the Mediterranean world, but their respective attitudes to vows is totally different.

Zech 9:11//Matt 26:28

The common link between the two passages that has been adduced as making the categorization of Matt 26:28 as an allusion to Zech 9:11 is the phrase in that verse, בְּדַם־בְּרִיתֵךְ. Despite Lindars' assertion that there is a clear connection between these two texts,[22] caution again should be exercised. Admittedly, there is an interesting parallel between the Zecharian reference to אַתְּ בְּדַם־בְּרִיתֵךְ and the Matthean phrase τὸ αἷμά μου τῆς διαθήκης. However, even here there is a difference in the possessive pronoun in both cases. Further, the notion of covenant blood is not unfamiliar in the OT, either being directly mentioned (cf. Exod 24:8), or being part of a narrative where blood (or sacrifice) and covenant are intrinsically linked (cf. Gen 15:9–18; 21:27). Also Hagner plausibly suggests that the background to Matt 26:27–8 must be understood in terms of the Passover meal, although Jesus is imbuing it with new significance.[23] By contrast, the text of Zech 9:11 offers little in the way of sacrificial language that may account for the tone of the Matthean reference. It seems more sensible to conclude that the reference בְּדַם־בְּרִיתֵךְ formed part of the wider conceptual framework of Jewish religious thought, and that 'blood' and 'covenant' were ideas that were often closely linked. However, it is almost certainly the case that while the synoptic tradition (Matt 26:28//Mk 14:24//Lk 22:20) depends on this wider body of concepts, it does not draw specifically upon any individual OT text. Therefore it is inappropriate to class Matt 26:28 as an allusion to the text of Zech 9:11.

Zech 12:10, 12, 14//Matt 24:30

There appears to be little doubt that in 24:30 Matthew has utilized material contained in Zech 12:10, 12, 14 albeit in a compressed form. Although not wishing to argue from silence, it is at least a little surprising that Matthew does not draw from Zechariah certain other elements contained in that verse.[24] Most significantly the reference to הַיָּחִיד (the only son) is not exploited. The potential Christological overtones surely would have been apparent to Matthew if he had been responsible for the creation of this short florilegium of citations. While it is obviously Matthew who has introduced this form of OT prophecy into the source material taken over from Mark, it is not impossible that he expanded the Dan 7:13 vision of the coming Son of Man not with his own redactional creation, but rather with a pre-existing collection of

OT scriptures that had already combined Dan 7:13 with elements from Zech 12:10f., such a combination being utilized as a prophecy of the parousia.[25] This argument is obviously strengthened by the fact that a similar association has already taken place in Rev 1:7. Aune, who notes the conflation in Rev 1:7, suggests that such a combination may also occur in both Mark and Luke:[26]

> It is quite possible that Dan 7:13 and Zech 12:10 are also conflated in Mark 13:26 and Luke 21:27, both of which read καὶ τότε ὄψονται τὸν υἱὸν τοῦ ἀνθρώπου ἐρχόμενον ἐν νεφέλαις [Luke: νεφέλῃ], 'and then they will see the son of man coming with the clouds [Luke: a cloud].'

It must however be noted that the argument for conflation in both the Markan and Lukan passages is weak since the only possible conflated term from Zech 12:10 is κόψονται which it must be argued has been reduced to ὄψονται in place of the interjection ἰδού contained in Dan 7:13.

This, however, is not the only evidence of conflation. Both in *Did.* 16:8, in a truncated form,[27] and in Justin's *Dial.* 14:8 similar combinations of Dan 7:13 and Zech 12:10–12 are present. Thus while Matt 24:30 obviously alludes to 'the weeping of all the tribes of the earth' as depicted in Zechariah, there are clear reasons to think that this is not due to the direct Matthean use of this OT source, rather the allusion has passed through at least one intermediate stage whereby the reference from Dan 7:13 had been combined with the material in Zechariah, but not necessarily in a standardized or fixed form.[28] This is not to suggest that Matthew is not dependent upon Mark for the Dan 7:13 citation, but rather that, when Matthew came to this quotation in Mark, he already knew this passage had been expanded with material from Zechariah. Therefore, without direct reference to the text of the prophet, Matthew integrated this larger complex of OT material into his Markan source material.

Zech 14:4//Matt 21:1

The shared element between these two verses is the geographical reference to the Mount of Olives. The Zechariah text could not be more different in content or context from Matt 21:1. The former depicts an apocalyptic vision of Yahweh appearing in glory on the Mount of Olives to look over Jerusalem and the might and majesty of his presence resulting in that mountain being rent in two. By contrast, Matt 21:1 contains nothing that could be conceived as remotely eschatological, rather it is a descriptive detail portraying Jesus' arrival with his disciples at the outskirts of Jerusalem. It cannot be seriously maintained that the Mount of Olives reference in Matt 21:1 is an allusion to Zech 14:4 simply on the basis of this geographical detail, any more than any other text that contains the term Jerusalem automatically alludes to Zech 14:4 simply because it also refers to the name ירושָׁלם.

Zech 14:5//Matt 25:31

There is a certain degree of parallelism between these verses, but probably not enough to warrant the conclusion that the Matthean text is alluding to Zech 14:5. The passage in Zechariah describes the Lord coming with his holy ones. The MT reads:

וּבָא יְהוָה אֱלֹהַי כָּל־קְדֹשִׁים עִמָּךְ (Zech 14:5b)

This is rendered quite faithfully in the LXX as καὶ ἥξει κύριος ὁ θεός μου καὶ πάντες οἱ ἅγιοι μετ' αὐτοῦ. In both cases those who accompany the Lord at his coming are described as 'holy ones' either using the term קדשׁים. or οἱ ἅγιοι. However, when the passage in Matt 25:31 is considered, the Son of Man is accompanied by οἱ ἄγγελοι. Apart from a different person described as coming, accompanied by different companions, the grammatical form used to describe the coming is different in both cases. In Zech 14:5 the future of ἔρχομαι is used, whereas in Matt 25:31 the preferred form is the aorist subjunctive of ἔρχομαι.[29] Since the picture of a kingly or messianic figure arriving with an accompanying train is not an uncommon image, it seems implausible to postulate any form of dependence.

Zech 14:7//Matt 24:36

Although Gundry references Zech 14:7 in his comments on Matt 24:36, he suggests that the principal dependence is the Greek version of Dan 12:13. He asserts: 'This saying [i.e., Matt 24:36] seems to rest on Dan 12:13 LXX (cf. Zech 14:7; *Pss. Sol.* 17:23; 2 *Apoc. Bar.* 21:8; 1QM 1:4–13).'[30] While not wishing to discuss Gundry's proposal that the Matthean text is based on Dan 12:13, it is noteworthy that he offers no reason for the comparison with Zech 14:7, rather it appears that he is simply presenting this verse because it is found in lists of OT allusions, probably the one given in NA26.[31] Matthew 24:36 relates the uncertainty concerning the time of the return of the Son of Man. After declaring the ignorance of all people in relation to this matter, including the angels and the son himself, the verse concludes by declaring the Father alone is aware of that day, εἰ μὴ ὁ πατὴρ μόνος (24:36c). Presumably (although it is far from clear), the point of contact with Zech 14:7 is taken to be the knowledge that the Lord has of the continuous day, without darkness, that he has appointed, הוּא יִוָּדַע לַיהוָה (14:7b).[32] Yet the differences are far more compelling. Whereas the Matthean reference focuses solely on the ignorance surrounding the return of the Son of Man, the text in Zechariah does not talk about ignorance of others in comparison to the Lord's knowledge, rather it announces the fact that the day of unending light is known to the Lord. Admittedly both texts are set in passages that deal with parousia expectations, that of the Lord God's return in Zechariah, and that of the Son of Man's return in Matthew. However, this in no way establishes a relationship between the two texts. In fact it is the dissonance in terms of content and language that makes any notion of allusion or dependence indefensible in the present context. Therefore the reference to the knowledge of the unending day cannot be seen as the basis for the reference in Matt 24:36 that depicts the Father's unique knowledge of the parousia.

Zech 14:21//Matt 21:12

The so-called cleansing of the Temple by Jesus undoubtedly parallels the hopes expressed by many of the prophets for a pure form of worship in their religious cultic centre. The MT of Zech 14:21 promises the purging of a certain group from the temple precincts in the following terms:

וּבִשְּׁלוּ בָהֶם וְלֹא־יִהְיֶה כְנַעֲנִי עוֹד בְּבֵית־יְהוָה צְבָאוֹת בַּיּוֹם הַהוּא

Here the term כְנַעֲנִי is used in its later sense denoting traders,[33] yet the LXX misses this nuance and translates literally as Χαναναῖος. If Matthew is echoing Zechariah at this point it can only be in relation to the MT, and he must also understand the association of כְנַעֲנִי with traders. While this is of course not impossible, the greater problem for those who would argue for some kind of allusion to the text of Zech 14:21 is the lack of verbal affinity between Matt 21:12 and either the MT or LXX forms of the OT text. Moreover, it becomes necessary to see the Greek word pair πωλοῦντας καὶ ἀγοράζοντας (both plural terms) as representing the single Hebrew term כְנַעֲנִי (used here in the singular). Rather Davies and Allison's comments on the relationship of this passage in Matthew to Mal 3:1ff. seem pertinent to the relationship that the Matthean text has to Zech 14:21:[34]

> It is possible that Matthew saw in Jesus' deed a fulfilment of Mal 3.1ff. ('Suddenly the Lord whom you seek will come to his temple ... he will purify the Levites', cf. Mt 11:10). But because this text is neither clearly cited or alluded to, it would be wiser to speak more generally of the (partial or initial?) fulfilment of the eschatological hope, found in several places, that the temple and/or its staff will be purified.

Such a comment fits the alleged allusion to Zechariah even more appropriately, since the text of Zech 14:21 has far less verbal affinity to Matt 21:12 than it does to Mal 3:1f.

The value of 'allusions' as a category

In their introductory volume to NA26 the Alands boast: 'Appendix III provides the fullest list of Old Testament quotations and allusions yet available in this edition of the New Testament.'[35] The 27th edition reproduces the same appendix, so that claim remains just as appropriate. This boast is no empty claim, as the thirty-seven pages of small font, closely compressed references clearly attest. However, it is the usefulness of such a list that needs to be questioned. As this foregoing study of the allusions to the book of Zechariah has shown, for the majority of cases there is little contact between the prophetic text and its supposed allusion in the first gospel. One wonders if a list of citations alone, where shared significant vocabulary was the primary indicator of dependence, would not bring more rigor to the study of the use of the Old Testament in the New, rather than this amorphous list of vague allusions. This indeed appears to be the case since the references contained in the list seem to reflect the wider background of Jewish religious thought during the first century CE but without making demonstrable contact with those texts from Zechariah that are considered as the basis of the allusions.

CITATIONS FROM ZECHARIAH

As has been noted previously, the relevant appendix in NA27 lists three citations from Zechariah contained in Matthew's gospel (Zech 9:9; 11:13; 13:7). However, it will be argued that one of the passages listed as an allusion (Zech 11:12), although having minor variations in wording, stands close enough to the text of Matt 26:15 in terms of significant shared words to warrant being classified as a citation.[36] These four quotations are now studied in the order that they occur in the text of Zechariah, to assess the way Matthew treats the OT passages he utilizes from Zechariah, as well as to see if any general conclusion can be drawn regarding which form of the text the evangelist is likely to have used.

Zech 9:9//Matt 21:5

The quotation of Zech 9:9 in the Matthean version of the triumphal entry into Jerusalem is unique to the first gospel. The addition comprises the introductory formula to the fulfilled prophecy (v. 4), followed by the quotation itself (v. 5). Cope classifies the Matthean scribal practice in this case as a *mid-point* text. By this he means that the text forms a central point in a large narrative block (with material arranged on either side in an almost chiastic fashion) and often as part of this process the storyline is made to conform to the citation rather than *vice versa*. He states:[37]

> A clear example of this is the citation of Zech 9:9 in Mt 21:5. The traditional story of the entry of Jesus in Jerusalem, into which this text is inserted in Matthew as a fulfillment citation has been reworked in order to conform to the citation. The reworking is apparent in the stress on two animals, the ass and her colt, both in the verses preceding the citation and in the verse following the citation ... Only in Matthew are there two animals involved, and only in Matthew does the citation text occur.

This observation is correct. It shows the importance of the fulfilment of scripture as a Matthean proof of the Christological claims he advances in his gospel.

The form of the citation is interesting in this case, for although Cope is correct that Matthew makes the story conform to the quotation, the words that comprise the prophecy in Matt 21:5 represent an abbreviated form of Zech 9:9 with certain terms not reflected in any known form of that text. The text of Matt 21:5 reads as follows:

> Εἴπατε τῇ θυγατρὶ Σιών· Ἰδοὺ ὁ βασιλεύς σου ἔρχεταί σοι πραῢς καὶ ἐπιβεβηκὼς ἐπὶ ὄνον καὶ ἐπὶ πῶλον υἱὸν ὑποζυγίου.

The most obvious change is the drastic way the first half of Zech 9:9 is reduced; only the address 'daughter of Zion' remains. It is possible that the evangelist has not simply abbreviated Zech 9:9, but has in fact conflated it with Isa 62:11 which contains verbatim agreement with Matthew in the LXX tradition (εἴπατε τῇ θυγατρὶ Σιων, 62:11ba).[38] Also it should be noted that instead of the charge spoken directly in Zechariah to the daughter of Zion to rejoice and shout aloud, another party is addressed and it is this group (note the plural form εἴπατε) which is called upon to speak to the daughter of Zion. Also the parallel appellative, בַּת יְרוּשָׁלַם, is omitted. If Matthew was concerned to make explicit the fulfilment of a prophecy relating to two animals, he was unaware of, or did not feel it necessary to mention, the two groups of addressees, בַּת־צִיּוֹן and בַּת יְרוּשָׁלַם.

There are also smaller changes in the second half of Zech 9:9. While some of these are probably merely stylistic, or perhaps represent a different translation from Hebrew into Greek, the omission of the phrase צַדִּיק וְנוֹשָׁע appears to be theologically motivated. By deleting these words the militaristic aspect of Zech 9:9 is removed, and the arrival of the humble king does not also approximate the triumphal procession of a victorious warrior.[39] The significance of a Christology centring on the image of a 'humble king' has been emphasized by Verseput in his study on Matt 11–12.[40] This point is recognized by Luz in relation to the deletion of the martial language from Zech 9:9, as it is cited in Matt 21:5:[41]

> Beherrschend im Mittelpunkt des Zitats steht das adjekiv πραΰς. Bei diesem sehr faccettenreichen Wort, dessen Grundbedeutung etwa »sanft, freundlich, mild« ist, lassen der Kontext und die Prophetenstelle zunächst an Friedlichkeit und Gewaltlosigkeit denken: Der Messias von Sach 9,9f kommt nicht hoch zu Pferde, er wird vielmehr Kriegswagen und Waffen abshaffen und den Völkern Frieden bringen.

As Tuckett also discusses, the notion of Jesus as 'meek and lowly of heart' (Matt 11:29) is a significant theme for the first evangelist and, moreover, 'It is also connected with Matthew's beliefs about Jesus as the fulfilment of other Old Testament texts'.[42] Apart from the use of Zech 9:9 in this context, Tuckett also cites the Matthean use of the Isaianic servant songs, Isa 53:4 in Matt 8:17 and Isa 42:1–4 in Matt 12:18–21.

While it is difficult to know whether Matthew was more likely to have been working with the MT or the LXX version of Zech 9:9, Soares Prabhu argues that the way Matthew refers explicitly to two animals makes it more likely that he was using a Septuagintal text form. The MT, using synonymous parallelism, refers to the animal as עַל־חֲמוֹר וְעַל־עַיִר בֶּן־אֲתֹנוֹת. While this double reference could perhaps be misunderstood as denoting two creatures, Soares Prabhu is correct that originally it denoted one and the same animal. He states that 'the Masoretic text is an obvious instance of synonymous parallelism, with both half verses referring to the same male ass'.[43] He continues by suggesting that the LXX, ἐπιβεβηκὼς ἐπὶ ὑποζύγιον καὶ πῶλον νέον, appears to have a higher degree of ambiguity, potentially making the misunderstanding about two animals more explicable.[44] However, the fundamental weakness of this argument is that the wording of Matt 21:5's reference to the second animal καὶ ἐπὶ πῶλον υἱὸν ὑποζυγίου stands closer to the MT (וְעַל־עַיִר בֶּן־אֲתֹנוֹת) than to the LXX (καὶ πῶλον νέον), especially in terms of the υἱός/בֶּן correspondence. Yet, ultimately, there is simply not enough evidence to determine which form stands behind the Matthean text, any more than it is possible to find a suitable explanation for Matthew's confusion over the number of animals. Thus we can conclude that in this instance we have a clear example of Matthew's use of a citation from Zechariah, we can see that it is used in line with the first evangelist's concern with showing that Jesus fulfils the prophecies of scripture thereby vindicating his messianic claims, but it is not possible to determine the form of the text that stands behind the quotation of Zech 9:9 in Matt 21:5.

Zech 11:12//Matt 26:15

The use of Zech 11:12 in the context of Matt 26:15 is better understood as a citation of scripture rather than just an allusion to the text of Zechariah as NA27 classifies this text. While the wording of Matt 26:15 deviates somewhat from both the MT and LXX forms of Zech 11:12b, the correspondence of these words is not dissimilar to the level of similarity between Zech 9:9 and Matt 21:5, discussed in the previous section. The phrase in question reads as follows in the MT:

וַיִּשְׁקְלוּ אֶת־שְׂכָרִי שְׁלֹשִׁים כָּסֶף (Zech 11:12b)

This is rendered in the LXX as καὶ ἔστησαν τὸν μισθόν μου τριάκοντα ἀργυροῦς. The points of contact with Matt 26:15 are the use of the same verb (ἔστησαν) agreeing in tense, number and person, the same numerical reference to the amount of money and the description of the money as silver although the passage in Zechariah uses the masculine plural ἀργυροῦς, whereas Matthew employs a neuter plural noun, ἀργύρια.[45] The differences stem partially from the fact that the Matthean account is a third person omniscient narration while in Zechariah it is a first person report of a financial agreement. This allows the money in Zechariah to be described as τὸν μισθόν μου. Such a detail simply would not fit the third person narrative perspective of the gospel, hence the evangelist describes the financial transaction not from the perspective of the one receiving payment, but from the standpoint of the narrator, οἱ δὲ ἔστησαν αὐτῷ τριάκοντα ἀργύρια.

The Markan source for this pericope (Mk 14:11) simply reads, οἱ δὲ ἀκούσαντες ἐχάρησαν καὶ ἐπηγγείλαντο αὐτῷ ἀργύριον δοῦναι, with no indication of the amount of silver that was agreed upon. Once again Matthew deviates from his Markan source to make a certain feature of the story correspond to his understanding of the prophetic intention of scripture. As Davies and Allison observe, 'Matthew's line, which anticipates 27:9, stands under the influence of Zech 11:12 ... This OT text, which also lies beneath the story in 27:3–10, shows that the betrayal is in accord with what God has foreseen.'[46]

A further reason for understanding this use of Zechariah as an intentional quotation, stems from the wider Matthean narrative. The evangelist's interest in Judas, and his actions as the fulfilment of scripture, is seen when the postscript to the betrayal is taken up in 27:3–10. In that version of Judas' suicide (cf. Acts 1:18–19), the prophecy of Zech 11:13 is taken up and applied to the actions of the priests and temple officials. However, the audience is expected to know that these events are a continuation of the payment of the silver in the previous chapter. This continuity is achieved not only at the level of the explicit story, but also at the level of both parts of the story fulfilling a prophecy that relates both the payment and the price set by those making the payment. Thus, to use a modern term, this short quotation functions as a 'sound bite'. That is, it alerts the reader to the wider context of the Zechariah citation, which in turn will be picked up in Matt 27:9–10. Its significance as a scriptural reference is therefore intrinsically linked with the use of Zech 11:13 in the following chapter, and at a literary level Matthew uses this pre-emptive quotation to generate resonances in that subsequent passage, thereby showing that the act of betrayal, from beginning to end, was anticipated by scripture and was in accord with the divine purpose.

Zech 11:13//Matt 27:9–10

Despite the fact Matthew prefaces this quotation as fulfilling the things spoken by Jeremiah, the majority of the reference is obviously drawn from Zechariah. Apart from the final four words of Matt 27:10 (καθὰ συνέταξέν μοι κύριος), there is no possibility of dependence on Jeremiah, and even those four words may more plausibly be seen as a loose rendering of Zech 11:13a ('And the Lord said to me'). Perhaps the mention of Jeremiah in the rubric is due to the allegorical story, related in Jer 18–19, referring to the potter's house and earthenware vessel, combined with Jer 32:6–25 where Jeremiah purchases the Anathoth field. However, the double reference in Zech 11:13 to 'the potter' (הַיּוֹצֵר) makes recourse to these passages in Jeremiah less necessary, and perhaps it is just a case of mistaken citation.[47] Knowles suggests another reason for the attribution of the citation to Jeremiah. He argues that Matthew would not 'have been likely to ascribe the quotation as a whole to "Jeremiah" without intending some identifiable reference to that prophet'.[48] It is then asserted that the fulfillment of scripture referred to in Matt 27:9a takes place at two levels:[49]

> What this amounts to, then, is 'fulfillment' in verbal detail from Zechariah, but 'fulfilment' in thematic substance from Jeremiah … It would appear, therefore, that Matthew refers to Jeremiah by name in his introductory formula as a means of drawing attention to an important allusion that could otherwise be easily overlooked.

It is suggested that this allusion at the thematic level is more than the rejection of a prophetic figure, but centres on Jer 19:3–4 and the phrase דַּם נְקִיִּם (LXX αἱμάτων ἀθῴων) which is seen not only as significantly echoed in Judas' description of Jesus as αἷμα ἀθῷον in Matt 27:4, but also recurs in the Matthean usage of the terms 'innocent' or 'righteous blood' (cf. Matt 23:30, 35; 26:28; 27:25). While this solution is admittedly ingenious, one cannot help but be troubled by the vagueness of some of the links that Knowles marshals in support of his thesis. Thus, despite Knowles' position that it is highly unlikely that Matthew would have confused his sources, this still appears as the most plausible solution and as Stendahl suggests this was probably due to 'a slip or rather a confusion of memory'.[50]

Like the quotation of the Zecharian text in Matt 26:15, Matthew again uses a citation from the same prophetic book in the context of his telling of the Judas story. However, unlike the pericope describing the negotiations between Judas and the temple authorities, this incident has no gospel parallels.[51] Moreover, as Harrington notes, 'This passage also carries on and adds to the "fulfillment of Scriptures" theme so prominent in the Gospel'.[52] For Matthew it is important to stress that not only was the betrayal foretold in the scriptures, but so too was the fate of the betrayer.[53] Although Gundry is keen to emphasize the Matthean redactional activity in this pericope, nonetheless he feels that it preserves a kernel of historicity.[54] However, while it is probably impossible to determine the historicity of this account, one can see typically Matthean traits in the way OT scripture has been used in 27:9–10.

The form of this citation is difficult to relate either to the MT or the LXX of Zech 11:13. However, despite this problem, the solution is not to be found in Lindars' four-stage reconstruction of the text's development as an apologetic prophecy. He argues that:[55]

> The original choice of a particular passage from the Passion prophecy of Zechariah (the Hebrew stage) is a straightforward matter ... The second (Palestinian Greek) stage is concerned with the correlation of details of the passage and the known facts about the fate of Judas. The method at this stage is to draw out the fullest implications of the text itself. The final exegete (using the Septuagint, but paying careful attention to the original Hebrew) introduces an allegorical element by seeing an equivalence, a mysterious identity, of Zechariah's prophecy and Jeremiah's transaction – not to mention the plague of boils. There is still a fourth stage. Matthew himself disregards the work of the final exegete, because he is only interested in the *pesher* text and its commentary from the point of view of his narrative. It is the second layer of exegesis which provides him with the information he wants.

Such a speculative reconstruction not only defies the evidence available from the text, but seems motivated by a desire in this case not to make Matthew responsible for the mistaken attribution to Jeremiah, as well as to account for the wide divergence of this quotation from either the MT or the LXX. The first part of Zech 11:13 ('Cast it into the treasury')[56] is not quoted in Matt 27:9–10, but has been anticipated in v. 5, which relates Judas in a state of remorse casting the money into the sanctuary, ῥίψας τὰ ἀργύρια εἰς τὸν ναόν. The remainder of Zech 11:13 forms the basis of the citation in Matt 27:9. Davies and Allison treat this material in three sections.[57] First, the Matthean clause, καὶ ἔλαβον τὰ τριάκοντα ἀργύρια is closest to the LXX, καὶ ἔλαβον τοὺς τριάκοντα ἀργυροῦς, with Matthew again using a neuter form for his reference to the money (cf. 26:15; 27:3, 5, 6; 28:12, 15). Second, the phrase τὴν τιμὴν τοῦ τετιμημένου reflects the MT אֶדֶר הַיְקָר אֲשֶׁר יָקַרְתִּי. Finally, the last clause of Matt 27:9, ὃν ἐτιμήσαντο ἀπὸ υἱῶν Ἰσραήλ, draws neither upon the LXX or MT forms of the text, rather it appears to be due to the redactional activity of the evangelist.[58]

Matthew appears more concerned with the idea of the scriptures being fulfilled, and the notion of the prophetic oracle finding its true significance in the events surrounding Jesus' ministry and passion, than in the accurate citation of those scriptures. That is, Matthew demonstrates that he is willing to nuance the wording of his quotations so that they better fit the events to which they are seen as providing testimony. As Davies and Allison state: 'when Matthew was the first to quote an OT passage we might expect him to offer a wording suitable to his purposes. In other words, it was the evangelist's wont to bring out from the storehouse of Scripture things both old and new'.[59] The form of Zech 11:13 used by the evangelist is neither fully based on the MT or LXX, nor is likely to represent some unknown form of the text. The reason for the latter is not simply to resist an argument from silence, but rather the positive evidence provided by the way even Zech 11:13 itself has been used by the evangelist, in particular the first part which has been taken up in Matt 27:5–6. Whereas both the Hebrew and Greek forms enjoin the one to whom the prophecy is directed to throw the money into the treasury, Matthew creatively reverses this tradition. He says Judas threw the money into the sanctuary, but the chief priests themselves prohibited the money to go into the treasury since it was blood money. Matthew continues this two-way process of conforming both facts and citation in v. 9 with the additional comment, ὃν ἐτιμήσαντο ἀπὸ υἱῶν Ἰσραήλ. Although there is no evidence for this piece of information in any known text form, its Christological relevance makes it far more likely to be the product of the early church than an unattested form of Zech 11:13. Thus Matthew's creative use of the prophecies of Zechariah is employed in his argument that the betrayal by Judas was in accord with the foreseen divine purpose.

Zech 13:7//Matt 26:31

Here Matthew is only secondarily dependent upon the text of Zechariah, his primary source is Mk 14:27. His modifications of the actual quotation taken from Mark are only two. First, he brings the verb διασκορπισθήσονται forward placing it in the post-positive position after the conjunction.[60] This in turn allows his second change, the addition of τῆς ποίμνης, to follow immediately the reference to 'the sheep', thus improving the syntax of the sentence. The addition of the reference to 'the flock' has some support in the LXX textual tradition of Zech 13:7. This arrangement of both the position of the verb and the addition of τῆς ποίμνης is found in the Alexandrinus (A) version of Zech 13:7. Although the first reaction might be to assume that Matthew preserves such a text form, this hasty conclusion should be resisted. Jobes and Silva describe the general textual quality of A in the following terms. 'Its text, which often shows signs of Hexaplaric influence, is mixed but valuable.'[61] This combined with the fifth century date of A, and the fact that (like all other substantial mss of the LXX) codex Alexandrinus is a 'Christian book', as the inclusion of the NT illustrates, leads one to ask about the direction of influence. It is perhaps more plausible that under the influence of Matt 26:31, the reference in Zech 13:7 was made to conform to the gospel text and not vice versa.[62] Such a process of textual assimilation was far from uncommon.

Lindars classifies what he calls the 'shepherd and sheep theme' of the NT into two categories. First, the *pastoral* references that reflect 'church order', with a prime example being the Miletus speech in Acts 20.[63] Second, there is the *redemptive* category. With this second group, it is argued that, 'it seems always to be possible to trace the phrases back to Isa 53 and Zech. 9–13.'[64] While the categorization of this second group appears to be somewhat circular, there is undoubtedly a redemptive, or at least a vicarious, aspect to the smiting of the shepherd both in the Matthean context as well as in the underlying quotation from Zechariah. However, Matthew himself appears to blur the distinction between the pastoral and redemptive categories. As Gundry recognizes, the phrase τῆς ποίμνης is an indication that Matthew 'may have wanted a figurative allusion to the church.'[65] This reason tends to undercut Davies and Allison's argument that the addition of τῆς ποίμνης must be under the influence of a

LXX A type reading, since no motivation can be found for the Matthean addition of these words. They state: 'we tend to think that LXX A, which is closer to the MT than LXX B, preserves a reading known to Matthew, for we are otherwise at a loss to explain Matthew's addition of "of the flock".'[66] However, Davies and Allison's observation about the general relationship of Alexandrinus to the MT is not relevant, since in this case the MT does not contain any phrase paralleling the Greek words τῆς ποίμνης. While its verbal form may be closer to the Matthean and LXX A verb διασκορπισθήσονται than the LXX B verb ἐκσπάσατε, this is hardly of relevance for deciding the origin of the phrase 'of the flock'.

Yet more importantly, contrary to Davies and Allison, it is possible to conceive a Matthean motivation for the addition of this reference in terms of the social setting of the group. In relation to the group's polemic against Jewish authority (cf. Matt 23), its alienation from synagogue life (cf. Matt 4:23; 9:35; 10:17; 12:9; 13:54; 23:34) and its struggle to redefine its own structures and organization (e.g., Matt 18:15–20), it is not surprising to find an inwardly focused reference to the shepherd being smitten for 'the sheep *of the flock*'. The liminal life being experienced by the community makes such a focus on the flock in relation to the shepherd a source of pastoral comfort in the face of their marginal existence. This being the case, it is highly likely that Matthew has added the words τῆς ποίμνης for his own pastoral purpose, but in the process has lessened the correspondence between his citation in 26:31 and the actual text of Zech 13:7.

CONCLUSIONS

Despite the impression given by the appendix of allusions and citations in NA27, Matthew does not make great use of the material in Zechariah. Of the eleven passages that have been analysed under the heading of allusions, all but one were found to lack the level of specificity that made a link with Zechariah probable. The one exception was Matt 24:30, where it appears to be beyond doubt that Matthew has utilized material contained in Zech 12:10, 12, 14. However, this dependence is not direct. It is highly probable that the material from Zechariah was combined with Dan 7:13 in the pre-Matthean tradition, and that the evangelist is using the catena of quotations rather than the OT text directly.[67]

The four passages that are treated under the heading of citations show a much closer verbal affinity with the material in Zechariah. However, one of these four passages is derived from Zechariah only secondarily. The use of Zech 13:7 in Matt 26:31 is dependent on the Markan material in 14:27 and not taken directly from the prophetic work itself. Efforts to explain the addition of the phrase τῆς ποίμνης in terms of Matthean dependence on a form of the Septuagint that reflects the reading found in codex Alexandrinus seem to run counter to the more plausible explanation, namely, that LXX A is itself dependent on Matt 26:31,[68] and not that Matthew has conformed his reading to a wording that is no longer preserved in the MT or any other form of the LXX textual tradition. The three remaining texts, Matt 21:5; 26:15; 27:9–10, do all draw directly on the text of Zechariah. However, the creativity the evangelist has exhibited in the two-way process of making event and citation parallel each other, means that it is no longer possible to recover the underlying text form with any certainty. The use of Zech 9:9 in the narrative of the triumphal entry (21:5) illustrates this process well. Not only has the evangelist omitted phrases from the verse he cites in order to present Jesus as a king without military inclinations, but he has also made the events, with the explicit mention of two animals, conform to his understanding of what the Zechariah text depicts. The other two citations from Zech 11:12 and 13 both are used in the context of the Judas story and seek to show that such an act of betrayal was both foreseen and in accord with the divine purpose. Thus Matthew is not so much concerned to use Zechariah accurately, or to use it because it is any more significant than other prophetic texts. Rather, Matthew exploits Zechariah in line with his own understanding that his portrayal of Jesus as a rejected figure and humble king is both vindicated and supported by the divine word in scripture.[69] In the process Matthew uses the few verses he quotes from Zechariah in a very haphazard manner. So perhaps in the first gospel it appears that the appropriate conclusion to draw is that Zechariah is not so much used by Matthew, but rather, is used minimally for the evangelist's own theological purpose. However, in this process the texts drawn from the OT prophetic book are not preserved with great accuracy, but are instead, at best, creatively misused.

NOTES

1 Aland, 1993, pp. 770–806.

2 See ibid., pp. 799–800.

3 By way of comparison, Gundry in his study of the use of the OT in the first gospel lists only eight references to Zechariah in his scriptural index: Zech 2:6, 10; 9:9; 11:12, 13; 12:10; 13:7; 14:5. Apart from the first reference, all the rest overlap with the list in NA27. The first reference, Zech 2:6, is, however, dealt with in the section treating 2:10 in this essay. It can only be considered as an allusion in the LXX form of the citation. Gundry himself treats it in association with 2:10, and does not consider it to be separate from the use of that verse in Matt 24:31: see Gundry, 1967, scriptural index.

4 Stanley, 1992, p. 32.

5 Thompson, 1991, p. 30.

6 This point is recognized by Thompson, 1991, p. 31, when he states: 'Aside from the presence of an explicit formula, the clearest sign of possible allusion is shared vocabulary. Obviously the greater the number of significant shared words in G[ospel] and E[pistle], and the greater their rarity in E and other Epistles by the same author, the higher the probability that there exists some kind of shared tradition. On the other hand, if the saying is commonplace or the author has chosen the only appropriate way to express the idea, the significance of the parallel diminishes.'

7 Perri, 1978.

8 Thompson, 1991, p. 29.

9 Stanley, 1992, p. 34.

10 Davies and Allison, 1997, p. 318.

11 In fact the opposite is the case, with Zechariah depicted as living on into fullness of years. The post-Biblical tradition contained in *The Lives of the Prophets* states: 'And he [Zechariah] died when he attained a great age, and when he expired and was buried near Haggai' (15:6). See *The Lives of the Prophets*, trans. D.R.A. Hare, in Charlesworth, 1985, vol. 2, p. 394.

12 Knibb, M. A., 'Martyrdom and Ascension of Isaiah', in Charlesworth, 1985, vol. 2, pp.

143–76. At best it could be asserted that Zechariah might be associated with the violence and rejection suffered by all the prophets, Q 11:49; 13:34. However, the lack of a specific reference to the OT prophetic figure Zechariah would nonetheless make this argument problematic.

13 Although it is of course theoretically possible that the reference υἱοῦ Βαραχίου was in Q and has been deleted by Luke, on balance it seems more plausible this detail has been introduced by Matthew. The reasons for this are twofold. First, Matthew also appears to have expanded reference to Abel with the phrase τοῦ δικαίου, second it is hard to see what Luke would have gained by deleting the reference to the Zechariah's father.

14 Harrington, 1991, p. 328.

15 However, this argument may be somewhat anachronistic. Not only is it uncertain that the canon of the OT had been closed when Q was written, but the argument, which seems to depend on Chronicles being known as the final book of such a canon, would appear to presuppose that the books of the OT were bound together in a fixed codex form. The evidence does not support this conclusion.

16 Steck comes to a similar conclusion in regard to the figure intended by the reference as it stood in the Q tradition: 'Meint Q Sacharja ben Jojada, so muß die schwierige Frage, ob die Chronikbücker schon in dieser Zeit ihre feste Stelle am Ende der Ketubim haben und somit das letzte Buch des hebräischen Kanons bilden, positiv entschieden werden, da sich nur so die nicht zeitlich bestimmte Markierung Abel-Sacharja verstehen läßt.' (Steck, 1967, p. 37.)

17 The MT of Zech 2:6 does, however, contain a reference to the four winds, but in that context it is a dispersion, not a gathering, that is envisioned.

18 Davies and Allison confirm this observation in general terms. In relation to Matt 24:30c–31 they state that these verses 'have close Markan parallels and are usually accounted for on the theory of Markan priority.' (Davies and Allison, 1997, p. 327). However, they do also note that the addition of the reference to the trumpet is due to Matthean redactional work in v. 31.

19 Hagner, 1995, p. 670.

20 Once again, Matt 19:26 in the first instance draws upon Mk 10:27 as its source. The deviations from the Markan material are so minor that they are best accounted for as stylistic alterations. For a discussion of the grammatical significance of such changes see Gundry, 1994, p. 390.

21 The most relevant OT sections describing the use of oaths are Lev 19:12; Num 30:3; Deut 23:22.

22 Lindars, 1961, pp. 132–3.

23 Hagner, 1995, p. 773. It has been argued by Jeremias that the most important OT background for the eucharistic words is to be found in Isa 53. He states: 'Without Is 53 the Eucharistic words would remain totally incomprehensible.' (Jeremias, 1966, pp. 218–37.)

24 Gundry tries to defend the Matthean version of the citation by arguing that the MT of Zech 12:10 is itself corrupt: 'The MT, which reads the first person, is inherently difficult and probably corrupt.' (Gundry, 1967, p. 53.)

25 The fact that NA27 sees Matt 24:31 as alluding to Zech 2:10 has already been discussed above. This material was already present in Mark 13:27, so Matthew cannot be responsible for introducing two Zechariah allusions and placing them either side of the citation from Dan 7:13. Rather, as has been argued, Matt 24:31 in fact makes the material taken over from Mark correspond less closely to the text of Zechariah.

26 Aune, 1997, p. 55.

27 Niederwimmer, 1998, p. 226, suggests that the *Didache* may be dependent on Mark 13:26: 'The text of the *Didache*, in the sequence of its elements, is closer to Mark 13:26

par. than to the text in Daniel.' However, he does not consider the possibility that this combination of Zech 12:10ff. and Dan 7:13 may reflect pre-synoptic traditions.

28 See Lindars, 1961, p. 123.

29 Davies and Allison, 1997, p. 421, baldly assert that Matt 25:31 'takes up LXX Zech 14:5 …, a verse also used in 27:51–3'. However, they fail to account for the striking differences between the two passages.

30 Gundry, 1994, p. 492.

31 Presumably at the date Gundry wrote the first edition of his commentary (1982) he was using the list of allusions printed in the NA26 (first printed in 1979). However, if the discussion in the commentary draws on his earlier work (Gundry, 1967), he could in fact be dependent on an even earlier addition of the Nestlé-Aland text. It is not possible to be precise because this monograph is a revision of his doctoral thesis.

32 Hagner, 1995, p. 716, sees the dependence to be based upon the LXX form of Zech 14:7. He states: 'The time of the coming of the Son of Man is in the keeping of "the Father alone" (ὁ πατὴρ μόνος; cf. Acts 1:7; for OT background, see the LXX of Zech 14:7: 'there will be one day, and that day is know to the Lord [γνωστὴ τῷ κυρίῳ]'; cf. 2 *Apoc. Bar.* 21:8).' It is hard to see what is to be gained from saying the allusion is based on the LXX as opposed to the MT, and moreover, how one would tell? The LXX is extremely close to the MT at the point Hagner cites the relevant section of Zech 14:7, and actually throughout the entire verse.

33 See *BDB*, p. 489.

34 Davies and Allison, 1997, pp. 138–9.

35 Aland and Aland, 1989, p. 259.

36 See Thompson, 1991, p. 31, for a discussion about 'significant shared vocabulary' to establish an allusion in the NT text.

37 Cope, 1976, pp. 86–7.

38 Hagner appears to support the notion that these two texts have been conflated. He writes 'εἴπατε τῇ θυγατρὶ Σιών is found verbatim in Isa 62:11, where the coming of ὁ σωτήρ, "the Savior," is announced in a passage similar to Zech 9:9'. The remainder of the quotation is drawn verbatim from Zech 9:9 …' (Hagner, 1995, p. 594). Davies and Allison are more circumspect in their evaluation. Having noted the possibility of conflation, they continue by suggesting other possibilities: 'Or do we have here a lapse of memory or the unconscious assimilation of like texts ("daughter of Zion" is common to both)? Origen satisfied himself by speaking of "abbreviation" (*Comm. on Jn.* 10:19).' (Davies and Allison, 1997, p. 118).

39 This suggestion is also made by Harrington, 1991, p. 293: 'Matthew omits from Zech 9:9 "righteous and victorious is he," leaving the emphasis on Jesus as the "meek" or humble king.'

40 Verseput, 1986.

41 Luz, 1997, p. 181.

42 Tuckett, 2001b, pp. 128–9.

43 Soares Prabhu, 1976, p. 158.

44 Ibid.

45 As McNeile, 1915, p. 307, notes: 'Both ἔστησαν and the sum named are due to Zach. xi.12'.

46 Davies and Allison, 1997, p. 452.

47 Soares Prabhu tries to resist this conclusion that Matthew is simply mistaken in his reference, but he fails to find a convincing alternative explanation. In relation to 27:9 he states, 'A mistaken attribution is unlikely on the part of an editor as familiar with the Hebrew Bible as the "author" of the formula quotations has shown himself to be. None of the many other solutions that have been proposed, ranging from a Jeremiah Apocryphon

to a copyist's error in an Aramaic original are completely satisfactory; and the complex text of the quotation, a free rendering of Zech 11:12f with a possible allusion to Jer 32:6ff further confuses the issue.' (Soares Prabhu, 1976, pp. 53–4).

48 Knowles, 1993, p. 59.

49 Ibid., pp. 76–7.

50 Stendahl, 1968, p. 123.

51 The version of the story in Acts 1:18–19 can hardly be classed as a parallel. Instead it uses the technique of a flashback narrating an entirely different account of the death of Judas, in order to explain the appointment of a replacement apostle.

52 Harrington, 1991, p. 386.

53 Lindars agrees that the purpose of the story was to demonstrate that what happened to Jesus was in accord with the foreordained plan of God. However, his reconstruction becomes unnecessarily speculative when he assumes that this argument had an apologetic focus aimed specifically at Jewish priests who were calling claims about Jesus' messiahship into question because he had unwittingly allowed himself to be betrayed by Judas. In regard to the polemic of the priests Lindars states: 'It would be very easy for them to object that it is unworthy of one who is said to be the Messiah, that he should be the dupe of such a scheme. If he had really been the Lord's Messiah, he would never have allowed this sort of thing to happen almost under his very eyes! This can be countered by adducing Zech 11.12f., which shows that what happened was already preordained in prophecy.' (Lindars, 1961, p. 116).

54 Gundry, 1994, p. 553, constructs his argument in the following manner: 'Because of Matthew's special diction, parallelism, heavy use of OT phraseology, and the absence of parallels in the other gospels, we might have thought that the story of Judas's end is a wholesale creation by Matthew himself. But the very different versions of Judas's end in Acts 1:15–20, one with signs of an early date (see esp. the Aramaic in Acts 1:19), favours that Matthew is working with historical tradition. His revisions, however, show how creatively he works with material at his disposal.' Yet despite Gundry's pleading, one wonders how the divergent account in Acts can lend any credence to the Matthean account apart from corroborate the view that Judas met a violent death shortly after his act of betrayal.

55 Lindars, 1961, pp. 121–2.

56 Compare Zech 11:13 α' σ'.

57 For their discussion, see Davies and Allison, 1997, pp. 569–70.

58 Davies and Allison describe this phrase as 'a targumizing interpretation' (Davies and Allison, 1997, p. 570).

59 Davies and Allison, 1997, p. 575.

60 Hagner suggests that the evangelist's motivation for moving the verb is as follows: 'Matthew puts the verb at the beginning of the clause to increase the parallel with the first clause and for emphasis.' (Hagner, 1995, p. 777).

61 Jobes and Silva, 2000, p. 59.

62 For arguments in favour of the originality of the LXX A reading see Stendahl, 1968, p. 81. Note also Allen's argument: 'Since Mt. does not elsewhere add extraneous words to Mk.'s quotations, and does add words that which are found in the LXX [Allen cites 19.5 and 22.32] … it is more probable that he here adds τῆς ποίμνης because he found it in a LXX text.' (Allen, 1912, p. 277).

63 See the discussion in Walton, 2000, esp. pp. 81–2.

64 Lindars, 1961, p. 128.

65 Gundry, 1994, p. 530.

66 Davies and Allison, 1997, p. 485.

67 This is not a new suggestion. Lindars, 1961, p. 123, commenting on the use of Zech

12:10–14, notes: 'Both Matthew and Revelation conflate the passage with the famous Parousia text, Dan 7.13. Both John and Revelation use the non-Septuagintal ἐξεκέντησαν, which is closer to the Hebrew, and found also in Aquila and Theodotion. These are surely more than coincidences, and indicate that here is another text selected for a special purpose in the Passion apologetic.' While not agreeing with Lindars' overall theory of a pre-existing Passion apologetic, it does appear highly likely that Dan 7:13 had already been combined with material from Zech 12:10–14 prior to its incorporation in 24:30 by the evangelist.

68 Gundry, 1967, p. 26, concurs with this idea in his analysis: 'LXX^{A} appears to have been assimilated to Mt in τῆς ποίμνης, but not in other respects.'

69 Lindars wishes to stress the eschatological dimension rather than the latent Christology derived from such citations. He asserts: 'The selection of scriptures for apologetic needs in the early Church is governed by a single factor, the established use of the prophets and Psalms in eschatological speculation.' (Lindars, 1961, p. 283).

Chapter 7

The Cleansing of the Temple in Mark 11:15 and Zechariah 14:21

Henk Jan de Jonge

Mark's account of the last week of Jesus' earthly ministry shows the influence of the book of Zechariah in about six passages. In three instances this influence can be established with absolute certainty or reasonable probability.[1] The most certain case is Mark 14:27, where Jesus before entering into Gethsemane says to his disciples: 'You will all become deserters; for it is written "I will strike the shepherd, and the sheep will be scattered." ' This is a clear reference to Zech 13:7, introduced with an explicit quotation formula, 'it is written'. It is also a reference which functions on the redactional level of Mark's narrative, for at the end of the Gethsemane episode Mark relates that 'all of (the disciples) deserted him (Jesus) and fled' (v. 50).

The influence of Zechariah is somewhat less evident in two passages in Mark 11, namely in the episodes of Jesus' triumphal entry into Jerusalem and the cleansing of the temple. According to vv. 7–11, Jesus entered Jerusalem on a colt. Matthew, in his reworking of this passage (21:4), adds the comment that 'this took place to fulfill what had been spoken through the prophet, saying "Tell the daughter of Zion, Look, your king is coming to you, humble, and mounted on a donkey, and on a colt, the foal of a donkey." '[2] This is a quotation from Zech 9:9, which does not yet occur in Mark. Yet many interpreters of Mark are of the opinion (rightly, I think) that Mark's account of Jesus' entry into Jerusalem alludes to Zech 9:9, even if Mark avoids quoting Zechariah explicitly at this point.[3] Not only in Matthew, but also in Mark, is the colt the riding animal mentioned in Zech 9:9.[4]

Quite a few scholars find another trace of Zechariah's influence in Mark 11, in the scene of the cleansing of the temple, Mark 11:15.[5] The passage in question may well be echoing the closing words of the book of Zechariah (14:21 end): 'There shall no longer be traders in the house of the Lord of hosts on that day' (NRSV). I intend to go into Mark's story about the cleansing of the temple and its relationship to Zech 14:21 presently, but let me mention first three further possible reminiscences of Zechariah in the final section of Mark's Gospel.

First, Mark's account of Jesus' entry into Jerusalem opens with a remarkable note indicating that what is going to happen took place: 'When they were approaching Jerusalem, at Bethphage and Bethany, near the Mount of Olives' (Mark 11:1). At this point in Mark's narrative, however, the Mount of Olives does not yet seem to play a role of any significance. It is understandable, therefore, that several exegetes have taken the mention of the Mount of Olives here as a reference to Zech 14:4,[6] where the prophet says that on the final day of judgement God will stand on the Mount of

Olives.[7] The geographical note in Mark 11:1 is so strange and, with no less than four geographical names, so excessive that the suggestion to see the Mount of Olives here as a reminiscence of Zech 14:4 is certainly worth considering. Another possibility is of course that this mention of the Mount of Olives is merely a redactional anticipation of the episodes that are explicitly said by Mark to have taken place on that mount: the eschatological discourse of Mark 13 (see 13:3) and the prediction of Peter's denial (see 14:26).[8]

Secondly, in his account of the Last Supper, Mark has Jesus say over the cup: 'This is my blood of the covenant, which is poured out for many' (Mark 14:24). The phrase 'my blood of the covenant' has often been taken to be an echo of Zech 9:11. It is true that Jesus' words of institution as recorded by Paul in 1 Cor 11:25 already include the phrase 'this cup is the new covenant in my blood' and that Paul's phrase 'the new covenant' seems to reflect primarily Jer 31:31 and perhaps 32:40. But the passages in Jeremiah do not specify that the restoration of the covenant will come about through blood. The mention of blood is a feature which Mark 14:24 and 1 Cor 11:25 have in common with Zech 9:11. It may well be due to the influence of Zech 9:11. This passage is the opening of an oracle that announces the release of Israel's and Judah's prisoners by God 'because of the blood of his covenant' with them.

Thirdly, it is quite possible that Mark's account of the centurion who was standing opposite the cross and 'saw how he died' is a remote echo of Zech 12:10: 'They will look upon the one whom they have pierced.' The prophetic passage is in any case referred to and quoted in John 19:37 and Rev 1:7.

This must conclude the present survey of the relationships between the final section of Mark, chs. 11–16, and the second part of Zechariah, chs. 9–14. There is no need to repeat that some of these relationships can be established with more certainty than others.

Apart from the question concerning the plausibility or probability with which the relationships mentioned can be established, there are two further questions with regard to each of the connections at issue individually. First, it should be asked at what stage in the tradition running from Jesus to Mark, the link between Jesus' words and actions, on the one hand, and the visions of Deutero-Zechariah, on the other, originated. In theory, the answer to this question can vary from the one extreme to the other. It has often been assumed, for instance, that Jesus himself chose to enter Jerusalem riding on a colt, in order to manifest himself as the triumphant but humble king announced in Zech 9:9–10, who would bring peace to the nations and reign to the ends of the earth. This is the position held, among others, by Robert M. Grant, now half a century ago. He argued that in Mark 11:1–23, in the stories of Jesus approaching the Mount of Olives, his entry into Jerusalem on a colt and the cleansing of the temple, it is not the evangelist, but the historical Jesus himself and the disciples around him, who effected the fulfilment of the prophecies of Zech 9.[9] Grant also thought that it was Jesus himself who in his words spoken over the cup at the Last Supper applied Zech 9:11 to himself, his death and his followers. Grant even went so far as to assert that the evangelist Mark, in writing his Gospel, was unaware of the relationships between his account in Mark 11 and Zechariah. To quote another example of the tendency to trace the origin of the links between Mark and Zechariah back to Jesus himself, the passage from Zech 13:7 on the shepherd being smitten and the sheep being scattered, quoted in Mark 14:27, induced F. F. Bruce to observe: 'According to

Mark, it is Jesus Himself who makes the identification [of the smitten shepherd with Jesus]. I [i.e., F. F. Bruce] have no doubt at all that Mark is right in ascribing this interpretation of the prophecy to Jesus; (...).'[10]

In contrast to this tendency to locate the link between Mark and Zechariah in the actions and words of Jesus himself, more recent interpreters of Mark's Gospel tend to see the connections between this Gospel and Zechariah rather as having originated in later stages of the tradition. It has been argued, for instance, that the words Jesus spoke over the cup at the Last Supper (Mark 14:24) originally contained no reference to the idea of covenant.[11] In that case, the echo of Zech 9:11 must have entered the tradition underlying Mark at some later stage. The story of the entry into Jerusalem was explained by R. Bultmann as a legend called forth by Zech 9:9, that is, as a Christian creation developed somewhere on the trajectory from Jesus to Mark.[12] Similarly, according to several commentators, the quotation on the shepherd and the sheep from Zech 13:7 has probably been added to the (older) prediction that the disciples would fall away.[13] Finally the possibility cannot be ruled out, at least in theory, that Mark himself was responsible for adding one or another reminiscence of Zechariah to the tradition he used.[14] A possible example of such a recent, redactional insertion of a reference to Zechariah is the quotation of Zech 13:7 on the shepherd and the sheep, included in Mark 14:27, but I shall not go into this possibility here.

The other question that should be asked with regard to every single allusion to Zechariah in Mark is whether or not Mark was *aware* of alluding to Zechariah. This question has to be distinguished from the one just mentioned. For it is quite possible for an author to take over from his source or tradition an allusion to some earlier authority without noticing that what he takes over *is* an allusion. This is Robert Grant's view of the relationship between Mark's account of the triumphal entry and the temple cleansing, on the one hand, and the corresponding passages in Zech 9:9 and 14:21, on the other. Grant argued that in these cases Mark's narrative does reflect the visions recorded in the book of Zechariah, but it was the historical Jesus who through his actions and words brought the correspondences about, whereas Mark remained unaware of them. I do not think that Grant is right in this, but it should be admitted that in principle such a view is defensible. Such a recent commentator as Professor Morna Hooker, for instance, is of the opinion that as regards Jesus' entry into Jerusalem, where the later evangelists, Matthew and John, made the link with Zech 9,[15] we cannot be sure that Mark had already done so.[16]

To summarize these introductory remarks, Mark's account of the final week of Jesus' earthly ministry seems to reflect traditions deriving from Zechariah in perhaps five or six passages. For each of these instances the question must be asked precisely at what stage of the tradition Zechariah's influence became effective, whether already in Jesus' own actions and utterances, or in a later phase of the forty years' tradition from Jesus to Mark, or only in Mark's redaction. Finally, if in a given passage of the Gospel of Mark Zechariah's influence can be established, it remains to be ascertained whether or not Mark was aware of this influence: did he refer to Zechariah on purpose or pass on an allusion without noticing?

With these considerations and questions in mind, let us turn now to Mark's account of the cleansing of the temple, especially Mark 11:15, examine its possible relations with Zechariah, and consider the consequences for the interpretation of Mark as well as those for the history of the interpretation of Zechariah.

MARK 11:15 AND ZECH 14:21

First I want to argue that Mark's cleansing of the temple (Mark 11:15) is indeed a working-out of the final sentence of the book of Zechariah, 14:21 end. This sentence reads: 'And there shall no longer be traders in the house of the Lord of hosts on that day'. My argument will consist of three successive steps. Before taking the first step, however, I must give some attention to the vocabulary of Zech 14:21.

Modern translations read 'there shall no longer be *traders* in the house of the Lord.' For 'traders' the MT has כנעני, originally the word for Canaanite. Now the LXX translates verbally, not to say slavishly, καὶ οὐκ ἔσται Χαναναῖος οὐκέτι ἐν τῷ οἴκῳ κυρίου παντοκράτορος ἐν τῇ ἡμέρᾳ ἐκείνῃ. However, already in biblical Hebrew the noun כנעני repeatedly has the meaning 'trader', 'trafficker', 'merchant'. This applies for instance to Isa 23:8, where the prophet, speaking about the merchants of the city of Tyre, uses the phrase 'her merchants', כנעניה. This is translated by the LXX as οἱ ἔμποροι αὐτῆς, 'her merchants'. It applies also to Prov 31:24, the ode to the dedicated and diligent wife. Here we read: 'She makes linen garments and sells them; she supplies the merchant with sashes.' For 'merchant' the Hebrew has כנעני, but here the LXX reads τοῖς Χαναναίοις. A further instances of כנעני meaning merchant or trader occurs in Job 40:25 (v. 30 MT, כנענים), where the LXX has Φοίνικες; compare Zeph 1:11 עם כנען, where the LXX has ὁ λαὸς Χανάαν. As to the meaning of כנעני in our passage Zech 14:21, here the word must be taken to mean 'trafficker,' 'trader,' rather than 'Canaanite'.[17] After all, the prophet has just invited 'all the families of the earth' to come up to Jerusalem for the Feast of Tabernacles, and there seems no reason for a last-minute exclusion of Canaanites.[18]

It is worth noting that Aquila (ca. 100 CE) translated the כנעני of Zech 14:21 by μετάβολος, which means 'huckster,' 'retail dealer'.[19] Jerome, who in his commentary on Zechariah records that Aquila's rendering of the Hebrew כנעני differs from that of the LXX, translates Aquila's reading (μετάβολος) by *mercator*, that is, 'merchant'.[20] The same interpretation of Zechariah's Hebrew is given by the Targum of the Minor Prophets, which translates עובד תגרא (*ᶜobēd taggᵉrâ*), that is, 'someone doing business', 'someone carrying on trade'.[21] It may be concluded that there was an ancient tradition, going back to the first century CE, which took the final sentence of Zechariah to mean that on the Day of the Lord there would no longer be traders in the temple. The reason why there would no longer be traders in the temple is that they would no longer be needed: on the Day of the Lord Jerusalem will be entirely sacred to the Lord and everything will be holy, even every ordinary cooking pot in Jerusalem (14:21a), nothing excepted. Consequently, traders will no longer be needed to sell ritually pure products used in the cultus, such as wine, oil, salt, sacrificial utensils, such as vessels, or animals without blemish, such as cattle, sheep and doves. Thus, the reason for the absence of traders is *not* that trading in itself would be a defilement of the temple: this somewhat moralistic idea may play a part in popular interpretations of the story of the cleansing of the temple, but it is not yet Zechariah's idea (nor Mark's for that matter).

It is now time to look at Mark 11:15–17, where Jesus is said to enter the temple and to drive out those who were selling and buying. He overturned the tables of the money changers and the seats of those who sold doves. Subsequently, he justified his action by explaining that the temple ought to have been a house of prayer for all nations, not a den of nationalist rebels. When evening came, Jesus and his disciples left the city. In a three-step argumentation, I shall now try to make a case for the idea that the Markan story of the temple cleansing reflects the influence of Zech 14:21.

First, as has been argued by other critics, in a pre-Markan stage of the tradition the entry into Jerusalem and the cleansing of the temple formed a literary unit.[22] As it stands now, the temple cleansing account is sandwiched between the two parts of the story of the cursing of the fig tree. This sandwich composition is notoriously characteristic of Mark.[23] It is Mark who inserted the first part of the cursing of the fig tree between the entry into Jerusalem and the temple cleansing. Originally, entry and cleansing were one story.

This view is confirmed by several observations. For instance, both Matthew (21:12) and Luke (20:45) put the cleansing episode back to Palm Sunday, the day of Jesus' entry into Jerusalem, in contravention of their common source Mark, who had moved the temple cleansing to the day *after* the entry into Jerusalem. Obviously, Matthew and Luke preferred to stick to a common older tradition according to which the temple cleansing was the immediate sequel to, and conclusion of, Jesus' entry into Jerusalem.

Furthermore, the final verse of the entry story in Mark's redaction, Mark 11:11, is a most peculiar and awkward anticlimax of the triumphal entry into Jerusalem.[24] The verse just says that Jesus went into the temple, looked around and left because it was already late: a very unsatisfactory end of the glorious entry into the holy city which had started so promisingly. It should also be noticed that on literary-critical grounds, this verse Mark 11:11 must be considered a purely Markan connecting link between the entry story and the scene of the temple cleansing.[25] Moreover, the entry story is continued in a smooth and natural way in verse 15, after the first part of the cursing of the fig tree, where we read: 'Then they came to Jerusalem. And he entered the temple and began to drive out those who were selling (etc.).' In brief, there is every indication that in the pre-Markan tradition Jesus' entry into Jerusalem and the cleansing of the temple formed a unit.

Second, I would like to point out that stories about kings who upon their accession to office proceed to the purging of the cult, form a traditional, clearly discernible genre both in the Hebrew Scriptures and Jewish literature.[26] For instance, 1 Macc 4:36–61 relates how Judas Maccabaeus, after assuming power in Judea and Jerusalem, cleansed and dedicated the temple and restored the cult. 2 Macc 10:1–8, too, records that Judas, on recovering Jerusalem and the temple, purified the sanctuary and erected a new altar of sacrifice. *Psalms of Solomon* 17 (ca. 40 BCE) expresses the hope that a new Davidic king will soon gain dominion over Israel; this ideal king is expected to 'purify Jerusalem with sanctity, as it was from the beginning' (v. 30).

Third, I wish to point out that in none of the earlier accounts of purifications of the temple, did the cleansing take the form of an expulsion of traders. We hear that idols are removed, sacrifices to other deities than Jahweh are discontinued, idolatrous priests are deposed, altars pulled down, temple furniture and vessels destroyed, the sanctuary is repaired and purified, new vessels are made and brought in, new priests appointed, new offerings and other rituals instituted, etc. We never hear that salesmen and their clients are driven out. Thus, the pre-Markan account of Jesus' entry into Jerusalem and the cleansing of the temple does seem to reflect the tradition of stories about new kings assuming their office and purifying the cult, but the expulsion of traders and buyers is a new element. This element cannot be explained by referring to the tradition of accounts of accessions to the royal office. Another explanation is called for. It is given by Zech 14:21, where, in a vision of the Day of the Lord, the prophet announces that 'there shall no longer be traders in the house of the Lord of hosts'. Just as the Markan story of Jesus' entry into Jerusalem borrowed the colt from Zech 9:9, the pre-Markan account of the temple cleansing borrowed the traders from Zech 14:21.

THE CLEANSING OF THE TEMPLE: A POST-EASTER TRADITION OF CHRISTOLOGICAL PURPORT

The next issue we have to discuss is at what moment the story of the temple cleansing and the expulsion of the traders came into being. Evidently it is of pre-Markan origin, for, as we have argued above, Matthew and Luke knew it in a version in which the temple cleansing was the conclusion of the entry into Jerusalem, and this is probably a more primitive version of the story, since it is closer to the traditional cleansing stories in Hebrew and Jewish literature. Moreover, it is most unlikely that Mark himself created the stories of Jesus' entry into Jerusalem and purging of the temple. In fact, both stories present Jesus as someone who did not fear to disturb public order. This is a presentation of Jesus which Mark normally tries to avoid. True, in Mark's view, Jesus is the Christ, the Son of David, the royal Son of God; but Mark does everything in his power to make it clear that Jesus had not been an agitator, not an insurgent, not a revolutionary in a social or political sense of the word.[27] For Mark, Jesus is the Son of God, but as a suffering righteous one and as the one who accepted death on the cross. The stories of Jesus' triumphal entry into Jerusalem and cleansing of the temple are not really consistent, therefore, with the tendency of Mark's own Christology. This inconsistency is an additional reason to see these stories as deriving from pre-Markan tradition.

On the other hand it seems to me impossible to trace this tradition back to an historical event in Jesus' lifetime. If a tradition can be accounted for satisfactorily on a more recent level, the principle of economy (Ockham's razor)[28] forbids us to look for an explanation on a level further back in time. Moreover, the story of the cleansing of the temple is full of historical improbabilities, often enumerated by the commentators: 'How could one person have overcome the resistance to which this action would obviously have given rise? Or, if we suppose that Jesus was assisted by his followers, why did the temple police or the Roman garrison do nothing to preserve the peace (contrast Acts 4:1ff), and why was the matter not raised at Jesus' trial? And how did Jesus gather an audience (v. 17) which included those responsible for the desecration of the temple?'[29] Furthermore, what was wrong with the trading in the temple? Was it not essential to the temple cult? Was it not necessary to provide animals without blemish and money of the right currency to pay the temple tax? Was it not strictly controlled and, on the whole, conducted fairly and in the interests of the pilgrims? In brief, it is difficult, if not impossible, to trace the story of the temple cleansing back to an event in the earthly ministry of Jesus.[30]

In a recent, extensive study of Jesus' attitude towards the temple, Jostein Ådna argues that Jesus' temple action is at least historically conceivable.[31] First, Ådna locates the scene of Jesus' cleansing of the temple, not in any of the temple courts, but in the royal portico, a basilica extending from west to east on the southern edge of the temple terrace. Then, on the basis of Mark 11:15 and John 2:15–16 (treated as independent of Mark), he gives a reconstruction of Jesus' temple action as an event of relatively limited, harmless scope, so that the non-intervention of temple police and Romans becomes understandable. Ådna concludes that the cleansing of the temple is historically imaginable.

It should be noticed, however, that Mark does not say that the temple action took place in a portico or basilica. On the contrary, Mark's words 'he (Jesus) would not let anyone carry anything through the temple' (Mark 11:16) rather suggests that the evangelist locates the event somewhere in the temple courts. Furthermore, there is definitely some reason to assume that John 2:13–17 is directly or indirectly dependent on Mark 11:15–17, especially because John concludes his story of the temple cleansing with the question about Jesus' authority (2:18) which is typically an element of Mark's plot (11:28). Consequently, Ådna's effort to present the temple cleansing as less violent and less drastic, and thus more conceivable, than the action narrated in Mark 11:15–16 fails to do justice to Mark, the only source of our knowledge of the tradition in question.

However, if (as we have argued) the cleansing of the temple story is a response in narrative form to the prophetic vision of Zech 14:21, any attempt to interpret it as an account of an historical event in Jesus' life becomes superfluous. The story can well be understood as an interpretation of the already highly valued person of Jesus in the light of Zech 14. This chapter is a vision of the Day of the Lord, when he will come to assume the kingship over all the earth (v. 9). According to Zechariah's vision, the Lord will appear 'on the Mount of Olives, which lies before Jerusalem on the east' (v. 4). When the Lord will appear, 'there shall no longer be traders in the house of the Lord of hosts' (v. 21).

Apparently, in the view of a number of Jesus' followers, sometime in a post-Easter situation, Zechariah's vision of the coming of the Lord had become true in the person and ministry of Jesus. They felt that in Jesus, God had come to the world in order to establish his kingdom on earth. They regarded Jesus as God's definitive representative, and, as a result, Jesus' appearance in the world as the appearance of God. In the words and actions of Jesus, his followers recognized the message and deeds of God intervening in history. Consequently, these followers of Jesus could sometimes speak about Jesus' ministry by appealing to the visionary language which the prophets had used for God and his future intervention in the history of Israel and the world. In other words, Christians sometimes applied the visions in which the prophets had spoken about the coming of God, to the earthly ministry of Jesus. An example of this phenomenon may be found in Mark 1:3, where the evangelist in his introductory remarks states that the coming of John the Baptist was in accordance with the words of Isaiah 'prepare the way of the Lord' (Isa 40:3). In the words of Isaiah, 'the Lord' is God. But in the context of Mark, 'the way of the Lord' which John the Baptist prepares is that of Jesus, or, if it is still the way of God, it is now also the way of Jesus. We would be pushing things too far if we said that Jesus here takes the place of God, but it is correct to say that, since Jesus is God's unique and definitive representative on earth, in the coming of Jesus it was God who came. 'God's advent in salvation and judgement has taken place in Jesus'.[32]

In sum, the idea underlying the story of the traders' expulsion from the temple is a specific Christological idea, namely, that when Jesus entered into Jerusalem, he came as God's representative, as judge and saviour on behalf of God. In Jesus, it was God himself who came to what was his own (John 1:11). With Jesus' coming to Jerusalem, the Day of the Lord had dawned, that is, the time when according to Zechariah there would no longer be traders in the temple. The story of the cleansing of the temple thus originated in a Christian environment to give expression to a specific Christology – a Christology which had much in common with the Christology of the Fourth Gospel, namely, that Jesus in his first coming was God's fully authorized representative on earth (compare, e.g., John 5:22, 26–27) and as such functionally one with God (compare, e.g., John 10:30, 37–38). In this view, Jesus is 'the one who enables God himself to be seen'.[33]

The idea behind the story of the cleansing of the temple then was that in Jesus' ministry God had begun to intervene in the history of mankind, the Day of the Lord had dawned. This idea was given a narrative form with the aid of the notion of the absence of traders from the temple, a notion found in Zech 14:21. After all, Zech 14 *is* about the Day of the Lord and the beginning of his reign on earth. If Jesus' followers believed him to be the one who had inaugurated God's reign on earth, it was quite natural for them to believe that on arriving in Jerusalem he had driven out the traders from the temple.

But in the story of the purification of the temple we not only get a glimpse into an early, pre-Markan Christology, but also into the early Christian use of Zechariah. In the second and third quarters of the first century CE, Christians believed that certain visions included in the book of Zechariah were relevant specifically to their time. These Christians interpreted the Christ event as the turn of the times about which Zechariah had spoken. Consequently, they interpreted Zechariah's visions as applicable to Jesus and felt free to depict Jesus with features borrowed from these visions. This explains how the traders from Zech 14:21 could turn up in a story about Jesus' appearance in Jerusalem.

THE CHANGE IN MEANING OF THE CLEANSING STORY IN MARK

The question that remains to be considered is whether or not Mark in editing the cleansing of the temple story, was still aware that it was related to Zech 14:21. The answer must probably be to the negative. I give two reasons for this answer.

First, by separating the cleansing of the temple from the entry into Jerusalem, Mark obscures the idea that the purification of the sanctuary was the act of a new king acceding to office and inaugurating a new order. In fact, if the cleansing of the temple is no longer seen as part of the inauguration of a new order, it has lost its link with Zech 14. For Zech 14:21 is about the new order to be established on the Day of the Lord.

Secondly, Mark places the cleansing of the temple within the framework of the cursing of the fig tree. This editorial intervention changes the meaning of the cleansing of the temple considerably. The temple is now cleansed, not because the Day of the Lord has come, nor because in Christ the Lord God has come to his people. The temple is cleansed because, in Mark's view, the Jewish cult has remained fruitless. In Mark's opinion Jesus condemned the temple cult, the heart of the Jewish religion, because it was as fruitless as a barren tree. It was fruitless as it had not recognized and accepted Jesus as God's unique and definitive envoy (cf. Mark 12:6) and, as a result, had not become a place of worship for *all* nations of the world. For Mark, the cleansing of the temple was a divine punishment for Israel's disobedience. By embedding the incident in the story of the fig tree, Mark shows clearly that he interprets it as a sign of God's condemnation of Israel because of her failure to bear fruit.[34] This suggests that Mark sees the temple cleansing as a symbol of the future destruction of the temple and the final cessation of worship (cf. Mark 12:9; 13:1–2).[35] Placed in the framework of the story of the barren fig tree, Jesus' words and actions in the temple are a condemnation of the Jewish religion for its failure to produce the fruit expected from it: belief in Jesus Christ. These words and actions imply judgement and destruction. They are thus a reference to judgement to come. Morna Hooker is thus right to comment that Mark, looking back on the events of the year 70 CE, saw the cleansing of the temple by Jesus as a symbol of forthcoming destruction. 'It is hardly surprising if Mark, writing at a time when the Jewish people appeared to have rejected the gospel (...), saw the story as pointing inevitably to the temple's destruction. Mark's community (...) would have found in these incidents the explanation of Israel's apparent rejection as the people of God.'[36]

If then the cleansing of the temple in Mark is meant as an adumbration of the temple's destruction and as a sign of God's disapproval of the traditional Jewish religion, it is highly questionable whether Mark did still see Jesus' action in the temple as related to the prophecy of Zech 14:21. In Zechariah, the absence of traders is a sign of the holiness of the temple and Jerusalem: traders will no longer be needed for selling products and animals used in the cult, for everything will be pure and holy. In Mark, the expulsion of the traders is symbolic of the condemnation of the Jewish cult as such. By driving out those who bought and sold in the temple, Jesus was interrupting the offering of sacrifices.[37] By not allowing anyone to carry anything through the temple (Mark 11:16), Jesus was bringing the temple cult to a standstill. For Mark, the traditional Jewish religion had failed. Mark's view of the temple cult is diametrically opposed to that of Zech 14. It is hard to believe, therefore, that Mark still saw any relationship between his cleansing story and Zech 14:21. The meaning of the Markan cleansing story is mainly determined by Mark's preoccupation with the historical destruction of the temple in 70 CE. This preoccupation is so strong that it seems to have obliterated any awareness of a link between the cleansing story and Zechariah.

Some attention should still be given to v. 17, in which Jesus is said to have explained his action in the temple by referring to two passages from the Jewish scriptures. First, Jesus says: 'Does not Scripture say "My house shall be a house of prayer for all nations?"', a quotation from Isa 56, where the context is concerned with the destruction of the temple. Then Jesus goes on to say: 'But you have made it a den of λῃσταί'. Elsewhere in Mark, λῃσταί means 'nationalist rebels', 'revolutionaries', 'insurrectionists'. So there is an a priori probability that this is the meaning intended by Mark here, too.[38] Barrett has argued that the meaning 'nationalist rebels' is confirmed by the fact that Mark contrasts the 'house of prayer *for all nations*' with the 'den of Jewish *nationalists*'. Barret has even gone so far as to argue that v. 17, which contains the two references to Isaiah and Jeremiah, is a secondary accretion to the story of the cleansing, replacing an earlier reference to Zech 14:21.[39] This latter hypothesis, namely that the quotations from Isaiah and Jeremiah replace one from Zechariah, is perhaps one step too far, but it is indeed very probable that v. 17 is more recent than the story of the temple cleansing. It is even probable that v. 17 stems from Mark's own redactional hand, seeing, for instance, the way he introduces here direct discourse with the qualifying verb ἐδίδασκεν (v. 17) the antithetic parallelism of the two quotations from the prophets, and the *inclusio* formed by ἐδίδασκεν and τῇ διδαχῇ αὐτοῦ (vv. 17–18).[40] In any case, on the level of Mark's redaction, Jesus' protest is not directed against selling and buying in the temple, nor against the existence of the temple market in itself, nor against disrespect for the holiness of God's house. In Mark, the protest is against the temple being a stronghold of Jewish nationalism, instead of being a place of prayer 'for all nations'. Clearly, this Markan protest is levelled against the temple of the year 70 CE as we know it from Josephus' account of the Jewish War, when the temple was indeed a stronghold of nationalists and zealots of all kinds.

It may now begin to become clear that the story of the cleansing of the temple has undergone a drastic change of meaning. At first, when the story was still connected with that of the entry into Jerusalem, it gave expression to the idea that, with and in Jesus, the Day of the Lord had come. Since, according to Zechariah, on the Day of the Lord there would be no traders any more in the temple, early Christians formed a story in which Jesus himself expelled the traders from the temple.

In Mark, however, the story of the cleansing of the temple announces the destruction of the temple in 70 CE. In changing the function and meaning of the story, Mark has Jesus justify his violent action by saying that the temple had failed to fulfil its destination: instead of becoming a religious centre for *all* nations, it had become a garrison of Jewish insurrectionists. This justification is remarkably anachronistic if put in the context of the year of Jesus' death, when the temple was not yet occupied by zealots, as it was in 70.

Obviously, the justification given in v. 17 mirrors Mark's own concerns about the fate of the temple, Jerusalem and Israel. In v. 17, Mark is so much concerned about the fate of Israel's temple that he loses sight of the original connection between the cleansing story and Zech 14:21. Mark is no longer aware of the link between the temple cleansing and Zechariah. He establishes new links between the cleansing story and the Jewish scriptures: no longer with Zechariah, but with Isaiah and Jeremiah. In Mark, the original, Christological function of the cleansing story seems to be forgotten; it is now a prediction concerning the end of the temple and God's judgement on Israel's traditional religion.

Remarkably enough, through the redactional work of Mark, the story of the temple cleansing, which had come into being to show that the prophecies of Zechariah 14 had come to fruition, lost its connection with Zechariah and became itself a *new* prophecy. In fact, the story of Jesus' action in the temple now became the account of a prophetic act which, according to Mark, foreshadowed the destruction of the Jewish temple in 70 CE.

CONCLUSIONS

The story of the cleansing of the temple originated as an expression of the idea that in Jesus Christ God's reign on earth had begun to break through. Followers of Jesus were convinced that, in a way, in the message and actions of Jesus the Day of the Lord had come. This conviction made it possible for them to narrate Jesus' arrival in Jerusalem in terms derived from Zechariah 9 and 14. Zechariah's promise that on the Day of the Lord there would no longer be traders in the temple, was now applied to the days of Jesus' visit to Jerusalem. As a Christian response to Zech 14:21, a story took shape in which Jesus, on his arrival in Jerusalem, drove out the traders from the temple. This story, which had a Christological purport, originated in post-Easter, pre-Markan tradition. Mark used this story to shape his account of the beginning of Jesus' passion week. In doing this, however, he was probably no longer aware that the story had been called forth by Zech 14:21. In Mark, the cleansing of the temple is no longer the actualization of Zechariah's vision; it becomes the foreshadowing of the destruction of the temple. It thus serves Mark's interpretation of the events of his own day.

NOTES

1 See Appendix, p. 100.
2 NRSV. Compare John 12:14–15, where Zech 9:9 is also quoted but in a different form.
3 Thus, e.g., Nineham, 1963, p. 291. The reason why I think that Mark was aware of alluding to Zech 9:9 is the following: Mark 11:1b–7 shows Mark's redactional hand to such an extent that the whole passage must probably be considered of Markan origin. In that case, it was Mark himself who introduced the element of the colt. But why would Mark have introduced the colt if not in response to Zech 9:9?
4 Lührmann, 1987, p. 188. Compare, however, Fitzmyer, 1985, 2.1244: 'The extent to which the earliest form of the story in Mark xi reflects Zech ix 9 is a matter of debate.'
5 See, e.g., Barrett, 1975, esp. pp. 19–20.
6 See for instance Hooker, 1991, p. 258, and Nineham, 1963, p. 291.
7 For the significance of the Mount of Olives in the ideology of first-century radical apocalyptic movements, see also Josephus, *J.W.* 2.13.5 and *Ant.* 20.8.6.
8 Thus, e.g., Lührmann, 1987, ad loc. In favour of the latter, more sober and mundane, interpretation it may be observed that the mention of Bethany in Mark 11:1 does not seem to have a function other than to prepare the reader for the visits Jesus is going to pay to that place in the following chapters; see 11:11–12 and 14:3. Jerusalem, Bethany and the Mount of Olives, mentioned together at the beginning of ch. 11, form the complete geographical stage of chs. 11–16.
9 Grant, 1948. The same view is held by Kümmel, 1957, pp. 116–17 ('There can be no doubt that Jesus consciously associated himself with Zech 9.9') and Roth, 1960.
10 Bruce, 1961, esp. p. 343.
11 Nineham, 1963, p. 385. Compare Hooker, 1991, p. 342: 'it seems impossible that Jesus himself could have used these words about the wine'.
12 Bultmann, 1979, pp. 281, 333. According to Bultmann, the legend may already have grown up in Palestinian Christianity.
13 Hooker, 1991, p. 344.
14 Just as Matthew added a reference to the thirty pieces of silver of Zech 11:13 to his account of the treachery of Judas; see Matt 27:9. The testimony from Zechariah is combined here with words from Jer 32:6–9. See Dodd, 1965, pp. 64–5.

15 Matt 21:5; John 12:15.

16 Hooker, 1991, p. 257. She continues: '(…), though he may well have had it in mind.'

17 I am aware that among Old Testament exegetes the meaning of כנעני in Zech 14:21 is debated. Yet I am inclined to think that those early interpreters who took it to mean 'trader' are right.

18 Dodd, 1955, p. 300.

19 Ziegler, 1943, p. 327, second apparatus. The sources for our knowledge of Aquila's reading μετάβολος include a marginal variant in MS. 86, the Syrohexapla, and Jerome (for whom, see n. 20). Field, 1875, 2.1030. For the meaning of μετάβολος, see LSJ, p. 1110: 'huckster', 'retail dealer'. The word occurs also in Isa 23:2 and 3 LXX, with the meaning 'merchant'.

20 Jerome, *Commentarii in Zachariam*, liber iii, cap. xiv, *PL* 25, 1540/1: 'Pro Chananaeo, Aquila interpretatus est *mercatorem*, quem et nos in hoc loco secuti sumus,' namely, in the Vulgate. The Vulgate has indeed: 'et non erit mercator ultra in domo Domini exercituum in die illo': Roth, 1960, p. 180. Interestingly, as Professor A. van der Kooij pointed out to me, Aquila is consistent in rendering כנען/כנעני by μετάβολος, 'trader'. He does so in Zech 14:21 and Hos 12:7, both times in accordance with the Targum, and in Zeph 1:11 in contravention of the Targum.

21 For the Aramaic text, see Sperber, 1992, p. 499. For the vocalization *tagg*^{e}*râ*, see Jastrow, 1903, p. 1647: s.v. *tagg*^{e}*râ*: 'business, trade. Targ Zech. XIV, 21.' Compare Cathcart and Gordon, 1989, p. 226: 'and there shall never again be a trader in the Sanctuary of the Lord of hosts at that time.' Gordon adds a footnote running: 'MT "Canaanite", probably here in the sense of "trader" (cf. *b. Pes.* 50a). The reference to the temple's degeneration into a "house of trade" in John 2:16 may contain an allusion to this verse as understood by *Tg.* (LXX, Syr have "Canaanite").' Compare Roth, 1960, p. 180; Bruce, 1961, p. 351. *b. Pesachim* 50a insists that כנעני in Zech 14:21 should be taken to mean 'trader,' not 'Canaanite'. See Goldschmidt, 1930, 2.456–457.

22 See, e.g., Telford, 1980, pp. 45–9.

23 Neirynck, 1988, p. 133, records the following instances of sandwich composition in Mark: Mark 3:20–21, 31–35 and 22–30; 5:21–24, 35–43 and 25–34; 6:7–13, 30 and 14–29; 11:12–14, 20–25 and 15–19; 14:1–2, 10–11 and 3–9; 14:53–54, 66–72 and 55–65.

24 Telford, 1980, p. 44.

25 Telford, 1980, p. 45, who rightly points out that Mark 11:11 contains several Markan characteristics in style and vocabulary.

26 2 Kgdms 18:1–4 on Hezekiah, king of Judah; 2 Kgdms 22:3–23:25 on Josiah, king of Judah; 2 Chr 29:1–36 on Hezekiah; 2 Chr 34:3–35:19 on Josiah; see also Neh 13:4–9. Furthermore, as mentioned in the text above, 1 Macc 4:36–61 and 2 Macc 10:1–8 on Judas Maccabaeus, and *Ps. Sol.* 17:33 on the future, ideal king, the son of David. I owe the list of passages just enumerated to Ms H. Nicole Roskam (Leiden), who is preparing a dissertation on the relationship between the character of Mark's Gospel as socio-political apologetics and its literary form.

27 De Jonge, 2000.

28 Entia non sunt multiplicanda sine ratione.

29 Nineham, 1963, p. 301.

30 *Pace* such authoritative critics as Bultmann, 1979, p. 59: 'Mk. 11:15–19 ist zwar die erzählte Handlung (Tempelreinigung) ein wahrscheinlich geschichtlicher Vorgang, doch wird er durch das angefügte Wort zur idealen Szene erhoben'; ibid. p. 36: 'altüberlieferte Szene V 15f' augmented with a „nachträgliche Deutung'; ibid., p. 66: Mark 11:18 is a Markan addition; Nineham, 1963, p. 301; Lührmann, 1987, p. 193: 'Historisch steht hinter dieser Geschichte und ihrer Parallele bei Joh sicherlich ein demonstratives Auftreten Jesu im Jerusalemer Tempel'; and Hooker, 1991, pp. 263–8.

31 Ådna, 2000, esp. pp. 300–33.

32 Hooker, 1991, p. 36. She rightly notes (pp. 35–6) that the use of 'the Lord' in Mark 1:3 is a significant Christological development. In my view, the same Christological development underlies the pre-Markan story of the temple cleansing.

33 Tuckett, 2001b, p. 116, in a chapter on the Christology of Mark.

34 Hooker, 1991, p. 265.

35 Ibid.; Barrett, 1975, p. 14.

36 Hooker, 1991, p. 266. See also Hooker, 1982. The view that Mark saw the cleansing of the temple as pointing to the temple's destruction is defended by Telford, 1980, pp. 58–9, on the redaction-critical ground that Mark added the logion on 'this mountain' that could be uprooted and cast into the see by anyone who believed in the efficacy of faith (Mark 11:23). Telford argues that, in the context, 'this mountain' is to be seen as the Temple Mount.

37 Hooker, 1991, p. 267.

38 Barrett, 1975, p. 16.

39 Barrett, 1975, p. 20: 'Thus the original Old Testament references [to Zech 14:21] were replaced by a composite quotation which may have been constructed for the purpose, or may (…) have already existed in another setting.' Barrett also suggests that it was the word כנעני of Zech 14:21 which elicited the word קנאנא = ληστής or ζηλωτής and thus the quotation from Jer 7:11.

40 Neirynck, 1988, pp. 123, 134, 174.

APPENDIX ZECHARIAH IN MARK

passage in Mark	*theme*	*passage in Zechariah*	*status*
Mark 11:1	appearance on the Mount of Olives	Zech 14:4	doubtful
Mark 11:2, 7	entry into Jerusalem riding on a colt	Zech 9:9	probable
Mark 11:15	cleansing of the temple	Zech 14:21	plausible
Mark 14:24	a new covenant through blood	Zech 9:11	probable
Mark 14:27	the shepherd smitten and the sheep scattered	Zech 13:7	certain
Mark 15:39	the centurion looking at Jesus on the cross	Zech 12:10	possible

Zech 14:21 MT
לֹא־יִהְיֶה כְנַעֲנִי עוֹד בְּבֵית־יְהוָה צְבָאוֹת בַּיּוֹם הַהוּא׃

Zech 14:21 LXX
καὶ οὐκ ἔσται Χαναναῖος οὐκέτι ἐν τῷ οἴκῳ κυρίου παντοκράτορος ἐν τῇ ἡμέρᾳ ἐκείνῃ

Zech 14:21 Aquila
Instead of Χαναναῖος Aquila reads μετάβολος, which Jeromes translates by *mercator*.

Chapter 8

Zechariah 13:7 and Mark's Account of the Arrest in Gethsemane

John Muddiman

The importance of the book of Zechariah as background for the interpretation of Mark's passion narrative is widely recognized,[1] but the only explicit scriptural citation, as distinct from passing allusions, is Zech 13:7a, quoted on the lips of Jesus at Mark 14:27. This singular fact probably indicates that the evangelist found in the Zecharian prophecy a key to his interpretation of the passion as a whole: the Shepherd-Messiah, smitten by God himself, would rise from the dead and gather his scattered flock in Galilee.[2] The repetition at 16:7 confirms this. The present context of the citation is the dramatic final scene in the upper room, before the departure (14:32) to the place called Gethsemane. But it is the proposal here that it is Mark himself who has thus promoted into greater prominence a prophecy which originally, that is in the oral or written traditions he was using,[3] had a more limited reference to a minor and surprising detail in the story of Jesus' arrest.

It may be helpful to offer at this point a summary of the argument in the following six sections:

1 The incident of the sword thrust at the arrest often plays a part in the broader discussion of the political aims of Jesus, but the significance of the episode is capable of opposing interpretations.
2 The present state of scholarly opinion with regard to the interrelationships of the canonical gospels permits almost any solution to that problem, but it is not unreasonable to defer consideration of the other gospels until we have read Mark on his own.
3 When the Markan passage is read without presuppositions derived from knowledge of the other gospels, certain textual difficulties emerge, the best solution to which is to suppose that Mark intended his readers to think that a sword was used in the garden *not* by one of Jesus' disciples at all, but by a bystander, one of the hangers-on who came out with the arresting party.
4 The reference to the scriptures at Mark 14:49 can best be explained on the hypothesis that pre-Markan tradition referred explicitly to some specific text which enabled the incident to be seen as the fulfilment of prophecy. Zechariah 13:7 is proposed as the text in question: it reads ' "Awake O Sword, against my shepherd – against the man who stands next to me", says the LORD of hosts. "Strike the shepherd that the sheep may be scattered" ' (RSV). Reasons for Mark's abbreviation and promotion of this text to its earlier position are given.

5 Two courses are open to the exegete at this point, either to suppose that the whole incident is a fictional construction based on the text of Zech 13:7, or to suppose that the narrative contains an element of historical reminiscence.

6 The other gospels may provide some evidence for the latter, in particular the name 'Malchus' and the curiosity that it was, according to Luke and John, his right ear that was severed, but the speculative nature of this part of the argument is acknowledged.

INCIDENT OF THE SWORD

The incident of the sword thrust in Gethsemane is sometimes used as evidence with which to associate Jesus with militant Jewish nationalism. To use it in this way it is often felt necessary to link it with the embarrassing instruction to buy a sword in the Lukan last supper narrative (Luke 22:35–8), and to posit a thorough reworking of the historical facts in the course of tradition before Mark and a toning down of the whole incident. To illustrate I refer to S. G. F. Brandon, the best known English exponent of the Zealot hypothesis. He introduces the evidence of an attempted armed resistance to arrest rather late in his book *Jesus and the Zealots*[4] and connects it firmly with the Lukan injunction on the purchase of weapons. He explains that Luke himself endeavoured to reduce the significance of Jesus' command by claiming that it was in order to fulfil prophecy (Isa 53:12), and that Jesus considered two swords quite enough for this symbolic purpose. Brandon then conjectures that, historically, it is scarcely likely that the disciples were so restrained. The extensive arming of the arresting party suggests that Judas had warned them that the disciples were well provided with weapons and that violent resistance could be expected. Of the incident itself Brandon says little; he admits that it is recorded as an isolated act and that Jesus, realizing that resistance was hopeless, intervened early on to prevent unnecessary bloodshed. This could be correct, he adds, but the possibility must be allowed in view of the apologetic concern of the gospel writers that the resistance was of a more serious nature, even though it proved ineffective.

In reply to this kind of case, Martin Hengel's book[5] is not untypical and illustrates the same method in reverse, i.e. the detachment of Luke 22:35 from the incident in Gethsemane and the minimizing of the latter. Of the Lukan instruction to buy a sword Hengel says that a sword is simply standard equipment of the Jewish traveller as protection against robbers and wild animals. And he cites a late rabbi who defends the wearing of a sword even on the Sabbath as part of a man's adornment. The sword thrust in Gethsemane becomes therefore, in Hengel's view, a solitary aberration and 'basically a sign that no meaningful organised resistance was offered'. Hengel clinches his argument with a point, which is, on its own terms, quite valid, by observing that 'the disciples were able after the event to flee without being apprehended. They leave, completely without punishment, and this would have been impossible in the case of an actual armed confrontation'.

These brief summaries of how the sword thrust in Gethsemane can be accommodated within the diametrically opposed reconstructions of the politics of Jesus may serve to illustrate the point that, despite the importance of the larger issue, our attention must first be directed to the details of the pericope itself. The historicizing methodology of both Brandon and Hengel, in any case, differs somewhat from the redactional and literary methods practised by most New Testament scholars today.

INTERRELATIONSHIPS OF THE CANONICAL GOSPELS

Despite attempts to revive the Griesbach hypothesis,[6] the majority view is still that it is more convincing to read Matthew as an expanded version of Mark, than to read Mark as a truncated version of Matthew. In this passage, for instance, in Matthew's account of the sword-blow, the solemn 'he stretched out his hand' (26:51) helps prepare the way for the Matthean addition 'put up again thy sword into its place'; furthermore 'in that hour Jesus said to the multitudes' (Matt 26:55a) is a typically Matthean addition, and 'I sat daily' (v. 55b) is a characteristic alteration of Mark's 'I was daily'; and finally, 'then all the disciples left him' (v. 56) replaces Mark's ambiguous 'they all left him'. Certain of these changes, as we shall see, clarify obscurities, the presence of which in Mark's account any readers of the text can verify for themselves quite independently.

The situation as regards Luke's use of sources is far more difficult and may be irrecoverable. Nevertheless, certain features of Luke's account, even where he is most distinctive vis à vis Mark, can be taken as editorial reaction to the problems of the Markan text, or a source closely similar to it. For instance, in Luke 22:49, instead of referring to the actual arrest which the evangelist delays till the beginning of the next pericope (22:54), Luke notes 'when they that were about him saw what would follow'; or again, v. 52a can plausibly be understood as editorial expansion of an ambiguity in Mark as to whom Jesus is addressing, which, as we have seen, Matthew may also have felt obliged to clarify.

The source-critical situation in the case of John's version is even more controversial. According to C. H. Dodd: 'The account of the assault on the High Priest's servant resembles Mark so closely that we could well believe it to be derived from Mark if it were not that the immediate context contains features resembling at one point Matthew (viz. the command to put up the sword) and at another Luke (viz. injury to the right ear) as well as other passages in Mark ... These phenomena seem to point to the kind of variation that arises within an oral tradition, rather than conflation of documentary sources.'[7] In contrast to Dodd, C. K. Barrett argues that the distinctive verbal contacts between John and Mark in the use of ἔπαισεν and ὠτάριον at John 18:10 'strongly suggest' that John knew Mark.[8] He considers the option that John and Luke are independently embroidering Mark but concludes, because of the mention of the right ear, that John was familiar with Luke as well as Mark. In the next verse however, despite the similarity between John and Matthew ('put up the sword ...'), he declares that 'it would be unwise to infer knowledge of Matthew on the part of John'. I think Barrett's judgement here must have been determined less by the evidence before him, and more by the comparative lack of evidence of contact between John and Matthew in the rest of the gospel.

The question of sources is still wide open. However, for our purposes here all that we need to agree upon is the following:

1 The theory of Mark's knowledge of and dependence upon Matthew and Luke would have in this pericope at least considerable difficulties to overcome.
2 More importantly, even supposing that Mark were secondary, it would still need to be proved (and it would be almost impossible to prove) that Mark assumed in his own readers knowledge of the more explicit versions of Matthew and Luke, as they read his text.
3 Finally the peculiar information in John's account which we shall look at later, and the similarities between John and Luke, may well indicate that there was a slightly different and fuller version of the incident of the sword thrust available in other circles, but there is no reason to believe that Mark was aware of this version or presumed knowledge of it in his readers.

READING MARK WITHOUT PRECONCEPTIONS

In the preceding section I hope to have provided justification for reading the Markan account (14:46–51) without presuppositions drawn from the other versions, and we can now proceed to list the six major difficulties of the narrative as they appear on such a reading.

First, the actual arrest is completed already by v. 46 ('they laid hands on him and took him'), that is, before the incident with the sword in v. 47. It is therefore not strictly correct to refer to Mark's account as an attempt to resist arrest; it is at most an attempt at rescue after arrest.

Secondly, the identity of the one who struck the blow is not disclosed, nor is he said to be a disciple: he is 'one of the bystanders'.[9] This is a well known problem, the solution to which is normally to harmonize Mark with the others[10] and to explain his failure to identify the assailant as an attempt to protect either his reputation or his person.[11] The only way that Mark identifies him is as 'one of the bystanders', a phrase that occurs four other times in the passion (14:69, 70; 15:35, 39) never of a disciple, but always of the somewhat hostile observers of the passion drama.

Thirdly, injury to an ear may in itself be a minor matter, but the presumptive intention of the act and the refusal to accept arrest are in principle much more serious offences. Mark says nothing of this but refers immediately to Jesus' reaction[12] to the incident which is surprisingly a rebuke not against one of his followers for resorting to violence, but against the arresting party for treating him as a brigand whose capture necessitated the use of swords.

Fourthly, the saying in v. 49a would more naturally be addressed to a more general audience than the official temple police: 'I was daily with you in the temple teaching, and you did not arrest me'.

Fifthly, the reference to the fulfilment of scripture in v. 49b is obscure: it could be a general motif or a more specific reference to some detail of the incident. (We shall look at this more closely later.)

Lastly, in v. 50, 'they all left him' cannot refer to the immediate antecedent which is the crowd with the arresting party; it must refer to his disciples. That there is a problem here is demonstrated by the clearly secondary reading of W et al. which rephrases 'then all his disciples left him and fled'.

To explain these incoherences, scholars such as Eta Linnemann would divide the passage into different parts, a biographical apophthegm against the use of violence, an arrest narrative including Judas' kiss and fragments of a narrative about armed resistance and the flight of the disciples.[13] But I believe that a more coherent reading is possible if we take the passage just as it stands. On such a reading, it was not a disciple but one of the crowd associated with the arresting party who drew his sword in the crush, nicking the ear of the high priest's servant who was standing too close to him in the darkness and confusion. The arresting party do not react to the sword-blow. Jesus reacts by objecting not to the action of the unnamed individual, but to the actions of the arresting group as a whole. In v. 48a we have to think of the bystanders as the addressees of Jesus' words. That the sword-thrust was a case of misdirected enthusiasm by someone in the crowd who came out to help in the arrest, explains the order of events. For in Mark the incident is not one of resisting arrest, but a piece of attempted police brutality after arrest. Furthermore, the minor injury to the ear is easier to understand as an accident perpetrated by one member of the crowd on another; it thus requires no official action to be taken and lends weight to Jesus' rebuke that they are using swords *against him*. We note that Mark specifically mentions the *drawing* of the sword[14] which itself caused the accident, it was not a sword thrust as such, not a deliberate blow aimed at the head of the high priest's servant. Mark refers to the injured member as an ὠτάριον which could imply not the whole organ but just the outer edge of the ear.[15]

If the above interpretation of Mark 14: 46–49a, when read as a unit without preconceptions derived from the parallels, is convincing, we have to ask why this trivial incident of the sword thrust in Gethsemane should have been recounted by Mark at all since it is an almost comic piece of bungling on the part of the arresting party, and especially since it invites the misunderstanding and reconstruction which we find in the other gospel narratives which solve one problem at the cost of raising so many others. We suggest an answer to this question in the next section.

FULFILMENT OF SCRIPTURE

We have already drawn attention to the problem of the reference to the fulfilment of scripture in Mark 14:49b. Many commentators refer to Isa 53:12: 'he was numbered with the transgressors', sometimes helped out with other texts.[16] Others take 'scriptures' in the plural to indicate a deliberately vague and generalizing appeal, and compare 1 Cor 15:3f.[17] But Paul is there referring to the whole salvation event, whereas Mark is describing one particular incident. The evangelist does not normally refer to scriptures in the plural; the only other example is Mark 12:24. But the plural does not imply a general appeal to scripture, for 12:24 is followed by a quotation of Exod 3:6 with the actual reference 'in the passage about the bush' being given.

A specific text is therefore probably in mind,[18] and either refers to the preceding action that precipitated Jesus' words in vv. 48b–49, namely the sword thrust, or else to the subsequent event of the flight of the disciples in v. 50. The difficulty with this suggestion is the problem I mentioned earlier that v. 50 'they all fled' follows on very badly from the address to the arresting party in the previous verse.

My suggestion, therefore, is that the specific text, which has been removed by the evangelist at this point, is Zech 13:7: ' "Awake O Sword against my shepherd, against the man who stands next to me", says the Lord of hosts. "Strike the shepherd, that the sheep may be scattered" '.[19] According to this prophecy, the sword blow meant for the shepherd, i.e. for the Messiah, was to land on the man standing next to the one who wielded it. An attempt was to be made to strike the shepherd, and the sheep would be scattered. If this whole verse stood in the pre-Markan form of the story, it would explain the non-sequitur of v. 50. 'They all fled' would then refer to the sheep in the text of scripture just quoted and not, of course, to the arresters. We asked earlier why an almost comic piece of bungling by those sent out to take Jesus was retained in church tradition. We have now, I think, a satisfactory answer: this strange incident fulfilled a text of scripture. And an interesting parallel emerges with another element of panic that almost verges on the comic in Mark's story of the arrest, namely Mark 14:51 (cf. Amos 2:16), where a young man loses his garment but saves his skin, the second instance of 'a close shave', as it were.

Why did Mark omit the reference to Zech 13:7 at v. 49? The answer is clear: it was because he had already quoted the second half of the verse, Zech 13:7b, at 14:27 and in a wider sense, referring it not to the abortive sword blow against the shepherd and the limited flight of the disciples in the Garden, but to the divine smiting[20] of the sacrificial son and to the scattering of all Jesus' followers after his crucifixion. Mark may have pondered the point that it was not, after all, a sword that would slay God's anointed but something far less humane, a Roman scourge and the cross. Using this text earlier gave Mark the opportunity to extend it (14:28 cf. 16:7) into a prediction of Jesus' resurrection, and having used it once in this larger meaning, he naturally omits it here[21] in its more restricted and surprising application.

FICTION OR HISTORY

The final two sections will be much briefer, for I have already said all that I can say with any confidence. Two courses are open to us if we wish to press on to a complete explanation of the Markan narrative of the sword thrust. We can suppose it to be a pre-Markan historicization of Zech 13:7a. This is an attractive option and would be compelling if it could ever be demonstrated that the other gospels are totally dependent on Mark as their source for this story. No longer able, after the removal of the text on which the incident is based, to understand its drift, they make the obvious but wrong assumption that the one who struck the servant of the high priest must have been acting on Jesus' behalf, and then all their other problems begin. I by no means discount this possibility.

However, given the evidence, as it appears, of some independent tradition in Luke and John, the alternative that an actual historical incident has been remembered here, which has been embroidered at a stage earlier than Mark with a scriptural proof text, and then for the reasons offered above stripped of the scriptural embroidery should not be dismissed.

THE RIGHT EAR AND THE NAME OF THE SERVANT

Let us speculate with a few loose ends: the right ear (in John and Luke) and the name of the servant (Malchus in John).

On the question of the right ear, there has been much learned debate. Rostovtzeff[22] found a second-century BCE Egyptian text, where a similar injury to the right ear occurred in a brawl. Benoit[23] thought that Peter deliberately chose the right ear, a more expensive injury according to the indemnity laws of the time, as a mark of defiance. Daube[24] referred to the slitting of a man's ear as disqualification for priestly office, which he supposes insults the high priest through the person of his servant. Marshall[25] commented on the Lukan version: 'The description is either a legendary accretion or a historical detail of interest to a doctor' (!). Bernard in his ICC commentary of 1928 commented that Peter cut off his right ear the blow missing the slave's head as he swerved to the left to avoid it; apparently the weapon arrested in mid-flight before it carved into his shoulder-blade. Nineteenth-century commentators, who knew more about fencing than most moderns do, were naturally sensitive about this kind of explanation for it would imply a murderous and ungentlemanly intent on Peter's part to split his enemy in two from top to bottom. This is an amusing game, and in the same spirit I would refer finally to R. E. Brown's reference to ingenious interpreters (which I have been unable to trace) who have observed that 'a right-handed man will normally strike at the left ear of an opponent who is facing him', so either Peter was left-handed or he was a cowardly right-hander striking from behind![26] But if the Markan scenario is as we have envisaged it, then the right ear fits perfectly. For a right-handed man with his sword slung on his left side, would put at risk precisely the right side of the man standing next to him. The sword would deal a glancing blow on the way up, and apart from damaging the ear would cause no other injury.

The name Malchus in John is a known Arabian name attested in this form in Josephus *Ant.* 13.131.[27] The mystery of Malchus does not end here in the Fourth Gospel for a relative of his is said to have confronted Peter with his crime in the denial scene in 18:26. I suppose it is conceivable that this sort of accidental injury inflicted on a special constable would naturally be blamed by his friends on the nearest Galilean suspect available, which he would equally vehemently deny.

So, finally, I leave the reader to decide whether to think of the severed ear in the garden of Gethsemane as an odd piece of history confirmed by prophecy or as an odd piece of prophecy turned into history. Either way this passage illuminates the importance of Zechariah both on the surface and beneath the surface of Mark's passion narrative, but it also underlines the point that this incident tells us nothing of any use concerning the political aims and methods of the Jesus movement, which need to be discussed on quite other and more solid ground.

NOTES

1 In addition to the commentaries, see e.g. Lindars, 1961, pp. 110–33; Marcus, 1993, pp. 153–63.

2 The scattering motif from Zechariah can be taken in different ways: negatively as the dispersal of the sheep and their abandonment of the shepherd, or positively as their escape and evasion of capture. In the positive sense there is no tension between Mark 14:27 and 14:28. Contrast Marcus, 1993, p. 154, who assumes a tension between the two verses and takes it to indicate that Mark added v. 48 to a source which already contained Zech 13:7 at this point. He notes that 'John 16:32 preserves an allusion to the Zecharian text in a similar context but the Johannine text seems to be independent of the Marcan one'. But apart from the use of the verb σκορπίζω (in Mark and Zechariah διασκορπίζω) there is nothing to connect John 16:32 with Zech 13:7; in particular, the sheep-shepherd imagery is lacking. More significantly, the theme of fulfilment is present in John's arrest scene (18:9), as it is in Mark's, though John seems to have replaced the idea of fulfilment of scripture with the idea of fulfilment of Jesus' own prophecies, that 'not one shall be lost' (see 6:39; 17:12).

3 It is difficult and perhaps impossible to decide between oral and written traditions underlying the Markan passion narrative. Since the passion would have been used frequently in mission preaching (Gal 3:1) and worship (1 Cor 11:26), it is likely to have assumed a standard form even in oral use. For further discussion, see Donahue, 1976; and for more recent contributions to the debate, Gundry, 1993, pp. 806–9.

4 Brandon, 1967, pp. 304f.

5 Hengel, 1973.

6 Discussed and rejected by Tuckett, 1983.

7 Dodd, 1963, p. 79.

8 Barrett, 1955, p. 435.

9 Compare Matthew 'one of those with him', Luke 'those who were about him', John 'Simon Peter'.

10 David Friedrich Strauss' strictures on this procedure are classic and are worth repeating: 'This supposition belongs to the justly exploded fictions of an exegesis framed on the false principle of supplying conjecturally all those links in the chain of natural causation which are wanting in the Gospels.' (Strauss, 1973, p. 652).

11 So most commentators on Mark, Gundry, 1993, p. 860, being a recent, notable exception who takes the view adopted here.

12 ἀποκριθείς, v. 48: for this sense of the participle cf., e.g., Mark 9:5.

13 Linnemann, 1970, pp. 41–54. The awkwardness in this analysis of having to posit odd fragments left over is pointed out by Schneider, 1972.

14 In the aorist participle, which may indicate action simultaneous with that of the main verb, as it does certainly at, e.g., Mark 7:33. Matthew in parallel clearly distinguishes the two actions of drawing the sword and striking with it.

15 It could also of course be an example of Mark's stylistic preference for diminutives; the word appears also in John; Matthew has ὠτίον and Luke οὖς.

16 Lane, 1974, p. 526 is typical: 'The comment that this was done that scripture might be fulfilled immediately calls to mind Isaiah 53:12', but he continues 'in the light of the disciples' flight in v. 50, it is appropriate to recall Zech. 13:7'.

17 Schweizer, 1971, pp. 318f., argues that the reference is deliberately vague as it is also in 1 Cor 15:3f. and comments: 'Therefore it is enough simply to assert here God's will which has been established throughout the ages is being done.'

18 The grammar of v. 49 is unclear; the choice is between supposing an ellipsis and a final clause (see Matthew) 'this was done in order that the scriptures be fulfilled', or supposing an imperatival use of ἵνα. In favour of the former is the strong adversative ἀλλά: 'you did not arrest me when I taught openly in the Temple, *but* now you have – by night, secretly, with a wounding kiss from a friend and an attempt at physical violence – in order to fulfil the scriptures.' See further Gundry, 1993, p. 880.

19 Perhaps I should add at this point that the Christian interpretation of Zech 13:7 is likely to be a misinterpretation. Meyers and Meyers, 1993, p. 384, agree that the term shepherd, and the explanatory phrase that follows 'a man, my neighbour', were intended ironically, i.e. this is what the ruler of the people should be and palpably is not. But that would not have prevented early Christian readers from taking the shepherd as a positive image for Jesus, the Messiah, God's right-hand man. Notice also that on this reading, the Hebrew phrase *geber amiti*, (in LXX 'my comrade', in Aquila 'my clansman', in Symmachus 'man of my people', in Theodotion 'my neighbour', in Jerome 'one who sticks close to me') is no longer an explanation of the word 'shepherd' but has a separate referent, i.e. the sword intended to hit the shepherd was to land on a bystander by mistake. That early Christian exegetes could so misconstrue the original meaning of a text from Zechariah in this way may seem improbable until one recalls Matt 21:5, where the colt and the foal of a donkey turn out to be two animals, on both of which the Lord, acrobatically, rides into Jerusalem!

20 Note the change from the LXX imperative 'Smite the Shepherd', to the future indicative, first person singular 'I will smite'.

21 Today, when intertextuality and the detection of OT echoes everywhere in Mark is all the rage, it may seem perverse to argue that the evangelist could have underplayed his intertextual hand and removed an explicit quotation. I am not worried by this objection, for I believe Mark does it quite frequently in the interests of making his story accessible to all his hearers, however great or however small their acquaintance with Jewish scripture. Quite often, Mark's references or allusions are parenthetical and, as it were, optional; see, e.g., 4:12, 29, 32.

22 Rostovtzeff, 1934.

23 Benoit, 1969, p. 43.

24 Daube, 1960, pp. 59–62.

25 Marshall, 1978, p. 837.

26 Brown, 1985, p. 812.

27 There is no need to suppose that it is a cryptic reference to Judas Iscariot (so Kreiger, 1957) or doubles for a reference to the king in that part of the synagogue lectionary parallel to this part of John (Guilding, 1960, pp. 164ff.). Brown, 1985, p. 812, comments reasonably that John sometimes adds names to add plausibility to his narrative. 'But since the tendency of legend-makers is to identify anonymous figures with better known ones, this explanation will work for Peter's name but not for that of Malchus.'

Chapter 9

Zechariah 12:10 and the New Testament

Christopher M. Tuckett

Zechariah 12:10 (and parts of its sequel in vv. 12 and 14) is a text which clearly influenced a number of early Christian writers. The verse in Zech 12 talks of people looking 'on one who is pierced';[1] these people will then 'mourn' for him, and the sequel in vv. 12, 14 refers to various groups who will mourn, including 'each family/tribe by itself' (v. 12) and 'all the families/tribes that are left' (v. 14). Zechariah 12:10 is explicitly cited in John 19.37 ('And again another passage of scripture says "they will look on the one whom they pierced" '). It is clearly alluded to in Matt 24:30 ('all the tribes of the earth will mourn [κόψονται]') and also in Rev 1:7 ('Every eye will see him, even those who pierced him, and on his account all the tribes of the earth will mourn [κόψονται]'). It is also referred to in some patristic texts, notably Barn 7:9 as well as a number of passages in Justin (*1 Apol.* 52:12; *Dial.* 14:8 (though there wrongly ascribed to Hosea); 32:2; 64:7; 118:1.)[2]

Although John 19:37 is the only place where Zech 12:10 is quoted as an explicit citation (i.e. with a clear signal in the text by means of an introductory formula),[3] it seems clear that this OT text was widely known and used as a Christian *testimonium*; moreover, it was apparently known and used in a relatively firm, but distinctive, text form. The text as cited in John 19:37 reads ὄψονται εἰς ὃν ἐξεκέντησαν. Revelation 1:7 shares with John the use of ἐκκέντεω as well as the use of οἴψεται/ὄψονται, as does Matt 24:30. A reference to 'all the tribes of the earth' (πᾶσαι αἱ φυλαὶ τῆς γῆς) who will 'mourn' (κόψονται) is also common to Rev 1:7 and Matt 24:30. Very similar wording is echoed in Justin, *1 Apol.* 52:12; *Dial.* 14:8 (including the rather unusual εἰς [as in John 19:37], though Justin also inserts the verb γνωρίζειν, resulting in a rather awkward γνωρίζειν εἰς: cf. too *Dial.* 32:2: ἐπιγνώσεσθε εἰς ὃν ἐξεκεντήσατε).[4] The verse is thus used by a wide range of Christian writers in closely related, but not identical, forms. Literary dependence between such a cross-section of writers seems unlikely.[5] There is thus widespread agreement that Zech 12:10 was known and used by Christians, probably substantially in the form as it appears in John 19:37: ὄψονται εἰς ὃν ἐξεκέντησαν. In addition there was probably a reference in the form of the citation as known and used to 'all the tribes of the earth' and 'will mourn' (κόψονται).[6]

In Matt 24 and Rev 1, the reference to Zech 12:10 is clearly combined with an allusion to Dan 7:13 as well and the combined allusion is related to the eschatological future. In John 19:37 the reference is applied to/at the time of the crucifixion. In terms of tradition history, the relative age of these different applications of the text is disputed.

EARLIEST APPLICATION: PASSION OR PAROUSIA?

A number of scholars have claimed that the reference to the crucifixion is the starting point of the development of the use of Zech 12:10 in early Christianity. Thus Lindars argued that the earliest use of the text was as part of a general 'passion apologetic', to account for Jesus' death by crucifixion (hence similar to John 19).[7] Subsequently the text was combined with Dan 7:13 and used in an eschatological context: thus Matthew took the initial ὄψονται at the start of the allusion to Dan 7:13 in Mark 13:26 as the first word of the Zech 12:10 in the form known to him, and hence worked in an allusion to that prophecy. Revelation 1:7 similarly combined the two texts (albeit in a slightly different form).

Perrin argued for a slightly more complex picture.[8] The original Christian form of the text resulted in a use of ὄψονται on the basis of a 'word play' with κόψονται and was used originally as a Christian *testimonium* about the cross. Subsequently a reference to Dan 7:13 was added so that 'the one they have seen crucified they will see coming as the Son of Man';[9] this then led to texts such as Rev 1:7 and Matt 24:30; in the former the two OT texts are separable, but in Matthew they have become fused so that the ὄψονται is now clearly linked with the Son of Man reference: 'they will see (Zech 12:10) the Son of Man coming … (Dan 7:13)'. According to Perrin, this last development is then reflected in Mark 13:26 and 14:62 where the ὄψονται/ὄψεσθε then represents a vestige of the Zechariah allusion, even though the other references ('tribes', 'mourning', 'piercing') have disappeared.

A very similar position appears to be adopted by J. D. Crossan in his book on Jesus.[10] Further, the discussion of the possible allusions to Zech 12:10 becomes an important part of his argument that the eschatological Son of Man sayings (as in Mark 13:26; 14:62 etc.) do not go back to the historical Jesus. Crossan refers to the fact that some of the earliest texts which talk of Jesus' return refer to him as 'Lord' not Son of Man (cf. 1 Thess 4:16–18 and perhaps Did 16:8). Reference to Jesus as Son of Man in this context only developed when Dan 7:13 was attached to the Zech 12:10 citation:[11]

> This whole stream of tradition, far from starting on the lips of Jesus, began only after his crucifixion with meditation on Zechariah 12:10, then moved on to combine Daniel 7:13 with that prophecy, and finally left only the barest vestige of those beginnings in the perdurance of the *see* verb for the apocalyptic judge.

So too Albl's recent study of possible *testimonia* collections argues that Matt 24:30 lets us see an earlier stage in the development of the tradition; Mark and Luke then drop the more explicit references to Zech 12 and have only the ὄψονται as the (tell-tale) allusion.[12]

There are a number of wide-ranging issues potentially raised here, especially when developed by Crossan in relation to a discussion of the historical Jesus. There is not enough time or space here to engage fully with the broad question of whether the eschatological Son of Man sayings, with their reference to Dan 7, might be dominical.[13] I consider here the more limited question of where and how Zech 12:10 might have entered the tradition and where its influence can be seen.

In relation to the theory of the development of the tradition as espoused by Perrin, Crossan, Albl and others, it must remain very doubtful whether one should see a vestige of an allusion to Zech 12:10 in the use of the verb ὁράω in Mark 13:26 or 14:62. The verb is a relatively common one in some respects, and on its own seems insufficient to establish the existence of an allusion to Zech 12 alongside the clear allusion to Dan 7.[14] Further, the line of development as postulated by Perrin and others seems a curious one in relation to the (normally accepted) relative chronology of the texts concerned. According to this line of development, Matthew's text must be the earlier one in terms of the tradition history, and Mark's the later; and yet on the usual theory of synoptic relationships, Mark's text is prior to Matthew and the source of Matthew. Any theory therefore which makes Matthew more original than Mark is inherently slightly implausible.[15]

In fact, although ὄψονται is not explicitly present in Dan 7:13, a very close verbal parallel exists in the opening 'I saw' (ἐθεώρουν in LXX and θ'). The number and the tense are different, but it is a verb from the same semantic domain. Hence a reference to 'seeing' with an allusion to Dan 7:13 can surely be adequately explained from within Dan 7:13 itself without going outside to Zech 12.

Overall, the evidence of the synoptics is probably best explained by a theory such as that of Lindars: Mark 13:26; 14:62 (and the Lukan parallels where appropriate) offer an allusion to Dan 7 alone; Matthew in his parallel to Mark 13:26 then adds the allusion to Zech 12:10, perhaps because of the 'trigger' provided by the ὄψονται of Mark 13:26.

What though of the development of the tradition as reflected in the other texts? Again the development postulated by Perrin and others fits rather uneasily with the normally accepted chronology of the texts themselves. Thus Perrin and Lindars argue that the earliest use of Zech 12:10 in early Christianity was in the context of a relatively unsophisticated passion apologetic, similar to John 19:37; this was then later expanded by Dan 7:13 to become a reference to the parousia. But once again the text often assumed to be later (John) is then posited as containing the earlier form of the tradition; and the earliest texts witness to the later tradition.[16] However, the claim that a use of Zech 12:10 was used originally as part of a passion apologetic is asserted rather than proved.[17] In fact a consideration of the text form may point in a rather different direction.

Text form of Zech 12:10

We have already seen that early Christian writers appear to know the text of Zech 12:10 in a fairly fixed text form. Moreover, this text form is rather distinctive and certainly not the same as that of the other Greek versions about which we have information. Much of the relevant evidence has been fully analysed by Menken and what follows is mostly a summary of his work. (However, some of the implications of his analysis are not quite so explicitly drawn out in his essay.)

All the Greek versions appear to be struggling to cope in various ways with the very difficult Hebrew text וְהִבִּיטוּ אֵלַי אֵת אֲשֶׁר־דָּקָרוּ, especially the apparent first person reference in the word אֵלַי. In context this must be a reference to Yahweh, who is then apparently said to be 'pierced'. Some corruption of the MT has been suspected,[18] though there is no real evidence in the versions that they are doing anything other than trying to make sense of the verse as it now stands in the MT. The LXX seems to have read רקדו as רקדו 'danced' (καὶ ἐπιβλέψονται πρός με ἀνθ' ὧν κατωρχήσαντο); Aquila appears to have taken the את as 'with' (συν), thus driving a wedge between the 'me' and the 'one who is pierced'. Symmachus is not fully extant. Theodotion is perhaps closest to the MT (ἐπιβλέψονται πρός με [εἰς] ὃν ἐξεκέντησαν).[19]

The form of the text as reflected by NT writers consistently has no obvious equivalent for the אֵלַי at all. This *may* be due to a different vocalization of the word (possibly reading it as אֱלֵי, a poetic form of the preposition אל and then 'translated' as εἰς).[20] But such an explanation seems over-subtle and unnecessary. The lack of any (obvious) reference to the אֵלַי of the MT may simply be due to the fact that Christians interpreted the verse as referring to Jesus and not to God: the one who is 'pierced' is the crucified Jesus, not God himself.[21] Thus this aspect of the text form may be due to the particular application of the verse by early Christians.

The Christian version of the phrase את אֲשֶׁר־דָּקָרוּ seems to be εἰς ὃν ἐξεκέντησαν. This agrees with θ' and α' is similar (σὺν ᾧ ἐξεκέντησαν); σ' uses a cognate verb (ἐπεξεκέντησαν). The LXX, as we have seen, has a totally different version, perhaps seeking to avoid the suggestion that Yahweh might have been 'pierced' and rewriting the Hebrew accordingly.

What though of the verb used for 'seeing'? All the Greek versions of Zech 12:10 have ἐπιβλέψονται for MT's הִבִּיטוּ whereas the Christian texts have, or presuppose, a version reading ὄψονται. Although the latter is not an impossible translation of the Hebrew,[22] it is not the most obvious verb to use, being somewhat vaguer and more general than the ἐπιβλέψονται of the other Greek versions.[23] Why then is this verb used – apparently so consistently – in the Christian texts?

Perrin suggested that the ὄψονται arose as a result of 'word play' with the verb κόψονται which occurs nearby in the verse; he argued that this was typical of 'pesher'-type exegesis as found at Qumran and hence he suggested that what we have here is a 'Christian pesher' tradition. Others too have followed the suggestion that what we have in the Christian texts is the result of some 'word play'.[24]

Perrin's argument is however not fully persuasive, at least in the form he presented it. The phenomenon he alluded to in Qumran texts might be described as one involving a certain *freedom* in relation to the text, if necessary at times even changing the text to fit with, or force, a particular interpretation.[25] But what is not evidenced is what Perrin appears to have postulated here, namely a substitution of what is virtually a simple synonym, perhaps on the basis of some apparent rhyming or similar sound. Of this there is no real parallel in the Qumran pesharim.[26] The suggestion then of 'word play', at least in the form proposed by Perrin, is really unproven and with little foundation or parallel.

Rather more convincing then may be Menken's suggestion that the use of the verb ὁρᾶν is to be related to the early Christian eschatological interpretation of Zech 12:10. Early Christians regularly used the verb ὁρᾶν of Christ's *parousia*, or the kingdom, or God, at the eschaton.[27] Thus Menken concludes:[28]

> This verb, not ἐπιβλέπειν which is found in other Greek versions of Zech 12:10, suggested itself for the translation of Zech 12:10 as applied to the *parousia* of Christ because it was already in use in connection with the *parousia*.

This then suggests that the Christian text form in using ὄψονται derived from a specifically Christian eschatological interpretation of the text.[29] But this in turn implies that the reference to the crucifixion alone may represent a secondary, not an original, use of the verse.[30] Rather than being the origin and basis of the citation in early Christianity, the use of the verse in relation to the passion narrative may then be a later development. In turn this suggests that Crossan's reconstruction of the development of the tradition is somewhat unconvincing. Zechariah 12:10 was thus not necessarily the original scriptural reference to which Dan 7:13 was later attached; rather, Dan 7:13 may have been earlier, Zech 12:10 (with an eschatological interpretation) was then attached to this (in Matt 24 and Rev 1), and subsequently applied to the passion narrative alone (John 19). This conclusion is the result in part of a consideration of the text form; but the reconstruction suggested for the development of the tradition history would also fit better with the (probable) relative dates of the texts in which the citations and allusions occur.

ZECH 12:10 IN JOHN 19:37

We have seen that Zech 12:10 was probably used initially by Christians with an eschatological interpretation. Nevertheless, the use of the word 'pierced' in the quotation itself led very naturally, if not inevitably, to its use more directly in relation to the passion narrative itself. Clearly we see this happening in John. But precisely how does John understand the text?

The citation has always caused some difficulty of interpretation, notably in relation to the ὄψονται. Who is the subject of this verb? Are those who 'see' the same as those who 'pierce'? And what exactly is that time reference: when 'will' they 'see' the pierced one?

Further, how precisely does John understand the text as functioning? Is it, for example, a simple fulfilment quotation, showing that with the piercing of Jesus' side by the Roman soldiers, the events of the passion narrative can be seen to be corresponding precisely with the words of a scriptural prophecy? This would be in line with what is said in v. 36a ('These things happened so that the scripture might be fulfilled'), this introductory formula being then taken as referring to both v. 36 and v. 37.[31]

On the other hand it is not entirely clear that the introductory formula of v. 36a is intended to apply to v. 37 as well. The two quotations (v. 36 and v. 37) are not connected by a simply καί or a πάλιν (as e.g. in Luke 4:10–11; Heb 2:13). Rather, v. 37 has its own extra introduction 'and again another scripture says'. This at least opens the possibility that the citation in v. 37 is not governed by the introductory formula in v. 36a, and may be functioning rather differently.[32]

Further, Menken points out that this interpretation of the verse as a simple 'fulfilment quotation', focuses almost exclusively on the reference to 'piercing' in the text and the event of the sword thrust, and as a result leaves the οἴψονται of the citation hanging in the air;[33] yet elsewhere John is not afraid to rewrite the grammar of a scriptural verse to make the main point he wants to emphasize correlate with the main clause of the form of the citation he uses.[34] Thus the fact that John has left 'they will see' as the main verb in the sentence suggests that as much stress, if not more, should be laid on the seeing as on the piercing. It is thus rather doubtful whether the main point of the citation is simply to show that the 'piercing' mentioned in Zechariah has been precisely fulfilled in the gospel story.

Who then does John have in mind as the subject of the verb ὄψονται? In one way the most 'obvious' way to read the text is to interpret the subject of the ὄψονται as the same as that of the ἐξεκέντησαν. The 'they' will then be the Roman soldiers. Alternatively one could extend this slightly to include the Jews present at the cross as well.[35] However, nothing is said in the immediate context of either the Roman soldiers or the Jews specifically 'looking at' or 'seeing' Jesus at this point. Given the fact that the sentence structure, with the 'seeing' rather than the 'piercing' as the main verb, has the former as the primary point of reference, such an interpretation has seemed to many to be too weak.

There is however at least one person in the immediate narrative context who is said to 'see': this is the person mentioned in v. 35 (probably the beloved disciple) as one who has 'seen' and has testified and whose testimony is assured by the writer of v. 35. Thus at least one person does 'see' the one who was pierced; but this 'seeing' is clearly regarded in a positive way, and the person who 'sees' in this way is not the same as those who have 'pierced' Jesus.

Partly with this in mind, a number of scholars have therefore separated the subjects of the 'seeing' and the 'piercing'. Further, a substantial body of opinion would connect the citation here with what is said in John 3:14–15, the comparison between Jesus as Son of Man who will be 'lifted up' and the serpent which was lifted up by Moses in the wilderness (cf. Num 21:8–9).[36] The effect of the sight of the one lifted up is to bring life to those who see. In Num 21, those who see the serpent will live. In John 3, this is paralleled by people 'believing in' Jesus. Thus the 'seeing' of Jesus may be meant in a positive sense, or rather those who see may be regarded by John positively: those who 'see' the one who is pierced are – at least potentially – those who believe.[37]

Further, it has been pointed out that a number of people do 'see' Jesus after his death – in the resurrection appearances of Jesus (cf. 20:18 [Mary Magdalene]; 20:20, 25 [the disciples]). Thus for Menken, 'to look on the pierced Jesus with belief coincided with seeing the risen Lord', thus fulfilling Jesus' own predictions in 14:19; 16:16–19.[38] As the disciples see Jesus, and the beloved disciple at the cross 'sees', so the prophecy is fulfilled. According to Menken too, the Thomas scene refers to a time when people will not 'see' physically (v. 29); but 'as believers who "see" the risen Jesus in the preaching of the church, they can be said to belong to those who "shall look on him whom they pierced"'.[39]

It is possible too that all this can be seen as part of John's 'realized eschatology'. As we saw, the earliest use of Zech 12:10 was an eschatological interpretation. Some have argued that the future ὄψονται is intended by John in a futurist eschatological sense (as in Rev 1:7): 'they will see' the pierced one at the eschaton when he comes in judgement.[40] But it could equally be interpreted as part of John's general attempt to reinterpret much of what is said in the tradition in terms of an eschatology realized in the present. Thus Menken concludes his essay as follows:

> The future looking on the pierced one is interpreted in John as taking place when people look in faith at the crucified Jesus as the risen Lord.[41]

> The quotation in its Johannine context refers primarily to the look in which believers will see the pierced Jesus as who he really is: the exalted Son of Man, the risen Lord. ... The eschatological look at the pierced one occurs when believers see in the crucified Jesus the risen Lord, and in the risen Lord the crucified Jesus.[42]

There is much that is suggestive in this interpretation. However, we should perhaps be a little cautious. Although the link with John 3:14f. is often adduced, one should note that there is nothing explicit in John 3 itself about 'seeing' the Son of Man as lifted up. It *may* be implied (and it is mentioned in Num 21: those who 'see' the serpent will live); but it is not explicit in John 3 itself.[43]

Further, it is somewhat unclear whether references to 'seeing' in relation to the risen Jesus are all meant positively in Johannine terms. It is true that Mary and the other disciples do 'see' the risen Jesus. But the Thomas scene (20:24–9) seems to imply quite clearly that 'seeing' Jesus is something quite exceptional for the majority of Christians. Thomas is granted the chance to 'see' Jesus; but Jesus then immediately says 'Blessed are those who have *not* seen and yet have believed' (20:29). The implication seems clear: those who come after Thomas will *not* be granted the chance to 'see' and yet they *are* summoned to 'believe'. Whether there is any personal antagonism to Thomas himself (or derivatively to a 'Thomas group' in early Christianity) may be doubted.[44] But it does seem that there is at least a hint of a critique of any who would claim that 'seeing' the risen Jesus is necessary or indeed possible (after the time of the initial eye-witnesses). However desirable such an experience might be, 20:29 seems to imply that such 'seeing' is not going to happen for the vast majority of post-Easter Christians.

How all this relates precisely to what is said in 14:19 ('you will see me') and the extended little discussion in 16:16–19 about the 'little while' when 'you will not see' and then 'will see me' is not clear. The sayings are notoriously ambiguous: is the time of 'seeing me' a reference to the time after the resurrection (the 'little while' when you 'will not see me' would then be the time between Jesus' death and his resurrection)? Or is it a reference to the eschatological future? As Brown points out, the concomitant references to the full understanding and joy of the disciples (14:23f.) are slightly odd if referring to the post-resurrection situation of the disciples.[45] It may be therefore that the reference is to the eschatological future, and that the post-resurrection period is covered by the clause 'a little while and you will *not* see me'. This is however Brown's interpretation of what the saying might have meant on the lips of Jesus. At the level of John, Brown claims that the reference *is* to the post-resurrection period as the time when the disciples will see Jesus. ' "Seeing" Jesus has been reinterpreted to mean the continued experience of his presence in the Christian, and this can only mean the presence of the Paraclete/Spirit.'[46] However, this interpretation seems to founder on the fact that the Paraclete in John is fairly consistently *not* simply a cipher for Jesus. However much continuity or identity in function there is between Jesus and the Paraclete,[47] John seems to emphasize that the Paraclete/Spirit is *different from* Jesus; he is 'another' Paraclete who can only come when Jesus goes (back to the Father in heaven).[48] In terms of the post-Easter situation, John presents primarily an *absentee* Christology: Jesus is *not* present but is in heaven and is *replaced* by the Paraclete/Spirit. So too Menken's attempt to reinterpret the 'seeing' of Jesus in 'the preaching of the church' (cf. above) seems somewhat forced and artificial. The model in John's thought is surely not that of a contemporary Lutheran theologian (Jesus as present where the word of the gospel is preached). Rather, as many passages in the gospel make explicit, Jesus has *departed* this world to his true home elsewhere.[49]

If then the post-resurrection period is for John a time when even believers will *not* 'see Jesus', it is perhaps worth reconsidering what *is* said in John 19:37. The verse as quoted states that 'they will see [on] *him whom they pierced*'. It may well be right to pay attention to what is the main verb in the sentence (cf. above). But equally one should perhaps note the *object* of the verb as well! In one sense it is probably right to say that the stress is not just on the fact of the piercing but on the act of seeing; but also there is the statement about who/what it is that people will look at/see: they will see – *the one who has been pierced*. Perhaps this, coupled with the verse in 20:29, may suggest a slightly different interpretation from the one suggested by Menken and others.

The reference by many to 3:14f. may indeed be apposite. However, its force may be a little more pointed and specific than some have allowed. John 3:14 is the first reference to the 'lifting up' of Jesus the Son of Man, a theme which, as many have pointed out, is developed and interpreted later in the gospel. The exact time and place of the 'lifting up' is left open in 3:14, but it is made absolutely clear later in the story that the 'lifting up' is identified with the lifting up on the cross (cf. 12:33 after 12:32). But equally as well, Jesus' 'lifting up' is his *glorification*, the time when he is 'glorified', and given the glory/status, that belongs to God alone.[50] The lifting of Jesus (on the cross) is the moment at which others will realize that 'I am' (8:28); thus the cross represents the supreme moment of the revelation of Jesus' identity as the one who manifests the divine glory. The part-verse in the Prologue in 1:14b 'we have seen his glory' should therefore perhaps be interpreted as a reference forward to the cross.[51]

It is perhaps against this Johannine background that the slightly negative references to 'seeing' the risen Jesus should be interpreted. The climax of the process of revelation, the moment of full revelation of Jesus' glory, i.e. the revelation of who he really is, is to be located in the cross, not in some wonderful post-Easter revelation scenes. Jesus as the revealer of God reveals himself, and his God, supremely in the moment of his *death* – as the crucified one.

If this is an appropriate interpretation of John, and of the significance of Jesus' death in John, then perhaps the citation of Zech 12:10 in John 19:37 gains added force. It is true that 'seeing' Jesus has been an important part of the narrative. And indeed it occupies a key role in ch. 20 as various people do 'see' Jesus; and yet, as we have seen, there is a strong hint that this kind of 'seeing', or perhaps seeing in this way, is not the most important thing about Christian existence. Rather, the only 'seeing' that may count in the post-Easter situation is the seeing *of the crucified one*, the one who *has been pierced*. It is this that shows Jesus in his true glory, which is the glory of God; hence it is this moment that marks the moment of climactic revelation.[52] It is arguably this that constitutes the 'greater things' promised in 1:51 as the making visible of the things of heaven to people on earth (symbolized in 1:51 by the ladder of Gen 28, now reinterpreted as the Son of Man, who provides the essential link between heaven and earth). Any other 'seeing' is implicitly denied by 20:29 and in turn this is all of a piece with the Farewell Discourses where the coming of the Spirit/Paraclete is clearly a substitute for Jesus' own *departure*.

The citation of Zech 12:10 may then be rather more important and climactic within John's passion narrative, and his gospel, than others have previously allowed. By emphasizing the fact that it is the pierced, crucified one whom others will 'see' in the future, the evangelist may then be seeking to shift attention away from the resurrection as some kind of happy ending that puts right the cross, and to emphasize the centrality of the cross as the supreme moment of revelation. That is what one sees – and that is all! In a way similar perhaps to Mark (cf. Mark 15:39), John presents his readers with a stark 'gospel' of a Jesus – and a God – who shows his truest colours as the crucified one. One may therefore agree with Menken's conclusion that 'the quotation in its Johannine context refers primarily to the look in which believers will see the pierced Jesus as who he really is: the exalted Son of Man, the risen Lord. … The eschatological look on the pierced one occurs when believers see in the crucified Jesus the risen Lord, and in the risen Lord the crucified Jesus.'[53] But maybe one should bear in mind too that the emphasis may be primarily on the first half of Menken's final sentence: one sees in the crucified Jesus the risen Lord. For John there is no other 'seeing' of the risen Lord which is on offer to believers here on earth. Any other 'seeing' of Jesus by believers is reserved for a future time and Christian followers of Jesus meanwhile are summoned to walk by faith not sight.

NOTES

1 The MT has 'on me, on one who is pierced'. On this see below.

2 Possibly too *Did.* 16:8.

3 For discussion of the problems of what can/should count as a genuine 'citation', see e.g. Thompson, 1991, pp. 28–36 (on the nature of 'allusions'); also Stanley, 1992, pp. 33–7 (Stanley refuses to accept as a 'citation' anything without a clear 'marker' in the text).

4 On this see Menken, 1993, p. 496; = 1996, p. 169.

5 The relation between John and Revelation is discussed by Frey, 1993, who argues that the agreement in text form is so striking that it cannot be coincidental and therefore demands some close relationship between the texts: 'Der auffällige Koinzidenz ein und derselben Lesart in Joh und Apk legt viel eher eine Verbindung beider Schriften bzw. der hinter ihnen liegenden Schriftaulegungstradition nahe' (p. 342). He is arguing primarily against Schnackenburg, 1984, pp. 164–73, who sees two separate streams of tradition based on Zechariah in early Christianity, one set in a passion context and the other eschatological. Frey is right to question the existence of two such separate streams; however, the existence of the allusion in Matthew (which I assume here to be independent of John) suggests that one should think of the second of Frey's alternatives rather than necessarily the first.

6 See Lindars, 1961, p. 124; Albl, 1999, p. 256; Menken, 1993, p. 497. For Perrin, see below. There is no need to see further allusion to Gen 12:3 in the phrase 'all the tribes of the earth'. (So Dodd, 1963, p. 132; Wilcox, 1988, p. 202; Schuchard, 1992, p. 142.) The exact phrase does not occur in any known version of Zech 12; but there is enough verbal similarity with other parts of the immediately adjoining context, especially vv. 12 and 14 (where 'tribes' and a reference to wide range of such tribes is specifically mentioned), to suggest that there is no need to look outside Zech 12 for the origin of this phrase.

7 Lindars, 1961, pp. 124–6; similarly Dodd, 1963, pp. 132f. However, Lindars argues that in the earliest tradition, the verse was applied to the piercing of Jesus' hands by the nails in crucifixion; John then reapplied the verse to the piercing of Jesus' side by the sword

thrust. (For Dodd, the latter is the original application and therefore shows that the sword thrust is part of the pre-Johannine tradition.)

8 Perrin, 1966.

9 Ibid., p. 153.

10 Crossan, 1991, esp. pp. 243–7.

11 Ibid., p. 247.

12 Albl, 1999, p. 257: 'Matthew's version can be seen as the most original of the three [synoptics]'.

13 On the broad issue, see Tuckett, 2001a.

14 Compare Menken, 1993, p. 496 n. 4 (= 1996, p. 168, n. 3): 'The use of this verb … seems, when taken alone, to be too narrow a basis for supposing influence of Zech 12:10.'

15 Unless of course one wishes to adopt an alternative solution to the synoptic problem and postulate Matthean priority. Alternatively, one might postulate common dependence of all three synoptic gospels on a common prior tradition: so Wenham, 1984, pp. 315–18, in relation to a supposed original eschatological discourse used independently by all three synoptics.

16 Especially in Crossan's detailed discussion involving 1 Thess as well: by the time the tradition reaches 1 Thess, the Dan 7 allusion (which Crossan agrees may be present there) has swamped the Zech allusion which has then disappeared. On this see Tuckett, 1999.

17 Compare Davies and Allison, 1997, p. 361, n. 228.

18 Compare too modern ETs which refuse to follow the MT here, e.g. RSV or NRSV.

19 There is some variation in the MS tradition concerning the presence or absence of the εἰς: see Menken, 1993, p. 501 (= 1996, p. 175). The agreement between John 19:37 and Zech 12:10 θ' in (perhaps) reading εἰς is however not sufficiently distinctive to warrant any theory of a relationship between the two readings. The (perhaps slightly unusual) use of εἰς with a verb of seeing is by no means unprecedented in Greek literature (cf. Homer, *Od.* 20.373; Liddell, Scott and Jones, 1968, s.v. ὁράω; Menken, 1993, p. 501 [= 1996, p. 175]); and in any case θ' reads ἐπιβλέψονται rather than ὄψονται. The differences thus seem to preclude any obvious link between the Christian texts and the Theodotian version: cf. Freed, 1965, pp. 110, 114.

20 Menken, 1993, p. 502 (= 1996, p. 176).

21 Compare Menken, ibid.; Schuchard, 1992, p. 148.

22 See Menken, 1993, p. 501 (= 1996, p. 175); also Schuchard, 1992, p. 145: cf. LXX Num 12:8; Job 6:19; Isa 38:11 (using the aorist ἰδεῖν); also 1 Sam 2:32 σ'.

23 Menken, 1993, p. 501 (= 1996, p. 175): 'a somewhat weak translation'.

24 Compare Schnackenburg, 1984, p. 170; also Moo, 1983, p. 216.

25 One example might be the apparent reading of the Hebrew of Zech 12:10 by the LXX translator, interchanging the consonants in order to enable a quite different interpretation.

26 In any case the pesharim are of a quite different form, giving an explicit citation of the text verse by verse, and then giving each verse's 'interpretation' (*pesher*).

27 Menken, 1993, p. 502 (= 1996, p. 175).

28 Ibid. Compare too Albl, 1999, pp. 257, 262.

29 In a sense then this is closer to the Qumran parallels which Perrin alluded to, by adapting the text *to make it fit with the interpretation*. It is this *exegetical* freedom which is evidenced in Qumran, not necessarily any love of rhyme or simple 'word play' in the sense of using synonyms almost for the sake of it.

30 Compare too Frey, 1993, p. 343.

31 Compare Bultmann, 1968, p. 524; Barrett, 1955, p. 464; Schuchard, 1992, pp. 141f.; also De Boer, 1996, pp. 92f. and others cited there (e.g. Fortna, Smith) at the level of the alleged Signs Source (or what De Boer calls 'John I'); also p. 301; Obermann, 1996, pp. 317f.

32 Menken, 1993, p. 506 (= 1996, p. 180).
33 Ibid. (= 1996, p. 179).
34 Menken refers to John 15:25 and the use of Ps 35:19/69:5, where the evangelist appears to have rewritten the grammar of the OT verse to be an independent clause: 'they hated me without cause'.
35 Compare e.g. De Boer, 1996, pp. 300f.
36 Compare those cited in Menken, 1993, 506f. n. 48 (= 1996, p. 180 n. 48); also Obermann, 1996, p. 318. John 3:14–15 should also be connected with 8:28 and 12:32.
37 Possibly though there is a double meaning. Compare e.g. Brown, 1985, p. 955: one can look with belief or unbelief.
38 Menken, 1993, p. 508 (= 1996, p. 182).
39 Ibid.
40 Compare Moule, 1959, p. 258 n. 3; Haenchen, 1984, p. 196; Moo, 1983, p. 213 (as a possibility); Hengel, 1989, p. 278.
41 1993, p. 510 (= 1996, p. 184).
42 1993, p. 511 (= 1996, p. 185).
43 Nor is it mentioned in 12:32. 8:28 does use the verb 'see' but in a rather different sense: the Jews will 'see' *that* 'I am'. 'Seeing' here means 'realizing'.
44 See Dunderberg, 1997, arguing in part against Riley, 1995.
45 Brown, 1985, p. 729.
46 Ibid., p. 730. And indeed most commentators agree: e.g. Bultmann, 1968, pp. 445, 478f.; Barrett, 1955, pp. 387, 410; Haenchen, 1984, p. 127; Lindars, 1972, pp. 480f.
47 Well brought out classically by Brown himself in Brown, 1967.
48 Hence Brown himself says, arguing against the theory of E. F. Scott, that the Paraclete in John is *not* to be identified with the risen Jesus: 'the patent thrust of the Paraclete passages is that the Paraclete and the risen Jesus have distinct roles in that Jesus will be above with the Father while the Paraclete continues the work on earth' (ibid., p. 128 n. 1). But then his claim (ibid., p. 128) that 'the Paraclete is the presence of Jesus when Jesus is absent' is somewhat paradoxical if not self-contradictory: if Jesus is absent, he is by definition *not* present!
49 See 7:33; 8:14; 8:21–2; 13:1, 3, 33, 36; 14:2, 5, 12, 28; 16:5, 7, 10, 17, 28; 17:11, 13. (Of course in the gospel story, the Jesus in the narrative points forward to what is still future in the narrative's terms.)
50 See De Boer, 1996, 176ff.
51 Hence not a reference to the whole of Jesus' incarnate life (so e.g. E. Käsemann's famous all-but-docetic interpretation of the Prologue and the gospel: see Käsemann, 1968).
52 Such an interpretation is of course much disputed; but for this, see e.g. Forestell, 1974, pp. 18–19; Lindars, 1990, p. 81; Smith, 1995, p. 121; De Boer, 1996, pp. 186–9 (with further references).
53 1993, p. 511 (= 1996, p. 185), cited earlier.

Chapter 10

The Attitude towards Christians who are Doubting: Jude 22–3 and the Text of Zechariah 3

Harm W. Hollander

One of the most characteristic features of the letter of Jude is the author's familiarity with OT and Jewish sources. Although he almost never quotes a passage explicitly, echoes of, and allusions to OT and Jewish texts and motifs are numerous. The author uses this source material to apply lessons from the past to the present situation, and thereby to convince his readers to stick to the true doctrine and to be wary of false teachers who try to deceive the members of the Christian community.[1] Consequently, we find a sharp distinction between 'you', i.e. the true believers, the readers of the letter, and 'they', i.e. the 'ungodly', the adherents of false beliefs.[2] As a matter of fact, the bulk of the letter consists of a warning to the readers to watch out for those false teachers who are depicted as a grave menace to the Christian community (vv. 3–19). They are 'causing divisions' (v. 19), but they will be punished by God at the end of time: for them, 'the deepest darkness has been reserved forever' (v. 13).[3] Their sins and final punishment are compared to the sins and the fate of the people of Israel who did not believe, to the 'watchers' or the 'fallen angels', and finally to the people of Sodom and Gomorrah. In addition, the warning passage is replete with references to other OT and Jewish figures of old, such as Moses, Cain, Balaam, Korah and Enoch; the archangel Michael is also mentioned.[4] From all this it is clear that the author of the letter of Jude was well acquainted with OT and Jewish tradition; he uses this source material without thinking it necessary to quote any passage explicitly.[5]

The main reason for writing the letter appears to have been the danger that the Christian community would be split up as a consequence of the activities of the false teachers. In the author's eyes, there was a strong possibility that community members might be impressed by those false teachers and might go astray. Therefore, he admonishes his readers to 'contend for the faith', to 'build themselves up on their most holy faith', to 'pray in the Holy Spirit', and to 'keep themselves in the love of God' (vv. 3, 20–21).

After the exhortations in vv. 20–21, and before the doxology at the end of the letter (vv. 24–5), there is a final instance of paraenesis in vv. 22–3. In these verses the readers are invited to 'have mercy on' or to 'save' some other people. In the history of New Testament research, this sentence has become a *crux interpretum*. Its meaning and function are still much discussed: who are the people on whom the readers are supposed to have mercy, or whom they should save? Is the author perhaps referring to two or three groups of people, one or two groups on whom the readers should have mercy, and another whom they should save? Who are the διακρινομένους, people who 'dispute' or people who 'doubt'? And last but not least, since there are quite a number of textual variants for this passage, what is the exact wording of vv. 22–3? In the following sections, I will first briefly discuss the textual difficulties, expressing my preference for the three-clause reading as found in א (and A) and printed in the 27th edition of Nestle-Aland. Next, I will analyse the passage in detail and show that also in these two verses the author of the letter of Jude has been influenced by OT source material, in particular the book of Zechariah. I hope to demonstrate that: (a) 'having mercy on' and 'saving' are in this context synonymous and are used to describe the same attitude; (b) by means of three parallel clauses the readers are exhorted to help one and the same group, viz. those doubting Christians, who are about to give in to the false teachers and their ideas; (c) the author adopts two images from Zech 3:2–4, viz. the 'fire' and the 'filthy clothes', and applies them to a new context to describe metaphorically the false teachers and their ideas, which Christians should avoid and hate.

TEXT OF JUDE 22–3

The text of Jude 22–3 has a number of variants which may be divided into two main categories, viz. a two-clause and a three-clause structure. The first, found in P^{72} it^{t} cop^{sa} sy^{ph}, reads:

οὓς μὲν ἐκ πυρὸς ἁρπάσατε,
διακρινομένους δὲ ἐλεεῖτε ἐν φόβῳ
  μισοῦντες καὶ τὸν ἀπὸ τῆς σαρκὸς ἐσπιλωμένον χιτῶνα
seize some from the fire,
but have mercy on those who dispute/doubt, with fear,
  hating the tunic defiled by the body.

Another example of the same category is found in C^2 sy^h, and, with many different variants, in many other manuscripts; it reads:

καὶ οὓς μὲν ἐλεᾶτε διακρινομένους,
οὓς δὲ σῴζετε ἐκ πυρὸς ἁρπάζοντες ἐν φόβῳ
  μισοῦντες καὶ τὸν ἀπὸ τῆς σαρκὸς ἐσπιλωμένον χιτῶνα
and have mercy on those who dispute/doubt,
but save others, seizing them from the fire, with fear,
  hating the tunic defiled by the body.

The second category, found in א and A, reads:[6]

καὶ οὓς μὲν ἐλεᾶτε (א; A: ἐλέγχετε) διακρινομένους,
οὓς δὲ σῴζετε ἐκ πυρὸς ἁρπάζοντες,
οὓς δὲ ἐλεᾶτε ἐν φόβῳ
  μισοῦντες καὶ τὸν ἀπὸ τῆς σαρκὸς ἐσπιλωμένον χιτῶνα

and have mercy on (א; A: rebuke) those who doubt,
save them, seizing them from the fire,
have mercy on them, with fear,
  hating the tunic defiled by the body.

Finally, B reads:

καὶ οὓς μὲν ἐλεᾶτε διακρινομένους,
  σῴζετε ἐκ πυρὸς ἁρπάζοντες,
οὓς δὲ ἐλεᾶτε ἐν φόβῳ
  μισοῦντες καὶ τὸν ἀπὸ τῆς σαρκὸς ἐσπιλωμένον χιτῶνα
and have mercy on those who dispute/doubt,
  save them, seizing them from the fire,
and/but have mercy on others, with fear,
  hating the tunic defiled by the body.

The text of B is identical to א except for the fact that the first οὓς δέ is lacking, as a consequence of which B is usually regarded as a representative of the two-clause reading.[7]

Although the text of vv. 22–3 is highly complicated from a text-critical point of view, the main question is, of course, whether the two-clause reading arose from the three-clause reading or the other way round. It is rather hard to imagine why a scribe changed a two-part structure into a sentence containing three clauses, the third of which is more or less a repetition of the first (ἐλεᾶτε … ἐλεᾶτε), in any case harder to imagine than the reverse operation. The two-clause reading looks like a deliberate attempt to smooth the (three-clause) text in order to introduce two different groups of people towards whom the readers should behave properly, for instance Christians who 'are doubting' and are to be helped and false teachers who must be avoided, or people who 'dispute' (= the false teachers) and fellow Christians who need to be helped in one way or another. An additional argument for the three-clause structure is the author's predilection for constructions with three members, as in vv. 4, 5–7, 8, 11, 12b–13, and 19.[8]

The main objection to the originality of the three-clause structure is that it is difficult to distinguish between the three groups of persons meant in the three clauses, in particular between the first and the third group of people.[9] The three-clause structure seems to make no sense and may therefore be regarded as the result of some mistake (conflation?). But suppose the three-clause reading is the original, does it really mean that the author of the letter is referring to three different groups of people? At first sight, the introductory words οὓς μέν … οὓς δέ … οὓς δέ seem to support the argument that the author refers to three different groups. However, Joel S. Allen has argued recently that there are numerous cases in which μέν … δέ (… δέ) 'indicate clause division rather than differentiation of groups'.[10] From passages in classical Greek literature (e.g., Thucydides, *Histories* 1.85.2; Plato, *Laws* 697D; Herodotus, *Histories* 1.45.3), the LXX (e.g., 2 Macc 11:18), and the NT (e.g., Rom 8:30–31; Jude 10), he concludes that μέν … δέ in series can serve to divide a sentence into several clauses without emphasizing a contrast. The same seems to be true for Jude 22–3: '… only one group is in focus. The descriptive force of the participle διακρινομένους is thus carried through the whole sentence so that the three clauses do not indicate distinct groups of persons, but amplification of the same group, i.e. those who doubt'.[11]

If Allen's interpretation is right, and I think it is, the main argument against the three-clause structure appears to be invalid. That means that the three-clause sentence, in particular the one found in א,[12] is to be regarded as the original text vis-à-vis the two-clause reading.[13] Thus, throughout the letter the author of Jude warns his readers against people who have 'stolen in' among the members of the Christian community (v. 4), who are 'flattering people to their own advantage' (v. 16), and who are 'causing divisions' (v. 19); the readers should not 'fall' (v. 24), that is, give in to these false teachers and their abject ideas. At the end of his letter, in three more or less parallel clauses, he summons his readers to 'have mercy on' or 'to save' those fellow Christians who 'are doubting', who are inclined to believe the words of the false preachers he is warning against. According to this interpretation, διακρινομένους should be translated as 'those who doubt', rather than 'those who dispute'.[14] An invitation to the readers to have mercy on or to save[15] the disputers, i.e. the false teachers, does not make much sense here: the author has argued earlier that the false teachers are sinners 'for whom the deepest darkness has been reserved forever' (v. 13). As a consequence, he does not ask his readers to help those ungodly people but to help their fellow Christians, whom the ungodly people are trying to persuade. For the author of the letter, there are three groups of people in this world: (a) people who believe, among whom the readers of the letter; (b) people who do not believe, among whom the false teachers; and (c) people who doubt. The first group must try to keep the third from joining the second. A thorough and detailed analysis of the wording of vv. 22–3 and its OT background will show that this interpretation is the correct one, and that, consequently, the three-clause structure not only makes perfect sense, but also has a strong claim to being the original reading.

ANALYSIS OF JUDE 22–3

Meaning of ἐλεᾶν and σώζειν

That the three clauses in vv. 22–3 refer to one and the same class of people is underlined by the use of the verbs ἐλεᾶν (in the first and third clauses) and σώζειν (in the second clause). Starting from the idea that in these verses the author refers to two (or three) different groups of people, scholars usually do their best to make a clear distinction between the two verbs. In that case, the author would have summoned his readers, for instance, 'to pity' the διακρινομένους (understood as 'those who dispute', i.e. the false teachers) and 'to save' each other.[16] However, an analysis of the use of the two verbs in OT (LXX), Jewish, and early Christian literature shows that both verbs are to a certain extent synonymous. They both refer to helping people who are in physical or spiritual need.[17] The verbs are often found together without any difference in meaning: see for instance Ps 86 (85):2–3: 'Preserve my life, for I am devoted to you; save (σῶσον) your servant who trusts in you. You are my God; be gracious to (ἐλέησον) me, O Lord, for to you do I cry all day long'; or *1 Clem* 59:4: 'We beseech thee, Master, to be our help and succour. Save (σῶσον) those of us who are in affliction, have mercy on (ἐλέησον) the lowly, raise the fallen, show thyself to those in need, heal the sick, turn again the wanderers of thy people, feed the hungry, ransom our prisoners, raise up the weak, comfort the faint-hearted …'.[18] These and other examples[19] point to the conclusion that ἐλεεῖν/ἐλεᾶν and σώζειν are interchangeable, both referring to the act of 'helping' people or 'saving' people from some kind of danger.[20] This strengthens the argument that in vv. 22–3 the author invites his readers to behave properly to one and the same class of people, that is to save their wavering fellow Christians from giving in to the false teachers and their dissenting opinions.

The image of 'seizing people from the fire' (ἐκ πυρὸς ἁρπάζοντες)

Whereas in the first clause the author of the letter of Jude indicates the group of people whom his readers should help, viz. those fellow Christians who are doubting, he continues by mentioning in the second clause the danger from which they should be saved. His readers should 'seize' their fellow Christians 'from the fire' (ἐκ πυρὸς ἁρπάζοντες, v. 23a). The common opinion is that with this phrase the readers are summoned to save people from the fire *of hell*, i.e. that they should protect them from being destroyed by the fire of hell at the end of time. The difficulty with this interpretation is that ἁρπάζειν ἐκ (or ἐξαρπάζειν) does not mean 'to save or to protect somebody or something from future danger' but 'to seize or to snatch somebody or something from present danger'.[21] It is found rather frequently in the context of rescuing people from dangers or helping them: see, for instance, Athenagoras, *Legatio* 21.2: 'when for all his grief he (= Zeus) cannot rescue him (= Sarpedon) from danger (ἀδυνατῇ δὲ ὀδυρόμενος τοῦ κινδύνου ἐξαρπάσαι)…';[22] or Plutarch, *Demetrius* 7.5: 'he (= Demetrius) helped and saved the city (βοηθήσας ἐξήρπασε τὴν πόλιν)'.[23] All this makes it plausible that the author of Jude is not referring to the fire of hell at the end of time from which the people who are in doubt must be saved by his readers but to some kind of danger which is threatening the doubters at this very moment.[24] But if πῦρ does not refer to the fire of hell, which danger is the author thinking of?

In order to answer this question we must first of all realize that in this verse the author is likely to have been influenced by a passage from OT, in this case Zech 3:2. In Zechariah 3, the prophet describes a visionary scene in the heavenly courtroom. The principal figure there is Joshua, the son of Jehozadak, who seems to have been the first chief priest after the exile. In Zech 3:1 LXX we are told that the prophet saw 'the high priest Joshua standing before the angel of the Lord, and the devil standing at his right hand to accuse him'. It seems likely that the accusations brought by the adversary were made against the election of Jerusalem, against the restoration of the priesthood, and against Joshua as the intended new high priest. In v. 2 we read that the Lord rebukes the accuser by defending Jerusalem and comparing Joshua to 'a brand plucked from the fire (LXX ὡς δαλὸς ἐξεσπασμένος ἐκ πυρός)'. Most probably, the simile serves to characterize the delicate situation in which the high priest Joshua found himself, namely as somebody who was about to fade away ('a brand'), but who had been rescued (by God) just in time ('plucked from the fire'). The words 'plucked from the fire' seem to refer to Joshua's narrow escape from a critical, dangerous situation: 'to pluck' stands for the action of saving, while 'the fire' stands for the peril that threatened Joshua.[25] The peril itself probably refers to God's wrath and Joshua's (and Judah's) experiences in exile.[26]

It is likely that the author of Jude took the image of somebody seized from the fire from Zech 3:2. That the wording is somewhat different (ἐκ πυρὸς ἁρπάζοντες instead of ἐξεσπασμένος ἐκ πυρός) is no argument against it. The use of another verb (ἁρπάζειν instead of ἐκσπᾶν) with a similar meaning is most probably due to the fact that the author of Jude quoted from memory.[27] When quoting or copying, people are inclined to replace (less frequent) words by more or less synonymous (and more common) terms.[28] Moreover, there is another theme in Zechariah's vision of the high priest Joshua that seems to have been adopted by the author of Jude, namely Joshua's filthy clothes; he uses this item to introduce a second image, that of the defiled tunic, mentioned at the end of v. 23. The occurrence of two similar images in Zech 3:2–4 and Jude 23 can hardly be accidental and has to be explained by assuming that the author of the letter of Jude was influenced by the passage in Zechariah.[29]

The author of Jude uses the image of the narrow escape from the fire to describe his readers' attitude towards fellow Christians who are doubting. They should 'seize them from the fire', that is, rescue them from grave danger. But, again, what kind of danger is the author thinking of? The danger, which the author considered a serious threat to the readers at the time, must have to do with the situation in which the doubters found themselves. Since they were people who were about to give in to the false teachers and their wicked ideas, the danger the author is mentioning here must refer to these false teachers themselves, and to their attempts to mislead Christians about the true faith.[30] The doubters were about to fall into sin and 'to be burnt by the fire' of the false teachers, but the readers should help them and rescue them before it is too late. In the author's view, the false teachers are 'the fire' from which the doubters should be seized by the faithful Christian readers.

The author's identification of the false teachers with a 'fire' has its roots in Jewish and early Christian tradition, according to which the good and pious man's adversaries are described as a burning flame or a fire. See, for instance, Sir 8:10: 'Do not kindle the coals of sinners, or you may be burned in their flaming fire (ἐν πυρὶ φλογός)'; 51:3–4: 'and [you] delivered me … from the hand of those seeking my life, from the many troubles I endured, from choking fire on every side, and from the midst of fire (ἀπὸ πνιγμοῦ πυρᾶς κυκλόθεν καὶ ἐκ μέσου πυρός) …'; *T. Jos.* 2:2: 'And I struggled against a shameless woman, urging me to transgress with her; but the God of Israel my father guarded me from the burning flame (ἐφύλαξέ με ἀπὸ φλογὸς καιομένης)'.[31] An interesting parallel is found in Justin Martyr's *Dialogue with Trypho* 115–16, where the author quotes Zech 2:14–3:2, followed by a kind of typological interpretation of the passage. He compares the Christians to the high priest Joshua: like Joshua, 'we', that is the Christians, 'have been plucked out as from fire, when we were purged from our former sins, and also from the affliction and the burning, wherewith both the devil and all his servants burn us' (116:2).[32] In this passage, 'fire' refers to the sin and affliction into which people have been plunged[33] and to those who are responsible, viz. the devil and his collaborators.

All this demonstrates that the author of Jude considers the false teachers to be the Christians' adversaries who try to make the believers go astray. His readers should arm themselves against them and rescue those who are about to be misled from their hands as from a fire.

The meaning of ἐν φόβῳ

In the first clause of Jude 22–3 the author mentioned the group of people strongly in need of help. The second clause deals with the danger from which those wavering souls should be saved, i.e. the false teachers and their wicked opinions. In the third clause, the author goes on to give some characteristics of the right attitude towards doubting fellow Christians, and he ends with a second metaphor taken from Zechariah 3 to describe the peril that threatens the Christians who are in doubt.

First the author summons his readers to have mercy on the doubters ἐν φόβῳ, 'with fear'. The question is, of course, what exactly does the author mean by the phrase 'with fear'? It may be interpreted as a reference to some feeling of fear or caution; but fear of what? Some scholars connect the phrase with the last words of the verse, and assume that the author wants to warn his readers to take care to avoid their own defilement. That means, the readers should avoid contact with the 'defiled tunic', that is with people having wicked religious ideas, in order not to be polluted by them.[34] A valid argument against this interpretation is that there is not a single indication that the spots on the tunic are to be understood as contagious or dangerous for those who touch them.

It is, therefore, more likely that the phrase 'with fear' serves to express something different, namely the attitude of good and pious men who act in a spirit of fear, that is fear *of God*, not in the sense of 'fear of God's judgment on sin'[35] but in the sense of respect or reverence for God. Both the term φόβος and the phrase ἐν φόβῳ, used absolutely, i.e. not followed by an objective genitive such as τοῦ κυρίου or θεοῦ, occur quite frequently in other early Christian writings to describe the disposition of people who are living in accordance with the will of God. Christians should act with fear and reverence for their Lord: see, for instance, 1 Pet 3:2: 'when they (= the husbands) see the purity and reverence of your (= their wives') lives (τὴν ἐν φόβῳ ἁγνὴν ἀναστροφὴν ὑμῶν)...'; *1 Clem* 51:2: 'For those who live in fear and love (μετὰ φόβου καὶ ἀγάπης) are willing to suffer torture themselves rather than their neighbours ...'.[36] Likewise, the readers of the letter of Jude are exhorted to help their fellow Christians who are doubting, in a spirit of 'fear', that is, as people who have a strong faith and show a deep reverence for God.

The image of the 'tunic defiled by the body' (τὸν ἀπὸ τῆς σαρκὸς ἐσπιλωμένον χιτῶνα)

At the end of vv. 22–3 the author gives another feature of the right Christian behaviour towards doubting Christians. The readers should help these waverers, should 'have mercy on them', not only 'with fear' but at the same time in a spirit of 'hatred' (μισοῦντες) for 'the tunic defiled by the body'.[37] This 'tunic' must represent something bad, for traditionally the pious man's hatred is directed towards people or things that are wicked and evil and are to be avoided. Pious men hate, for instance, 'the company of evildoers', 'iniquity', 'injustice', 'arrogance', 'evil desire', 'hypocrisy', 'telling lies', in short anything evil in the eyes of God.[38]

But what does the author mean by 'the tunic defiled by the body'? To what does it refer? Like the image of the 'fire' from which the doubters should be seized, the author of Jude has taken the metaphor of the dirty tunic from the prophet Zechariah's vision of the high priest Joshua in the heavenly courtroom as told in Zechariah 3.[39] Not only is Joshua compared to 'a brand plucked from the fire', but he is also depicted as somebody who 'was dressed with filthy clothes (LXX ἦν ἐνδεδυμένος ἱμάτια ῥυπαρά) as he stood before the angel' (v. 3). We read how the angel ordered that 'the filthy clothes (τὰ ἱμάτια τὰ ῥυπαρά)' should be taken off and how one put a clean turban on his head and clothed him with new clothes. This ceremony is accompanied with the words, 'See, I have taken your guilt away from you, and I will clothe you with festal apparel' (vv. 4–5). This statement makes clear that Joshua's dirty clothes, which are to be removed, symbolize his guilt. The state of iniquity in which Joshua finds himself is most probably not the result of his own actions; it is rather the consequence of his having lived in exile, and includes the contamination he has suffered in Babylon as an unclean country.[40] Since the exile was God's punishment for the Judahites' apostasy, Joshua as one of them, or rather as one of their representatives, should be 'cleansed' in order to be fit to become the first high priest after the exile.[41]

The author of Jude took the motif of the filthy clothes from Zechariah 3, just as he did with the image of the fire. The wording is different: he replaced the words (τὰ) ἱμάτια (τὰ) ῥυπαρά by the words τόν ... ἐσπιλωμένον χιτῶνα, which is another example of the replacement of words with a more or less similar meaning.[42] Moreover, the cause of the tunic's defilement is mentioned explicitly: the tunic is defiled 'by the body' (ἀπὸ τῆς σαρκός). All this supports the assumption that the author quoted the OT (LXX) from memory.[43]

Whereas in Zechariah's vision Joshua's dirty clothes are symbolic of the high priest's uncleanness or guilt, the author of Jude uses the image as a metaphor to describe something his readers should find insufferable. It seems, however, methodologically correct first to look for the literal sense of the phrase, before interpreting the meaning of the metaphor in the context of the letter of Jude. That means that, on the non-metaphorical level, one should presume that both χιτών and σάρξ are to be understood literally. As a consequence, σάρξ does not refer to, for instance, 'the sinful worldly environment', the evil desires of the false teachers, or the perverseness of people in general.[44] Nor should one interpret the word σάρξ on the basis of its (metaphorical) meaning in the letters of Paul. The word usually refers to the human body,[45] and there is nothing against assuming that in Jude 23, too, it refers to the human body.[46] This means that, literally, the 'tunic defiled by the body' refers to a garment stained by its contact with the body.[47] Since the χιτών was the article of clothing which was worn next to the skin, it could easily become dirty and stained by blood, sweat and other bodily fluids.[48] All this leads to the conclusion that the author of Jude took the motif of Joshua's dirty clothes from Zech 3:3–4 and paraphrased it, in order to explain and to stress the filthiness of the garment ('defiled by the body').

The author of Jude uses the motif of a 'defiled tunic' as a metaphor[49] to describe the 'filthiness' of the things or persons his readers should hate. But what things or persons is he thinking of? In early Christian literature, 'stains' are used metaphorically to refer to sins or sinners. See, for instance, Eph 5:27: 'so as to present the church to himself in splendour, without a spot or wrinkle (μὴ ἔχουσαν σπίλον ἢ ῥυτίδα) or anything of the kind – yes, so that she may be holy and without blemish'; 2 Pet 2:13: 'They (= false teachers) count it a pleasure to revel in the daytime. They are blots and blemishes (σπίλοι καὶ μῶμοι), revelling in their dissipation while they feast with you'.[50] This metaphorical use of words for 'stains' or 'filthiness' in early Christian literature makes it likely that the author of Jude, too, uses the metaphor of the 'tunic defiled by the body' to describe a specific class of sins or sinners. This conclusion is substantiated by the similar metaphorical interpretation of the 'filthy clothes' in Zech 3:3–4 that is found in Justin's *Dialogue with Trypho* 115–16.[51] There, we are told that 'we (= the Christians) who formerly lived in fornication, and, in fact, every kind of filthy action, have ... put off all the filthy garments (τὰ ῥυπαρὰ πάντα) wherewith we were clothed ... we stripped off our filthy garments (τὰ ῥυπαρὰ ἱμάτια), that is to say, our sins ...' (116:1–3).[52]

Since the author of Jude used the first image, that of the 'fire', to refer metaphorically to the false teachers and their wicked ideas, the same must be assumed for the second image. The 'defiled tunic', which the readers of the letter must hate when they help their fellow Christians who doubt, represents the false teachers and their attempts to mislead innocent Christians. The author does not call upon his readers to fear, i.e. to try and avoid people with wicked ideas in order not to be polluted by them;[53] he rather exhorts them to hate these adversaries, the false teachers with their unorthodox doctrines and actions who try to mislead Christians and to split the Christian church.[54]

CONCLUSION

From the analysis of the terms and images found in Jude 22–3, it has become clear that the three-clause reading as found in א (and A) and printed in Nestle-Aland 27 makes perfect sense. After some harsh words about people who try to divide the Christian community with their wicked ideas, and some exhortations to his readers to stick to the real Christian faith, the author urges the addressees to 'help' (ἐλεᾶτε ... σῴζετε ... ἐλεᾶτε) their fellow Christians who are doubting (διακρινομένους). In the second and third clauses of vv. 22–3 he uses two metaphors to describe the danger from which the doubters are to be saved. Both originate from images and phrases in Zechariah's vision of Joshua the high priest standing in the heavenly courtroom, as told in Zechariah 3 LXX. The author of Jude does not repeat them verbatim but quotes them from memory, replacing some words by more or less synonymous terms. Thus he uses the image of Joshua being like 'a brand plucked from the fire' to compare the false teachers to a 'fire' from which the doubters should be saved (ἐκ πυρὸς ἁρπάζοντες). Next, he takes the theme of the 'filthy garment' in which Joshua was clothed, in order to introduce a second image to describe once more the danger of the adversaries of the Christian community, whom the readers of this letter should hate (μισοῦντες καὶ τὸν ἀπὸ τῆς σαρκὸς ἐσπιλωμένον χιτῶνα); helping fellow Christians who are in danger of losing their faith implies hating those who are responsible for bringing ruin on them. This way of using OT phrases shows us how early Christian writers could use the OT/LXX: they were so well acquainted with the OT that they could echo OT phrases or quote them from memory, whether literally or not, and adapt them to new needs. They felt free to use them in any way they wanted, and even did not always find it necessary to mention their sources explicitly.

NOTES

1 See esp. Charles, 1991, 1993; Heiligenthal, 1992.
2 See ὑμεῖς, 'you' (vv. 17, 20; cf. vv. 2, 3, 5, 12, 18, 24), versus οὗτοι, 'they', 'these people', or τινες ἄνθρωποι, 'certain individuals' (vv. 4, 8, 10, 12, 16, 19).
3 The OT and NT quotations are usually taken from the NRSV.
4 See esp. Charles, 1990.
5 The only exception seems to be vv. 14–15, where we find an explicit citation from *1 Enoch* 1:9. On Jude 9, see n. 29.
6 This translation assumes that the author does not intend to distinguish between three classes of people but refers to one and the same group, viz. those who doubt: see below.
7 For details and discussions of all the variants, see Metzger, 1971, pp. 727–9; Bauckham, 1983, pp. 108–11; Vögtle, 1994, pp. 102–5; Landon, 1996, pp. 131–4; and esp. Kubo, 1981, pp. 239–53.
8 So, e.g., Metzger, 1971, p. 728, and Kubo, 1981, p. 250, though the latter, joining Mayor, 1965, pp. cxc, lvi, rightly indicates that the author of Jude also uses constructions with two members.
9 Vögtle opts for three different groups of Christians who are all influenced by the doctrines of the false teachers, but one more than the other (see 1994, pp. 104–7); the text itself, however, does not offer any indication that such a distinction was meant by the author.
10 See Allen, 1998, esp. p. 137.
11 Ibid., p. 143.
12 The variant ἐλέγχετε in A instead of the first ἐλεᾶτε seems to be an attempt to vary between the verbs in the three clauses and is therefore secundary. Kubo, too, is in favour of the text of ℵ, but prefers to read ἐλεεῖτε instead of ἐλεᾶτε (1981, p. 253).
13 Compare, e.g., Windisch, 1930, p. 47; Metzger, 1971, pp. 727–9; Kubo, 1981, pp. 239–53 (but see Kubo, 1965, pp. 89–92); Vögtle, 1994, pp. 102–5; Paulsen, 1992, pp. 84–6; *pace* scholars such as Schelkle, 1961, pp. 170–2; Birdsall, 1963; Reicke, 1964, pp. 215–16; Osburn, 1972; Balz and Schrage, 1973, pp. 230–1; Bauckham, 1983, pp. 108–11; Winter, 1994; and Landon, 1996, pp. 131–4 who support a two-clause text.
14 For διακρίνεσθαι in the sense of 'to doubt', see also, e.g., Mark 11:23; Matt 21:21; Rom 4:20; 14:23; Jas 1:6; Pseudo-Clement, *Homilies* 1.20.6; 2.40.3. These passages make clear that this meaning was well known in the early church.
15 Schelkle, 1961, p. 171, Balz and Schrage, 1973, p. 231, and Vögtle, 1994, p. 106, assume that in v. 23 the verb ἐλεᾶν or ἐλεεῖν means 'to pray for' (the false teachers or sinners in general); but this interpretation is rather forced and cannot be substantiated.
16 So, e.g., Winter, 1994, pp. 217–18. Most scholars who opt for a two-clause division prefer the text of either P^{72} or B; likewise, they either make a distinction between the actions of 'seizing (ἁρπάσατε) from the fire' and 'having mercy' (ἐλεεῖτε) in the case of P^{72}, or between the first ἐλεᾶτε and the second ἐλεᾶτε in the case of B. Both attempts are rather arbitrary and lack any conclusive evidence (see also n. 15).
17 See also Allen, 1998, p. 141: 'The verb ἐλεάω in the NT and LXX does not simply mean "to extend empathy toward", but includes the appropriate response, namely, the response which brings about and ensures salvation, deliverance or healing'.
18 Translation according to Lake, 1912.
19 See also Ps 6:3–5; 86 (85):16; Isa 59:1–2; Hos 1:6–8; Tob 6:18; *2 Clement* 1:7; *Acts of Andrew* 1.
20 It is, therefore, not surprising that there are also many passages in which the verbs ἐλεεῖν and ῥύεσθαι ('to save') occur together without any difference of meaning: see, e.g., Ps 6:3–5; *Acts of John* 42; *Acts of Philip* 112; *Acts of Thomas* 38.

21 See, e.g., 2 Sam 23:21 ('Benaiah … snatched the spear out of the Egyptian's hand [ἥρπασεν τὸ δόρυ ἐκ τῆς χειρὸς τοῦ Αἰγυπτίου] …'); Job 29:17; *Joseph and Aseneth* 12:8, 10; Philo, *Quis heres* 71; John 10:28–9; Acts 23:10; Hermas, *Vis.* 2.1.4; Athenagoras, *Legatio* 21.2; Plutarch, *Pompeius* 81.6; *Demetrius* 7.5; *Cato* 23.2; *Crassus* 11.6.

22 Text and translation according to Schoedel, 1972.

23 See also Plutarch, *Pompeius* 81.6 (ἐξήρπασε … βοηθῶν).

24 Compare also Vögtle, 1994, p. 105.

25 The same imagery is found in Amos 4:11. In this verse, the rescue of some of the Israelites, who were in a situation comparable to the destruction of the people of Sodom and Gomorrah, is described in similar terms: 'I overthrew some of you, as when God overthrew Sodom and Gomorrah, and you were like a brand snatched from the fire (LXX ὡς δαλὸς ἐξεσπασμένος ἐκ πυρός); yet you did not return to me, says the Lord'. That is, their destruction was not total, so that a return to God remained a viable possibility.

26 See, e.g., Van der Woude, 1984, p. 64; Reventlow, 1993, p. 53; VanderKam, 1991, pp. 555–6 (= VanderKam, 2000, pp. 159–60); but cf. Rudolph, 1976, pp. 95–6; Petersen, 1985, pp. 192–3; Meyers and Meyers, 1987, pp. 186–7.

27 *Pace* Bauckham, 1983, who is of the opinion that 'it was the Hebrew Bible with which Jude was really familiar. When he wished to allude to it he did not stop to find the Septuagint translation, but made his own translation …' (p. 7). The (few) arguments presented by Bauckham to confirm this statement are far from convincing. The author's command of the Greek language and of good Greek idiom (so also Bauckham, 1983, p. 6) makes it much more plausible that he, like (almost) all the other early Christian writers, knew the OT in its Greek version, the LXX. See also Gerdmar, 2001, esp. pp. 158–9.

28 We find a similar substitution of the verb ἐκσπᾶν by ἐξαρπάζειν in the manuscript tradition in Job 29:17 LXX (ἐξέσπασα versus ἐξήρπασα).

29 So also Bauckham, 1983, pp. 114–15. A third argument may be found in Jude 9. The words 'May the Lord rebuke you', together with the story about the discussion between Michael and the devil concerning the body of Moses, are most likely adopted from *Ass. Mos.* (see esp. Tromp, 1993, pp. 271–81). Nevertheless, there is a good possibility that the words spoken by the archangel Michael to the devil in *Ass. Mos.* reminded the author of Jude of the identical words spoken by the Lord to the adversary in Zech 3:2.

30 Compare Vögtle, 1994, p. 105, who argues that the fire refers to 'die Verführung durch die häretische Lehre und Lebenspraxis', although he thinks that 'der Gedanke an das Höllenfeuer mitschwingen mag'.

31 Translation according to Hollander and De Jonge, 1985. See further Sir 8:3; 28:22–3; 4 Macc 18:14–15; and cf. Hollander, 1994, esp. pp. 99–102.

32 Translation according to Williams, 1930.

33 Compare also Job 31:12; Isa 9:17–19; Sir 23:16; 40:30; Philo, *Somn.* 2.181; *Decal.* 49; 173; Jas 3:6; Ignatius, *Trall.* 2:3; *Rom.* 7:2.

34 Compare e.g., Schelkle, 1961, p. 171; Reicke, 1964, p. 216; Balz and Schrage, 1973, p. 231; Kubo, 1981, p. 252; Heiligenthal, 1992, pp. 93, 164; Paulsen, 1992, p. 85.

35 So Bauckham, 1983, p. 116; cf. Vögtle, 1994, p. 106.

36 Translation according to Lake, 1912. See further 1 Pet 1:17; *1 Clem* 19:1; 64:1; *Barn.* 2:2; 11:11; Hermas, *Mand.* 6.1.1; 7; and cf. Ps 2:11 (and Polycarp, *Phil.* 2:1; 6:3); *Aristeas* 95; Phil 2:12.

37 Grammatically, καί after μισοῦντες is somewhat pleonastic; its function here is to connect the two feelings of fear (ἐν φόβῳ) and hatred (μισοῦντες) with each other. For similar cases of a pleonastic καί (after a preposition, a relative pronoun, a comparative conjunction such as καθώς, or a participle), see, e.g., Rom 1:13; 15:7; 1 Cor 1:8; 2:13; 10:6; 1 Thess 4:5, 8, 13; Phil 4:3.

38 See, e.g., Exod 18:21; Ps 26 (25):5; 36 (35):3; 45 (44):8; 97 (96):10; 101 (100):3; 119 (118):104, 113, 128, 163; Prov 8:13; 13:5; 28:16; Amos 5:15; Heb 1:9; *Did.* 4:12; *Barn.* 4:1, 10; 19:2, 11; Hermas, *Mand.* 12.1.1; *T. Dan* 5:1.

39 As a consequence, the image of the dirty tunic should not be interpreted against the background of the Jewish and early Christian motif of 'the garments of glory' worn by the righteous and the ones who are elected by God (*pace* Heiligenthal, 1992, pp. 74–5).

40 For a similar imagery, see the *Hymn of the Pearl* 29, 62–3 (*Acts of Thomas* 109 and 111): 'I clothed myself in garments like theirs [= the Egyptians], so that I would not be seen as a stranger… And I took off the dirty clothing (ἀποδυσάμενος τὸ ῥυπαρὸν ἔνδυμα) and left it behind in their land. And directed my way forthwith to the light of our Eastern home' (translation from Elliott, 1993).

41 See, e.g., Van der Woude, 1984, pp. 65–6; Petersen, 1985, pp. 193–6; Meyers and Meyers, 1987, pp. 187–9; cf. Reventlow, 1993, pp. 53–4; VanderKam, 1991, pp. 555–8 (= 2000, pp. 159–62).

42 Compare 2 Sam 15:32 LXX, where A reads τὰ ἱμάτια instead of τὸν χιτῶνα.

43 See above. The very fact that the source of the defilement is mentioned makes it rather improbable that the author used the Hebrew Bible and made his own translation (*pace* Bauckham; see n. 27).

44 So, e.g., Reicke, 1964, p. 216; Schelkle, 1961, pp. 171–2; Balz and Schrage, 1973, p. 231; Paulsen, 1992, p. 85; Vögtle, 1994, pp. 106–7.

45 Compare Liddell, Scott and Jones, 1968, s.v. σάρξ; Bauer and Aland, 1988, s.v. σάρξ sub 2. Compare also Jude 7 and 8.

46 Compare the *Sentences of Sextus* 449: 'Keep spotless your body, the garment of the soul given by God, just as you keep spotless your coat, the garment of the flesh (ὡς καὶ τὸν χιτῶνά σου τηρεῖς ἀσπίλωτον ἔνδυμα ὄντα τῆς σαρκός)' (text and translation according to Edwards and Wild, 1981).

47 It seems obvious that ἀπό here means 'by' in a causal sense (see Blass, Debrunner and Rehkopf, 1990, § 210, 2), and not 'of' or 'from' in the sense of the material from which something is made (*pace* Winter, 1994, p. 219).

48 Compare Bauckham, 1983, p. 116. Bauckham thinks that the author of Jude interprets the 'filthy clothes' in Zech 3:3–4 in this way because of the connotations of the Hebrew word for 'filthy' (צואים) and its cognates, words which are often used in the OT to refer to human excrement; this argument, however, is not valid since it is more likely that the author of Jude used the Septuagint and quoted it from memory. In order to understand the author's interpretation of the OT/LXX text together with his rewording of the phrase, it is not necessary to assume that he used the Hebrew Bible (see also above and n. 27).

49 Compare Philo who uses Joseph's tunic ('a coat of many colours'; cf. Gen 37:3 LXX) as a metaphor to describe the life of the politician (*Somn.* 1.220–25; *Jos.* 32).

50 Compare also Jas 1:27; 2 Pet 3:14; Hermas, *Vis.* 4.3.5; *Sim.* 9.6.4; 9.8.7; 9.26.2; Justin, *Dial.* 110:6; *Apoc. Peter* 30; *T. Asher* 2:7.

51 On this passage see also above.

52 Translation according to Williams, 1930.

53 A rather common interpretation; see above.

54 A final argument in favour of this interpretation may be the use of the term σπιλάς in v. 12. In this verse, the author gives a description of the false teachers who are threatening the Christian community: 'These are blemishes (σπιλάδες) on your love-feasts, while they feast with you without fear, feeding themselves …'. Although the word σπιλάς usually means 'reef' ('rock') or 'storm', another meaning seems to be 'stain' (cf. Bauer and Aland, 1988, s.v. σπιλάς, and Liddell, Scott and Jones, 1968, s.v. σπιλάς). It is interesting that the author of 2 Peter calls the false teachers who threaten the unity of the communities to which he writes, 'blots and blemishes (σπίλοι καὶ μῶμοι)' (2:13; see also above).

Chapter 11

Why Would a Pagan Read Zechariah? Apologetics and Exegesis in the Second-century Greek Apologists

Jeremy S. Boccabello

Christians in the second century were still trying to decide exactly what to do with the Jewish scriptures. On the one hand, they were affirming their continued connection to these texts and the traditions they represented. On the other hand, the newness of the Christian message was often in tension with these very traditions. Those who saw themselves in continuity with these texts were compelled to draw upon a wide variety of interpretive techniques in order to achieve the complex task of assimilation. The second-century Greek apologists (a somewhat arbitrary grouping usually referring to Aristides, Athenagoras, Justin Martyr, Tatian, and Theophilus of Antioch) faced the further difficulty of working all of this out in polemical contexts as they defended Christianity against pagan and Jewish detractors.

The relationship between the exegetical task and the apologetical task of these authors is a complex one, and is linked to our perceptions regarding the readership which they had in mind. For whom did the apologists exegete the Jewish Scriptures? Although all are willing to see an internal Christian readership, and some a Jewish, few take seriously the idea that the apologists would consider an exegesis of the Septuagint as a useful way of commending Christianity to pagans.[1] In fact, the presence of large portions of LXX interpretation, considered by most to be of no interest to a pagan reader, is often taken as a clear sign that *real* pagans were far from the author's mind. Did Christians in the second century fight to retain the LXX only as an act of internal self-definition, or was it important as well for their self-presentation to the wider culture (here gathered under the oversimplifying term 'paganism')?

The book of Zechariah constitutes an interesting test case for this question, because it is used in works by the apologists ranging from those which are clearly Christian-Jewish debate to those claiming to address pagans directly. In this paper I will argue that the second-century Greek apologists make a distinctive use of Zechariah in contexts in which they at least claim to be addressing pagans, and that this use differs in identifiable ways from the use which they make of Zechariah when addressing questions raised by their continuing interaction with Judaism. In this way I would like to provide some limited support to the idea that the apologists thought of the Septuagint as useful in apologetics with pagans, and show in the case of Zechariah *why* they thought it was useful.

There are good reasons to ask why a second century-pagan would be interested in

Zechariah. For instance, there is the issue of comprehensibility – this criterion is often used to ask if a particular text assumes a prior familiarity on the part of its readers with certain texts or ideas. This can often help identify the cultural or educational background of an author's apparent addressees. By this criterion, the more references to the LXX which are included in an apologist's work, the less likely it is that he is truly expecting to be understood by an audience outside the biblically literate thought world.

Take for example Justin Martyr: his *Dialogue with Trypho* is a work nearly as long as the four gospels combined, consisting almost entirely of discussions involving the Septuagint. The *Dialogue* deals with issues between Jews and Christians and thus involves debate over these commonly held texts. By contrast, Justin's two *Apologies*, which are more focused on the Christian reply to paganism, use the Septuagint much less often (though they still use it to a significant extent). Tatian's *Address to the Greeks* uses the Septuagint even more rarely than Justin's *Apologies*. It would seem that the Septuagint, being of 'barbarian' origin, was thought to be useful for in-house discussions within the Judeo-Christian thought world but less useful in addressing pagans.

Nor does it seem that all pagans met the Septuagint with enthusiasm. Celsus, a second-century pagan whose response to Christianity was preserved in detail by Origen, calls the Christian search into the meaning of Jewish prophecy a search for the 'shadow of an ass'.[2] Theophilus of Antioch, also writing in the second century, repeatedly tries to convince his pagan friend Autolycus that these books were at least worth the effort required to read them, and there is no indication that he ever did so.[3] The Greek literary tradition, although not 'canonical' in the sense that would later be applied to the Bible, was nevertheless a stable tradition deeply integrated into the educational system and considered indispensable to an educated status. One clear distinction which it made was the superiority of the Greek literary tradition to the writings of the barbarians.

Since Christianity was embracing the Septuagint, and pagans were embracing Christianity, eventually some pagans would read it, but it seems unlikely on first examination that the Septuagint had a place in apologetics with unconvinced pagans.

What has caused me to re-examine this case are statements by former pagans who say that the Septuagint was *decisive* in their conversion to Christianity. These former pagans are the apologists themselves. It is of course possible to be drawn by the apologists into a circularity here: perhaps these former pagans had little or no contact with these 'barbarian' texts prior to their conversion and only began to value them after being thoroughly persuaded through other means. Then, faced with the insurmountable difficulty of generating pagan interest in texts which they had come to see as crucial, they put the best possible face on a bad situation by adding to their own biographies a conversion which included an encounter with the prophets.[4]

Even if this all amounts to little more than a brave façade, it is certainly a widespread phenomenon. Justin gives an account of his conversion in the *Dialogue:* the old man who introduces him to Christianity does so in part by encouraging him to read the prophets. Justin describes his subsequent conversion: 'immediately a flame was kindled in my soul; and a *love of the prophets*, and of those men who are friends of Christ, possessed me.'[5] Likewise Theophilus of Antioch says that he was an unbeliever until he 'met with the sacred scriptures of the holy prophets'.[6] Tatian portrays his chance encounter with the 'barbarian' writings valued by the Christians during his search for truth as central to his own conversion:[7]

> … while I was giving my most earnest attention to the matter, I happened to meet with certain barbaric writings, too old to be compared with the opinions of the Greeks, and too divine to be compared with their errors; and I was led to put faith in these … my soul being taught of God, I discern that the former class of writings lead to condemnation, but that these put an end to the slavery that is in the world.

Not to multiply examples, but to show just how widespread and clear this claim to a decisive role for the Septuagint in conversion to Christianity is among the apologists, we can also see that Aristides seems to have been persuaded in some potent way by these writings:[8]

> Take, then, their writings, and read therein, and lo! you will find that I have not put forth these things on my own authority, nor spoken thus as their advocate; but since I read in their writings I was fully assured of these things as also of things which are to come. And for this reason I was constrained to declare the truth to such as care for it and seek the world to come.

This quotation from Aristides also provides a good example of another widespread phenomena among the apologists regarding the Septuagint: in addition to claiming a key role for the Septuagint in their own conversions, the apologists go to great lengths to encourage pagans to delve into these writings for themselves, seemingly confident that it would have a persuasive effect if they did. Athenagoras assumes that his hearers are at least familiar with Moses and the other prophets and encourages them to examine these writings and judge for themselves.[9]

Once again we must evaluate this posture carefully: it is possible that the apologists are so committed to the importance of the LXX in the face of the rejection of it by Marcion and others that, even though it is of little use in the witness to pagans, they feel they must put the best possible face on a bad situation by featuring the LXX prominently in their writings. It could also be that these works, ostensibly addressed to pagans, have only to do with internal self-definition on the part of Christians and therefore have nothing to tell us about what they thought might be useful in persuading real pagans.

Despite these possibilities, it could be that these apologists actually thought of the Septuagint as useful for apologetics with pagans for some reason or reasons. To give some limited support to this idea I would like to show the way in which the apologists used Zechariah when claiming to address pagans in order to see if it can help reveal in what this usefulness might lie. A clear difference in the use of Zechariah in these contexts which makes sense in light of the issues at stake in pagan–Christian interaction can at least provide some guidelines for understanding exegesis in this apologetic context.

We will consider the use of Zechariah in the three Greek apologetic works in which it appears, two by Justin Martyr and one by Theophilus of Antioch. First, Justin Martyr in his *Dialogue with Trypho* (c. 155–65) claims to be reflecting a conversation with a Jewish exile from Palestine which took place just after the Bar Kochba War (c. 135). In the *Dialogue* Justin deals with issues largely internal to Jewish–Christian debate and uses numerous references to Zechariah to support his arguments. By contrast, his *First Apology* written c. 155–61, is addressed to the Roman emperor Antoninus Pius and addresses many issues raised by the Christian contact with paganism. The *First Apology* uses Zechariah much less than the *Dialogue*, but still makes use of it. Helpful for our purposes is that most of the material from Zechariah used in the *First Apology* is used in the *Dialogue* as well, and thus allows us to compare use of the same material in different contexts – one addressing Christian–Jewish issues, and the other claiming to address pagans. Finally, we have two uses made of Zechariah by Theophilus of Antioch in his *Ad Autolycum*, written in the 180s CE and also claiming to be written to a pagan.

In order to see what is distinctive about the use of Zechariah by these second-century Greek apologists in their address of paganism, we will therefore first compare directly the use which Justin makes of certain passages of Zechariah in his *Dialogue with Trypho* and then see what changes when these same passages are used in the *First Apology*'s address of paganism. Then we will consider the case of Theophilus' use of Zechariah in his letter to his pagan friend Autolycus.

In *Dialogue with Trypho* Justin makes use of Zech 12:10–14, particularly v. 10, which in the LXX reads 'then they will look on me whom they pierced. Yes, they will mourn for Him as one mourns for his only son, and grieve for Him as one grieves for a firstborn.' Justin implicitly takes the piercing, as does John 19:37, as referring to the crucifixion, but his emphasis throughout the *Dialogue* is on the prediction of mourning by the tribes of Israel. This he takes as referring to a second advent of Christ, in which the Jews will recognize the messianic kingship of Jesus.[10] This division of advents enables Justin to respond to the Jewish objection that Jesus was dishonourable in his death and did not have an everlasting kingdom.[11] Zechariah 12:10 also serves as a warning of judgement by which Justin calls for repentance for the rejection of the messiah.[12] In the *Dialogue* therefore, Justin uses a Christian interpretation of this passage in Zechariah which addresses issues internal to Jewish–Christian debate: whether Jesus is to be identified as the messiah of Jewish prophecy, and what the Jewish response to that identification ought to be.

How does the use of this passage shift when it moves into an address of paganism? Zechariah 12:10 also appears in Justin's *First Apology*. Here it also serves as an argument of proof from prophecy, but on a much different level. It is important at the outset to recognize that fully *one-third* of the text of this apology, which is at least formally addressed to pagans, is dedicated to a discussion of the Jewish scriptures. It begins with a discussion of their inspiration by the prophetic Spirit, their preservation by Jewish kings, and their translation into Greek under Ptolemy.[13] Justin explains many details in the text that would be unfamiliar to a pagan hearer, such as the location of Bethlehem.[14] Although this significant use of the LXX might be used to argue for an intended audience in the biblically literate thought world, the additional presence of this quite basic explanatory material is reminiscent of that which the gospel authors used to present Jewish terms and customs to those unfamiliar with these traditions.

The persuasive function of these prophecies in the *First Apology* is much more simple than the complexities of messianic claims made in the *Dialogue*, where biblically literate Jews are in mind. Justin uses them simply to show that things which were predicted by the prophets have in fact occurred. This represents a different use by Justin of biblical prophecy. He must in this context argue for things which were already accepted by anyone who had embraced the LXX. Justin identifies both his problem in persuading pagans and the way in which his use of the prophecies addresses this problem in the *First Apology*:[15]

> We do not make mere assertions without being able to produce proof, like those myths that are told of the so-called sons of Jupiter. For with what reason should we believe of a crucified man that He is the first-born of the unbegotten God, and Himself will pass judgment on the whole human race, unless we had found testimonies concerning Him published before He came and was born as man, and unless we saw that things had happened accordingly.

Zechariah 12:10 therefore serves the purpose of the proof that prophecies were fulfilled and thus reinforces Christian claims about Jesus. This differs from Justin's use of the passage in the *Dialogue* precisely in that the veracity of the prophecies themselves is also in question in this discussion.

Specific interpretations of this passage found in the *Dialogue* also show up in the *First Apology*. The idea of the two advents shown in the future mourning of Israel which defends the messianic identity of Jesus in the *Dialogue* is used in the *First Apology* primarily to tell of a coming resurrection and judgement of the wicked. This judgement is not aimed at Israel alone, as is the judgement which underlies Justin's call for Jewish repentance using Zechariah in the *Dialogue*. The call to repentance now applies to all of the nations, and Justin uses the description of Israel mourning 'tribe by tribe' in Zechariah as a reference to a repentance by all the tribes of the earth.[16]

When addressing paganism Justin uses Zech 12:10 as a source of general proofs through fulfilled prophecy, and expands interpretations directed at Israel in the *Dialogue* to apply to the nations at large. Interpretations which are peculiar to Jewish–Christian dialogue fade into the background.

This shift in use can be seen vividly in Justin's use of Zech 9:9: 'Rejoice greatly, O daughter of Sion; proclaim it aloud, O daughter of Jerusalem; behold your King is coming to you, just, and a Saviour; he is meek and riding on a donkey, and a young foal.' In his *Dialogue with Trypho*, Justin finds a great deal for use in this passage for Jewish–Christian dialogue. First, the parallel echo of the word 'donkey' with 'a young foal' allows him to associate this verse with Gen 49:11 which speaks of Judah as 'binding his foal to the vine, And his donkey's colt to the choice vine.' This passage about the future of Judah is subject to messianic interpretation in Jewish literature,[17] and Justin may therefore be reflecting Jewish interpretation at this point. The double occurrence of donkeys in both of the passages forms the basis for an allegorical interpretation for Justin: the nations were 'like an unharnessed foal, which was not bearing a yoke on its neck',[18] that is, they did not obey God, until Christ came and they willingly 'bore the yoke of His word, and yielded the neck to endure all, for the sake of the good things promised by Himself, and expected by them'.[19] By contrast, Jewish converts to Christianity are represented by the harnessed donkey, because they already possessed the law. Altogether this allegory shows the bringing in of the new people of God, both Jewish and Gentile, by the messiah. Despite this allegorical treatment, Justin also avails himself in the very same passage of the literal interpretation: Jesus sending his disciples for the foal before his triumphal entry is a fulfilment of this prophecy.

These machinations are gone when Justin uses this passage in the *First Apology* to address paganism – and understandably so: such an audience would be utterly unfamiliar with midrashic interpretation and without appreciation for the messianic import of the texts. In fact, we might wonder if this 'double donkey' interpretation is exactly what Celsus was referring to when he talked about Christians searching for the 'shadow of an ass'. Justin therefore uses Zech 9:9 differently: it is found within a cluster of prophecies designed to show the veracity of the prophets and consequently the validity of the one to whom Justin says they refer. Gone are the elaborate discussions of salvation history comprehensible within the biblical thought world. Here the emphasis is on the specificity with which the prophetic books, when properly interpreted of course, were able to point to events in the life of Christ: his birth in Bethlehem, his crucifixion, and, in this case, his riding into Jerusalem on a donkey. These prophecies are used in this context not only to confirm the validity of Christian claims regarding Christ, but also to show the veracity of the prophets in general. This veracity has continuing implications because the prophets also predict future events which Justin wishes to impress on his hearers – the second advent and the coming judgement. This represents a significant shift in the use of Zechariah by Justin when moving between these two contexts.

The only other second-century Greek apologist to make use of Zechariah is Theophilus of Antioch. Theophilus was the sixth bishop of Antioch in Syria. He probably died some time in the 180s. Very little is known about his life; he was possibly born in Syria, he received at least a basic Hellenistic education and was converted to Christianity as an adult in a process which, as we saw above, involved in some decisive way the reading of the Septuagint.

He is otherwise unknown to us except through his writings. Although he is widely reported to have been a prolific author, all of his works are lost, with the exception of his *Ad Autolycum*, a collection of three treatises addressed to a pagan friend named Autolycus. Whether Autolycus was real or a merely a literary creation, for my purposes it is important that Autolycus is portrayed by Theophilus as a pagan with whom he has had a series of discussions on Christianity. A key element of this discussion is a comparison of the Greek literary tradition with the Septuagint,[20] so Theophilus spends a great deal of effort developing arguments to persuade his correspondent to read these writings.

The issue of the audience of *Ad Autolycum* is a difficult one. Theophilus was known to have written catechetical literature as well as anti-heretical works and works which expounded scripture.[21] As a bishop, he would have had primary responsibility for catechetical education, so a work like *Ad Autolycum* which engaged pagan thought and literature might have been useful to the Christian community in Antioch. On the other hand, Theophilus' presentation of these letters as written to a pagan friend, their warm personal manner of address, and their references to specific conversations outside of the world of the text make it possible that a real pagan recipient is in view.[22] Without reaching a specific conclusion as to audience, we can say that this letter represents what Theophilus felt was useful either to a pagan who is a potential convert to Christianity, or to a Christian community whose ongoing participation in the culture gave these issues continued relevance.

There is a large amount of material from and about the Septuagint in *Ad Autolycum*. It also presents itself as a correspondence between a Christian and a pagan, with the former trying to convince the latter to read the LXX. Theophilus is apparently convinced that Autolycus would find it persuasive if he did so. This brings us to the same question again: what use does Theophilus wish to portray the Septuagint as having to a pagan reader like Autolycus – one who knows virtually nothing about the Septuagint, is apparently quite indifferent to reading it, and is instead an avid reader of the Greek mythological tradition?[23]

In the case of Zechariah, Theophilus uses two passages which are not used by Justin or any other second-century Greek apologist. They are also not shared with the New Testament, like many of Justin's references are. What do they reflect about the use to a pagan reader which this apologist might have seen in Zechariah? The first passage used by Theophilus appears a bit unpromising at first: 'In the eighth month, in the second year of the reign of Darius, the word of the Lord came to Zacharias, the son of Barachias, the son of Addo, the prophet' (Zech 1:1). The task for which Theophilus uses this opening line, however, is important both for him and for the other apologists: it is the task of establishing the chronological priority of the 'prophets' over Greek writings. One of Theophilus' major goals in these three treatises is a commendation of the Septuagint to Autolycus. Autolycus thinks that these writings are recent and therefore not possessed of a venerable ancient tradition.[24] Theophilus calls Zechariah the 'last of the prophets'[25] and points out using this verse that the prophet was a contemporary of Darius. Theophilus then uses this dating to align Zechariah with Solon the Athenian (who was actually elected magistrate in 594 BCE, about 70 years before the opening of Zechariah was written), and so asserts that the latest writings of the prophets are contemporaneous with the earliest period of known Greek history.

This sort of chronological comparison to argue for the notoriety of a so-called barbarian culture is seen elsewhere, in Manetho, in Berossus, and, most notably in this case, Josephus, whose *Contra Apionem* forms an important model for Theophilus in this regard. Zechariah is thus used by Theophilus as evidence for the antiquity of the prophetic writings for the purpose of giving them greater credibility to pagans who know little about them.

Theophilus' second use of Zechariah reflects quite a different agenda. Theophilus is eager to convince Autolycus that the charges of immorality levelled against Christians (specifically incest and cannibalism) are false.[26] This results in a long discourse in book 3 on the comparative morality of Christians and pagans. Theophilus' assertion of the morality of the Christians includes a collection of sayings from Isaiah, Jeremiah, Hosea, Joel and Zechariah; each concerned with the subject of true righteousness. Here he quotes Zech 7:9–10:[27]

> Thus says the Lord Almighty, Judge a judgement of truth, and show mercy and pity each to his neighbour, and do not oppress the widow and the orphan and the sojourner, and let each one not bear malice to his brother in your hearts.

Here the moral teaching on the proper expression of devotion to God and Torah by a sixth-century BCE Jewish prophet is used as a proof of Christian morality. This represents to some extent a *combination* of on the one hand Theophilus' defence of

Christian morals and, on the other, his ever-present defence of the Septuagint as a book worth pagan notice. Theophilus challenges Greek mythological literature as a rival standard of moral teaching, which because of the immoral acts of the heroes and gods inculcates vice in those who study them.[28] By contrast, Theophilus contends, the Septuagint can be shown to be a superior source of moral teaching using passages on true righteousness such as Zech 7:9–10. Because the Septuagint is a source of moral teaching superior to Greek literature, the Christians who have embraced it therefore have a superior ethical constitution.

What then has the evidence told us about our central question? We have been using Zechariah as a test-case to see if there are distinctive uses made of this book by the apologists when they are addressing paganism. I have been attempting to provide some limited support to the idea that the apologists thought of the Septuagint as useful in apologetics with pagans by showing in these contexts what that usefulness might have been.

The evidence from Justin has been particularly helpful by allowing us to see what stays the same and what changes when passages used in a context of Christian–Jewish debate are put to use in an address of paganism. Theophilus' use of Zechariah gives us further examples in a context claiming to address a pagan friend.

Why, then, would a pagan read Zechariah? Judging by this evidence, we can see several reasons why the apologists considered it useful for just that purpose. First, there is a proof from prophecy. When addressing Jewish questions, Justin uses Zechariah as a part of his efforts to show that Jesus was the Jewish messiah, and engages in elaborate exegesis using allegorical and even midrashic interpretive paradigms in order to show this to be the case. When addressing paganism, Justin also engages in a proof from prophecy using Zechariah, even in service to his claims regarding Jesus. This proof from prophecy differs however: it is on a more basic level which assumes disagreement not just over the interpretation of the texts, but over the validity of the texts themselves. He presents these texts as culturally foreign and in need of arguments of support. The veracity of the prophetic texts is tied up with the truth of Christian claims about Jesus, and both are at stake.

The apologists are therefore concerned to show the veracity of the prophets. This also serves the purpose of supporting their contentions about the future fulfilment of other prophecies which they see in the scriptures, such as a final conflagration. They try to persuade others that the Septuagint is worth reading, first because it represents an ancient venerable tradition (for which Zechariah is used as a dating marker), and also because it is a superior source of moral instruction (for which Zechariah serves as a source of teaching on the law applied to Christians). The presence of a culturally dominant literary tradition among pagans makes it necessary for the apologists to contrast the writings of the prophets with those of the Greeks to convince them that they are worth reading.

Justin uses Zechariah's predictions of a future repentance of Israel to speak of the two advents of Christ. When addressing Jewish challenges, he uses this eschatology to address the dishonourable state of Jesus and the apparent end of his claim to kingship. He also uses it to encourage repentance by the Jews because repentance has been predicted and is thus inevitable. Justin takes this same passage with its interpretation into an address of paganism, and builds on the same eschatology of two advents. But here, both the future repentance and the future judgement no longer refer only to Israel. They are universalized, and expand to include the idea of a transnational and transethnic eschatology.

Several tasks involving Zechariah are therefore evident which are more than just Christian self-definition vis-à-vis Judaism. These tasks are only comprehensible in the context of an address of paganism: (a) the need to prove the basic veracity of the Septuagint prophecies, its value as a source of moral instruction, and its superiority to Greek literature in terms of its antiquity and truthfulness; (b) the need to integrate this bolstering of the Septuagint with claims about Jesus to an audience unfamiliar with both Jewish texts and messianic ideas; (c) the shift to a universal application of biblical prophecies in a structure of transethnic eschatology. Zechariah is put to use in service of each of these tasks, and this can give us some idea of what use the apologists saw in these texts when dealing with paganism.

We are still left with uncertainty about the intended and actual audience of these works, particularly how often they were actually read by pagans. Because of this, it is probably best to draw rather limited conclusions – the apologists saw Zechariah as useful in addressing issues which were clearly raised by the Christian interaction with paganism. This is true regardless of the extent to which these texts themselves represent just such an interaction. We can see perceived usefulness whether they are talking to pagans or merely talking to each other about pagans.

However, the combination of the apologists' own claim to the decisive role of the Septuagint in their own conversions, their constant use of it in contexts which claim to address pagans, and their apparent efforts to convince reluctant pagan hearers to read it – all of this taken together with what we have seen here in their use of Zechariah – a particular, discernable difference in their use of the same texts when moving from a Christian–Jewish context to a Christian–pagan context – might allow us to go further. It is at least probable that Zechariah and much else from the Septuagint actually made its way significantly into the self-presentation of Christians to pagans.

NOTES

1 For example, Manlio Simonetti in his helpful introduction to exegesis in the early church says of the second-century apologist Justin Martyr that he was 'interested in the Old Testament only in terms of disagreement with the Jews' (Simonetti, 1994, p. 22).

2 Origen, *Contra Celsum*, 3.2.

3 Theophilus of Antioch, *Ad Autolycum*, 1.14; 3.1. If Autolycus is merely a literary construction, it is even more telling that Theophilus shows him as recalcitrant and ultimately unwilling to read the LXX despite Theophilus' repeated efforts to present it in a favourable light.

4 'The prophets' is a favourite designation among the apologists for the writings accepted by the Christians, and can refer to any part of the Jewish scriptures. See for example Justin Martyr, *First Apology*, 23; 31; Athenagoras, *Legatio*, 7; 9; Theophilus of Antioch, *Ad Autolycum*, 1.14; 2I.9; Tatian, *Address to the Greeks*, 20; 36.

5 *Dialogue*, 7–8, emphasis mine.

6 *Ad Autolycum*, 1.14.

7 Tatian, *Address to the Greeks*, 29.

8 Aristides, *Apology*, 16. Aristides' claim is found in the Syriac version but not in Robertson's reconstruction of the Greek text.

9 Athenagoras, *Legatio*, 9.
10 *Dialogue* 14.8; 126.1.
11 *Dialogue* 32.2.
12 *Dialogue* 118.1.
13 *First Apology*, 31.
14 *First Apology*, 34.
15 *First Apology*, 53.
16 Justin may also hint at a more universal interpretation of 'tribe by tribe' in *Dialogue*, 121.
17 For example, see Gen 49:10–12 in Targums Neophyti, Onkelos, and Pseudo-Jonathan.
18 *Dialogue*, 53.3.
19 Ibid.
20 Theophilus of Antioch, *Ad Autolycum* 3.1.
21 Eusebius, *H. E.*, 4.24; Jerome, *De Viris Illustribus*, 25.
22 *Ad Autolycum*, 1.1, 14; 2.1, 38; 3.1, 15.
23 *Ad Autolycum*, 2.1; 3.1.
24 *Ad Autolycum*, 3.1.
25 *Ad Autolycum*, 3.23.
26 *Ad Autolycum*, 3.4.
27 Zech 7:9–10 as quoted in *Ad Autolycum*, 3.12.
28 *Ad Autolycum*, 3.8.

Bibliography

Ackroyd, P. R. (1968), *Exile and Restoration* (Old Testament Library), London: SCM.

Ådna, J. (2000), *Jesu Stellung zum Tempel. Die Tempelaktion und das Tempelwort als Ausdruck seiner messianischen Sendung* (WUNT 2.119), Tübingen: Mohr Siebeck.

Aland, K. et al. (eds) (1993), *Nestle-Aland Novum Testamentum Graece* (27. Auflage), Stuttgart: Deutsche Bibelgesellschaft.

Aland, K. and Aland, B. (1989), *The Text of the New Testament* (German original 1981), Leiden: Brill/Grand Rapids: Eerdmans.

Albl, M. C. (1999), *'And Scripture Cannot Be Broken'. The Form and Function of Early Christian Testimonia Collections* (NovTSup 96), Leiden: Brill.

Allen, J. S. (1998), 'A New Possibility for the Three-Clause Format of Jude 22–3', *NTS* **44**, 133–43.

Allen, W. C. (1912), *A Critical and Exegetical Commentary on the Gospel according to St Matthew* (ICC; 3rd edn), Edinburgh: T. & T. Clark.

Amsler, S. (1981), *Aggée, Zacharie 1–8* (CAT 11c), Neuchâtel and Paris: Delachaux & Niestlé.

Aune, D. E. (1997), *Revelation 1–5* (WBC 52A), Dallas: Word.

Baldwin, J. G. (1972), *Haggai, Zechariah, Malachi* (Tyndale Old Testament Commentaries), Leicester: Inter-Varsity.

Balz, H. and Schrage, W. (1973), *Die katholischen Briefe* (NTD 10), Göttingen: Vandenhoeck & Ruprecht.

Barr, J. (1977), *Fundamentalism*, London: SCM.

Barrett, C. K. (1955), *The Gospel according to St John*, London: SPCK.

— (1975), 'The House of Prayer and the Den of Thieves', in Ellis, E. Earle and Grässer, E. (eds), *Jesus und Paulus. Festschrift für Werner Georg Kümmel zum 70. Geburtstag*, Göttingen: Vandenhoeck & Ruprecht, pp. 13–20.

Barstad, H. M. (1984), *The Religous Polemics of Amos* (VTSup 34), Leiden: Brill.

— (1996), *The Myth of the Empty Land* (SOFS 28), Oslo: Scandinavian University Press.

— (1997), *The Babylonian Captivity of the Book of Isaiah. "Exilic" Judah and the Provenance of Isaiah 40–55* (Instituttet for Sammenlignende Kulturforskning), Oslo.

Barthélemy, D. (1992), *Critique textuelle de l'Ancien Testament, 3. Ezechiel, Daniel et les 12 Prophètes* (OBO 50/3), Göttingen: Vandenhoeck & Ruprecht.

Barton, J. (1984), *Reading the Old Testament: Method in Biblical Study* (revised edn 1996), London: Darton Longman & Todd.

— (1986), *Oracles of God: Perceptions of Ancient Prophecy in Israel after the Exile*, London: Darton Longman & Todd.

— (2001), *Joel and Obadiah: A Commentary* (Old Testament Library), Louisville KY – London – Leiden: Westminster John Knox Press.

Bauckham, R. J. (1983), *Jude, 2 Peter* (WBC 50), Waco: Word.

Bauer, W., Aland, K. and B. (1988), *Griechisch-deutsches Wörterbuch zu den Schriften des Neuen Testaments und der frühchristlichen Literatur* (6th edn), Berlin – New York: de Gruyter.

Benoit, P. (1969), *The Passion and Resurrection of Jesus Christ*, New York: Herder & Herder.

Beuken, W. A. M. (1967), *Haggai-Sacharja 1–8. Studien aur Überlieferungsgeschichte der frühnachexilischen Prophetie*, Assen: Van Gorcum.
Bič, M. (1962), *Das Buch Sacharja*, Berlin: Evangelische Verlagsanstalt.
Birdsall, J. N. (1963), 'The Text of Jude in P^{72}', *JTS* **14**, 394–9.
Blass, F., Debrunner, A., Rehkopf, F. (1990), *Grammatik des neutestamentlichen Griechisch* (17th edn), Göttingen: Vandenhoeck & Ruprecht.
Blenkinsopp, J. (1984), *A History of Prophecy in Israel*, London: SPCK.
— (1995), *Sage, Priest, Prophet. Religious and Intellectual Leadership in Ancient Israel*, Louisville: Westminster John Knox Press.
Boda, M. J. and Floyd, M. H. (eds) (2003), *Bringing Out the Treasure: Inner Biblical Allusion and Zechariah 9–14* (JSOTSup 370), Sheffield: Sheffield Academic Press.
Brandon, S. G. F. (1967), *Jesus and the Zealots*, Manchester: Manchester University Press.
Bright, J. (1960), *History of Israel*, London: SCM.
Brown, R. E. (1967), 'The Paraclete in the Fourth Gospel', *NTS* **13**, 113–32.
— (1985), *The Gospel according to John XIIIi –XXI* (AB 29A), New York: Doubleday.
Bruce, F. F. (1961), 'The Book of Zechariah and the Passion Narrative', *BJRL* **43**, 336–53.
Bultmann, R. (1968), *Das Evangelium des Johannes* (19th edn), Göttingen: Vandenhoeck & Ruprecht.
— (1979), *Die Geschichte der synoptischen Tradition* (9th edn; FRLANT 29), Göttingen: Vandenhoeck & Ruprecht.
Butterworth, M. (1992), *Structure and the Book of Zechariah* (JSOTSup 130), Sheffield: Sheffield Academic Press.
Calvin, J. (1849), *Commentaries of the Twelve Minor Prophets. Vol. 5 Zechariah and Malachi* (transl. J. Owen), Edinburgh.
Carroll, R. P. (1979a), *When Prophecy Failed. Reactions and Responses to Failure in the Old Testament Prophetic Traditions*, London: SCM.
— (1979b), 'Twilight of Prophecy or Dawn of Apocalyptic?', *JSOT* **14**, 3–35.
— (1986), *Jeremiah: A Commentary* (Old Testament Library), London: SCM.
Cathcart, K. J. and Gordon, R. P. (1989), *The Targum of the Minor Prophets* (The Aramaic Bible 14), Edinburgh: T. & T. Clark.
Charles, J. D. (1990), ' "Those" and "These": The Use of the Old Testament in the Epistle of Jude', *JSNT* **38**, 109–24.
— (1991), 'Jude's Use of Pseudepigraphical Source-Material as Part of a Literary Strategy', *NTS* **37**, 130–45.
— (1993), *Literary Strategy in the Epistle of Jude*, Scranton: University of Scranton Press; London/Toronto: Associated University Presses.
Charlesworth, J. H. (ed.) (1985), *Old Testament Pseudepigrapha*, 2 vols, New York: Doubleday.
Chary, T. (1969), *Aggée, Zacharie, Malachie*, Paris: Gabalda.
Childs, B. S. (1974), *Exodus* (Old Testament Library), London: SCM.
Coggins, R. J. (1987), *Haggai, Zechariah, Malachi*, Sheffield: Sheffield Academic Press.
Collins, J. J. (1993), *Daniel* (Hermeneia), Minneapolis: Fortress Press.
Conrad, E. W. (1999), *Zechariah*, Sheffield: Sheffield Academic Press.
Cope, O. L. (1976), *Matthew: A Scribe Trained for the Kingdom of Heaven* (CBQMS 5), Washington: Catholic Biblical Association of America.
Cowley, A. E. (1910), rev. edn of Kautzsch, E., *Gesenius' Hebrew Grammar*, Oxford: Clarendon Press.
Crossan, J. D. (1991), *The Historical Jesus. The Life of a Mediterranean Jewish Peasant*, Edinburgh: T. & T. Clark.
Daube, D. (1960), 'Three Notes having to do with Johanan ben Zaccai', *JTS* **11**, 53–62.
Davies, W. D. and Allison, D. C. (1997), *The Gospel according to Saint Matthew* Volume III (ICC), Edinburgh: T. & T. Clark.

De Boer, M. C. (1996), *Johannine Perspective on the Death of Jesus*, Kampen: Pharos.
De Jonge, H. J. (2000), 'Joden tegen Marcaanse christenen in Galilea kort na 70' [Jews versus Markan Christians in Galilee shortly after 70 CE], in Frishman, J., Jenner, K. D., Wiegers, G. A. (eds), *Godsdienstvrijheid en de religieuze identiteit van joden, christenen en moslims; verwachting en realiteit*, Kampen: Kok, pp. 64–88.
Delcor, M. (1952), 'Les sources du Deutéro-Zacherie et ses procédés d'emprunt', *RB* **59**, 385–411.
Dodd, C. H. (1955), *The Interpretation of the Fourth Gospel*, Cambridge: Cambridge University Press.
— (1963), *Historical Tradition in the Fourth Gospel*, Cambridge: Cambridge University Press.
— (1965), *According to the Scriptures*, London: Collins.
Dogniez, C. (1998), 'La Bible d'Alexandrie, II. Select passage: Sophonie (Zephaniah) 3,8–11', in Taylor, B. A. (ed.), *X Congress of the International Organization for Septuagint and Cognate Studies*, Oslo (SCS 51), Atlanta: Society of Biblical Literature, pp. 199–216.
Donahue, J. (1976), 'From Passion Traditions to Passion Narrative', in Kelber, W. H. (ed.), *The Passion in Mark*, Philadelphia: Fortress Press, pp. 1–20.
Duhm, B. (1911), 'Anmerkungen zu den zwölf Propheten', *ZAW* **31**, 1–43, 81–110, 161–204.
Dunderberg, I. (1997), 'John and Thomas in Conflict?', in Turner, J. D. and McGuire, A. (eds), *The Nag Hammadi Library after Fifty Years. Proceedings of the 1995 Society of Biblical Literature Commemoration* (NHMS 44), Leiden: Brill, pp. 361–80.
Edwards, R. A. and Wild, R. A. (1981), *The Sentences of Sextus* (SBLTT 22), Chico, CA: Scholars Press.
Ego, B. (1999), 'Buch Tobit' in H. Lichtenberger et al. (eds), *Unterweisung in erzählender Form* (JSHRZ Bd II), Gütersloh: Gütersloher Verlagshaus.
Ehrlich, A. B. (1912), *Randglossen zur Hebräischen Bibel* 5, Leipzig.
Eichorn, J. G. (1783), *Einleitung in das Alte Testament* (3rd edn), Leipzig.
Eisenbeis, W. (1969), *Die Wurzel* שלם *im Alten Testament* (BZAW 113), Berlin: de Gruyter.
Elliger, K. (1959), *Das Buch der zwölf kleinen Propheten*, II (ATD), Göttingen: Vandenhoeck & Ruprecht.
Elliott, J. K. (1993), *The Apocryphal New Testament: A Collection of Apocryphal Christian Literature in an English Translation*, Oxford: Clarendon Press.
Field, F. (1875), *Origenis Hexaplorum quae supersunt* (2 vols), Oxford: Clarendon Press.
Fishbane, M. (1985), *Biblical Interpretation in Ancient Israel*, Oxford: Clarendon Press.
Fitzmyer, J. A. (1981, 1985), *The Gospel according to Luke* (2 vols; AB 28, 28A), New York: Doubleday.
Floyd, M. H. (2000), *Minor Prophets, Part 2* (The Forms of Old Testament Literature 22), Grand Rapids/Cambridge: Eerdmans.
Forestell, J. T. (1974), *The Word of the Cross. Salvation as Revelation in the Fourth Gospel* (AnBib 57), Rome: Pontifical Biblical Institute.
Freed, E. D. (1965), *Old Testament Quotations in the Gospel of John* (NovTSup 11), Leiden: Brill.
Frey, J. (1993), 'Erwägungen zum Verhältnis der Johannesapokalypse zu den übrigen Schriften des Corpus Johanneum', in Hengel, M., *Die johanneische Frage. Ein Lösungsversuch* (WUNT 67), Tübingen: Mohr Siebeck, pp. 326–429.
Gaide, G. (1968), *Jérusalem, voici ton roi (Commentaire de Zacharie 9–14)* (LD 49), Paris: Cerf.
Gerdmar, A. (2001), *Rethinking the Judaism-Hellenism Dichotomy. A historiographical case study of Second Peter and Jude* (CB NT 36), Stockholm: Almqvist & Wiksell International.
Goldschmidt, L. (1930), *Der babylonische Talmud* (9 vols), Berlin: Jüdischer Verlag.
Goodblatt, D. W. (1994), *The Monarchic Principle* (TSAJ 38), Tübingen: Mohr Siebeck.
Grant, R. M. (1948), 'The Coming of the Kingdom', *JBL* **67**, 297–303.

Guilding, E. (1960), *The Fourth Gospel and Jewish Worship*, Oxford: Clarendon Press.
Gundry R. H. (1967), *The Use of the Old Testament in St. Matthew's Gospel* (NovTSup 18), Leiden: Brill.
— (1993), *Mark: A Commentary on his Apology for the Cross*, Grand Rapids: Eerdmans.
— (1994), *Matthew: A Commentary on his Handbook for a Mixed Church under Persecution* (2nd ed.), Grand Rapids: Eerdmans.
Haenchen, E. (1984), *John 2*, Philadelphia: Fortress Press.
Hagner, D. A. (1995), *Matthew 14–28* (WBC 33B), Dallas: Word.
Hanson, P. D. (1975), *The Dawn of Apocalyptic*, Philadelphia: Fortress Press.
Harrington, D. J. (1991), *The Gospel of Matthew* (Sacra Pagina), Collegeville, MN: Liturgical Press.
Heiligenthal, R. (1992), *Zwischen Henoch und Paulus. Studien zum theologiegeschichtlichen Ort des Judasbriefes*, Tübingen: Francke Verlag.
Hengel, M. (1973), *War Jesus Revolutionär?*, Stuttgart: Calwer Hefte.
— (1989), 'Die Schriftauslegung des 4. Evangeliums auf dem Hintergrund der urchristlichen Exegese', *JBTh* **4**, 249–88.
Ho Fai Tai, N. (1996), *Prophetie als Schriftauslegung in Sacharja 9-14. Traditions- und kompositionsgeschichtliche Studien* (Calwer Theologische Monographien A 17), Stuttgart: Calwer.
Holladay, W. L. (1989), *Jeremiah II: A Commentary on the Book of the Prophet Jeremiah Chapters 26–52* (Hermeneia), Phildelphia/London: Fortress Press/SCM.
Hollander, H. W. (1994), 'The Testing by Fire of the Builders' Works: 1 Corinthians 3.10–15', *NTS* **40**, 89–104.
Hollander, H. W. and De Jonge, M. (1985), *The Testaments of the Twelve Patriarchs. A Commentary* (SVTP 8), Leiden: Brill.
Hooker, M. D. (1982), 'Traditions about the Temple in the Sayings of Jesus', *BJRL* **65**, 78–99.
— (1991), *The Gospel according to St Mark* (BNTC), London: Black.
Horst, F. (1954), 'Nahum bis Maleachi', in Robinson, T. H. and Horst, F., *Die zwölf kleinen Propheten* (3rd ed.; Handbuch zum Alten Testament 14), Tübingen: Mohr, pp. 153–275.
Huffmon, H. B. (1983), 'Priestly Divination in Israel', in Meyers, C. L. and O'Connor, M. (eds), *The Word of the Lord Shall Go Forth. Essays in Honor of David Noel Freedman*, Winona Lake: Eisenbrauns, pp. 355–9.
Husser, J.-M. (1994), *Le songe et la parole. Etude sur le rêve et sa fonction dans l'ancien Israël* (BZAW 210), Berlin – New York: de Gruyter.
Jansma, T. (1950), 'Inquiry into the Hebrew Text and the Ancient Versions of Zechariah IX–XIV', *Oudtestamentische Studiën* **7**, 1–142.
Jastrow, M. (1903), *A Dictionary of the Targumim, the Talmud Babli and Yerushalmi, and the Midrashic Literature*, Brooklyn, N.Y.: Traditional Press Inc.
Jepsen, A. (1945/48), 'Kleine Beiträge zum Zwölfprophetenbuch III', *ZAW* **61**, 95–114.
Jeremias, C. (1977), *Die Nachtgesichte des Sacharja. Untersuchungen zu ihrer Stellung im Zusammenhang der Visionsberichte im Alten Testament und zu ihrem Bildmaterial*, Göttingen: Vandenhoeck & Ruprecht.
Jeremias, J. (1966), *The Eucharistic Words of Jesus*, London: SCM.
Jobes, K. H. and Silva, M. (2000), *Invitation to the Septuagint*, Grand Rapids: Baker Books.
Jones, B. A. (1985), *The Formation of the Book of the Twelve. A Study of Text and Canon* (SBLDS 149), Atlanta: Scholars Press.
Joosten, J. (1998), 'Exegesis in the Septuagint Version of Hosea', in J.C. de Moor (ed.), *Intertextuality in Ugarit and Israel* (OTS 40), Leiden: Brill.
— (2001), 'On the Translators' Knowledge of Hebrew', in Taylor, B. A. (ed.), *X Congress of the International Organization for Septuagint and Cognate Studies*, Oslo (SCS 51), Atlanta: Society of Biblical Literature, pp. 165–79.

Joüon, P. (1923), *Grammaire de l'hébreu biblique*, Rome: Institut Biblique Pontifical.
Käsemann, E. (1968), *The Testament of Jesus*, London: SCM.
Keil, C. F. (1888), *Die zwölf kleinen Propheten* (BKAT), Leipzig.
Knowles, M. (1993), *Jeremiah in Matthew's Gospel: The Rejected-Prophet Motif in Matthaean Redaction* (JSNTSup 68), Sheffield: JSOT Press.
Kreiger, N. (1957), 'Der Knecht des Hohenpriesters', *NovT* **2**, 73–4.
Kremer, J. (1930), *Die Hirtenallegorie im Buche Zacharias*, Münster: Verlag der Aschendorffschen Verlagsbuchhandlung.
Kubo, S. (1965), P^{72} *and Codex Vaticanus* (SD 27), Salt Lake City: University of Utah.
— (1981), 'Jude 22–3: Two-division form or three?', in Epp, E. J. and Fee, G. D. (eds), *New Testament Textual Criticism. Its Significance for Exegesis*, Oxford: Clarendon Press, pp. 239–53.
Kümmel, W. G. (1957), *Promise and Fulfilment. The Eschatological Message of Jesu* (SBT 23), Naperville, IL: Allison.
Lacocque, A. (1981), 'Zacharie 9–14', in Amsler, S., Lacocque, A. and Vuilleumier, R., *Aggée, Zacharie 1–8, Zacharie 9–14, Malachie* (CAT 11c), Neuchâtel and Paris: Delachaux & Niestlé, pp. 127–216.
Lake, K. (1912), *The Apostolic Fathers* (Loeb Classical Library), London: Heinemann.
Lamarche, P. (1961), *Zacharie IX–XIV. Structure littéraire et messianisme*, Paris: Gabalda.
Landon, C. (1996), *A Text-Critical Study of the Epistle of Jude* (JSNTSup 135), Sheffield: Sheffield Academic Press.
Lane, E. W. and Lane-Poole, S. (1863), *An Arabic-English Lexicon*, London.
Lane, W. L. (1974), *The Gospel of Mark* (NLCNT), London: Marshall, Morgan & Scott.
Larkin, K. J. A. (1994), *The Eschatology of Second Zechariah. A Study of the Formation of a Mantological Wisdom Anthology* (CBET 6), Kampen: Kok Pharos.
Leske, A. M. (2000), 'Context and Meaning of Zechariah 9.9', *CBQ* **62**, 663–78.
Liddell, H. G., Scott, R. and Jones, H. S. (1968), *A Greek-English Lexicon* (9th edn), Oxford: Clarendon Press.
Lindars, B. (1961), *New Testament Apologetic*, London: SCM.
— (1972), *The Gospel of John*, London: Marshall, Morgan & Scott.
— (1990), *John*, Sheffield: JSOT Press.
Linnemann, E. (1970), *Studien zur Passionsgeschichte* (FRLANT 102), Göttingen: Vandenhoeck & Ruprecht.
Lipiński, E. (1962), 'Les psaumes de la royauté de Yahwé dans l'exégèse moderne' in De Langhe, R. (ed.), *Le Psautier: Etudes présentées aux XIIe Journées Bibliques*, Louvain, pp. 133–272.
— (1970), 'Recherches sur le livre de Zacharie', *VT* **20**, 25–9.
Lührmann, D. (1987), *Das Markusevangelium* (HNT), Tübingen: Mohr Siebeck.
Luz, U. (1997), *Das Evangelium nach Matthäus*, 3. Teilband *Mt 18–25* (EKK), Benzinger: Neukirchener Verlag.
McNeile, A. H. (1915), *The Gospel According to St Matthew*, London: Macmillan.
Marcus, J. (1993), *The Way of the Lord*, Edinburgh: T. & T. Clark.
Marshall, I. H. (1978), *The Gospel of Luke* (NIGTC), Exeter: Paternoster.
Marti, K. (1904), *Das Dodekapropheton* (Kurzer Hand-Commentar zum Alten Testament 13), Tübingen: Mohr.
Mason, R. A. (1973), 'The Use of Earlier Biblical Material in Zechariah IX–XIV: A Study in Inner-Biblical Exegesis', unpublished dissertation, University of London.
— (1976), 'The Relation of Zechariah 9–14 to Proto-Zechariah', *ZAW* **88**, 227–39.
— (1977), *The Books of Haggai, Zechariah and Malachi* (Cambridge Bible Commentary), Cambridge: Cambridge University Press.

— (1982a), 'Some Examples of Inner Biblical Exegesis in Zech. IX–XIV', *Studia Evangelica* 7 (TU 126), Berlin: Akademie Verlag, 343–54.
— (1982b), 'The Prophets of the Restoration' in Coggins, Richard, Philips, Anthony and Knibb, Michael (eds), *Israel's Prophetic Heritage: Essays in Honour of Peter Ackroyd*, Cambridge: Cambridge University Press, 137–54.
— (1984), 'Some Echoes of the Preaching in the Second Temple? Tradition Elements in Zechariah 1–8', *ZAW* **96**, 221–35.
— (1990a), *Preaching the Tradition: Homily and Hermeneutic after the Exile*, Cambridge: Cambridge University Press.
— (1990b), 'Inner-Biblical Exegesis', in Coggins, R. J. and Houlden, J. L. (eds), *A Dictionary of Biblical Interpretation*, London: SCM, pp. 312–14.
— (1997), *Propaganda and Subversion in the Old Testament*, London: SPCK.
Mayor, J. B. (1965), *The Epistle of St. Jude and the Second Epistle of St. Peter* (reprint of 1907 edn), Grand Rapids: Baker.
Menken, M. J. J. (1993), 'The Textual Form and the Meaning of the Quotation from Zechariah 12:10 in John 19:37', *CBQ* **55**, 494–511 (reprinted in Menken, 1996, pp. 167–85).
— (1996), *Old Testament Quotations in the Fourth Gospel. Studies in Textual Form*, Kampen: Pharos.
Metzger, B. M. (1971), *A Textual Commentary on the Greek New Testament*, London/New York: United Bible Societies.
Meyers, C. L. and Meyers, E. M. (1987), *Haggai, Zechariah 1–8* (AB 25B), New York: Doubleday.
— (1993), *Zechariah 9–14* (AB 25C), New York: Doubleday.
Milgrom, J. (1991), *Leviticus 1–16* (AB 3), New York: Doubleday.
Miller, J. W. (1955), *Das Verhältnis Jeremias und Hesekiels sprachlich und theologisch untersucht mit besonderer Berücksichtigung der Prosareden Jeremias*, Assen: Van Gorcum & Co. Ltd.
Mitchell, H. G. (1912), *Haggai, Zechariah* (ICC), Edinburgh: T. & T. Clark.
Moo, D. (1983), *The Old Testament in the Gospel Passion Narratives*, Sheffield: JSOT Press.
Moule, C. F. D. (1959), 'The Influence of Circumstances on the Use of Christological Terms', *JTS* **10**, 247–63.
Muraoka, T. (1983), 'Hosea IV in the Septuagint Version', *AJBI* **9**, 24–64.
— (1986), 'Hosea V in the Septuagint version', *Abr-Nahrain* **24**, 120–38.
— (1989), 'In Defence of the Unity of the Septuagint Minor Prophets', *AJBI* **15**, 25–36.
— (1993), *A Greek-English Lexicon of the Septuagint (Twelve Prophets)*, Louvain: Peeters.
— (1995), 'Hosea III in the Septuagint version', in Davies, J., Harvey, G. and Watson, W. G. E. (eds), *Words Remembered. Texts Renewed. Essays in Honour of John F. A. Sawyer*, Sheffield: Sheffield Academic Press, pp. 242–52.
— (2002), 'Introduction générale aux Douze Prophètes', in *La Bible d'Alexandrie 23.1: Les Douze Prophètes, Osée*, Paris: Cerf.
Neirynck, F. (1988), *Duality in Mark. Contributions to the Study of the Markan Redaction* (rev. edn), Leuven: Leuven University Press & Peeters.
Niederwimmer, K. (1998), *The Didache*, Minneapolis: Fortress Press.
Nineham, D. E. (1963), *The Gospel of St Mark*, Harmondsworth: Penguin.
Noth, M. (1962), *Exodus* (Old Testament Library), London: SCM.
Nowack, W. (1922), *Die kleinen Propheten* (GHAT), Göttingen: Vandenhoeck & Ruprecht.
Nurmela, R. (1996), *Prophets in Dialogue. Inner-Biblical Allusions in Zechariah 1–8 and 9–14*, Åbo: Åbo Akademi University Press.
Obermann, A. (1996), *Die christologische Erfüllung der Schrift im Johannesevangelium* (WUNT 2.83), Tübingen: Mohr Siebeck.

Ollenburger, B. C. (1996), 'The Book of Zechariah', *The New Interpreters' Bible* 7, Nashville: Abingdon, 733–840.

Orelli, C. von (1908), *Die zwölf kleinen Propheten* (KKANT), München.

Osburn, C. D. (1972), 'The Text of Jude 22–23', *ZNW* **63**, 139–44.

Otzen, B. (1964), *Studien über Deuterosacharja* (Acta theologica danica 6), Copenhagen: Munksgaard.

Paul, S. M. (1991), *Amos* (Hermeneia), Minneapolis: Fortress Press.

Paulsen, H. (1992), *Der zweite Petrusbrief und der Judasbrief* (KEK XII.2), Göttingen: Vandenhoeck & Ruprecht.

Perowne, T. T. (1908), *The Books of Haggai and Zechariah*, Cambridge: Cambridge University Press.

Perri, C. (1978), 'On Alluding', *Poetics* **7**, 289–307.

Perrin, N. (1966), 'Mark xiv. 62: The End Product of a Christian Pesher Tradition?', *NTS* **12**, 150–6.

Person, R. F. (1993), *Second Zechariah and the Deuteronomic School* (JSOTSup 167), Sheffield: Sheffield Academic Press.

Petersen, D. L. (1985), *Haggai & Zechariah 1–8* (Old Testament Library), London: SCM.

— (1995), *Zechariah 9–14 and Malachi* (Old Testament Library), Louisville: Westminster John Knox.

Petitjean, A. (1969), *Les oracles du Proto-Zacharie. Un programme de restauration pour la communauté juive après l'exil*, Paris–Louvain: Gabalda.

Porten, B. (1968), *Archives from Elephantine*, Berkeley: University of California.

Porter, B. N. (2000), 'The Anxiety of Multiplicity. Concepts of Divinity as One and Many in Ancient Assyria', in *eadem* (ed.), *One God or Many? Concepts of Divinity in the Ancient World* (Transactions of the Casco Bay Assyriological Institute 1), *s.l.*, pp. 211–71.

Rabenau, M. (1994), *Studien zum Buch Tobit* (BZAW 220), Berlin: De Gruyter.

Redditt, P. L. (1992), 'Zerubbabel, Joshua and the Night Visions of Zechariah, *CBQ* **54**, 249–59.

— (1995), *Haggai, Zechariah, Malachi* (New Century Bible), London: Marshall Pickering.

Reicke, B. (1964), *The Epistles of James, Peter, and Jude* (AB 37), New York: Doubleday.

Reventlow, H. Graf (1993), *Die Propheten Haggai, Sacharja und Maleachi* (ATD 25.2), Göttingen: Vandenhoeck & Ruprecht.

Rignell, L. G. (1950), *Die Nachtgesichte des Sacharja*, Lund: Gleerup.

Riley, G. J. (1995), *Resurrection Reconsidered: Thomas and John in Controversy*, Minneapolis: Fortress Press.

Rooke, D. W. (2000), *Zadok's Heirs. The Role and Development of the High Priesthood in Ancient Israel*, Oxford: Oxford University Press.

Rose, W. H. (2000), *Zemah and Zerubbabel. Messianic Expectations in the Early Postexilic Period* (JSOTSup 304), Sheffield: Sheffield Academic Press.

Rostovtzeff, R. (1934), 'Οὖς δεξιὸν ἀποτέμνειν', *ZNW* **33**, 196–9.

Roth, C. (1960), 'The Cleansing of the Temple and Zechariah', *NovT* **4**, 174–81.

Rothstein, J. W. (1910), *Die Nachtgesichte des Sacharja. Studien zur Sacharjaprophetie und zur jüdischen Geschichte im ersten nachexilischen Jahrhundert* (BWAT 8), Leipzig.

Rudolph, W. (1976), *Haggai–Sacharja 1-8–Sacharja 9-14–Maleachi* (KAT XIII.4), Gütersloh: Gerd Mohn.

Rylaarsdam, J. C. (1962), 'Day of Atonement', *IDB* **1**, Nashville, p. 314.

Sæbø, M. (1969), *Sacharja 9–14. Untersuchungen von Text und Form* (WMANT 34), Neukirchen-Vluyn: Neukirchener Verlag.

Schelkle, K. H. (1961), *Die Petrusbriefe/Der Judasbrief* (HTKNT XIII.2), Freiburg – Basel – Wien: Herder.

Schenker, A. (2000), 'Die zweimalige Einsetzung Simons des Makkabäers zum

Hohenpriester', in *idem*, *Recht und Kult im Alten Testament. Achtzehn Studien* (OBO 172), Freiburg: Universitätsverlag/Göttingen: Vandenhoeck & Ruprecht.

Schmidt, B. B. (1996), *Israel's Beneficent Dead. Ancestor Cult and Necromancy in Ancient Israelite Religion and Tradition*, Tübingen: Mohr, 1994, repr. Winona Lake: Eisenbrauns, 1996.

Schnackenburg, R. (1984), *Das Johannesevangelium* IV. Teil (HTKNT 4/4), Freiburg – Basel – Wien: Herder.

Schneider, G. (1972), 'Die Verhaftung Jesu. Traditionsgechichte von Mk 14,43–52', *ZNW* **63**, 188–209.

Schoedel, W. R. (1972), *Athenagoras, Legatio and De Resurrectione*, Oxford: Clarendon Press.

Schuchard, B. G. (1992), *Scripture within Scripture. The Interrelationship of Form and Function in the Explicit Old Testament Citations in the Gospel of John* (SBLDS 133), Atlanta: Scholars Press.

Schultz, R. L. (1999), *The Search for Quotation: Verbal Parallels in the Prophets* (JSOTSup 180), Sheffield: Sheffield Academic Press.

Schweizer, E. (1971), *The Good News according to Mark*, London: SPCK.

Sellin, D. E. (1930), *Das Zwölfprophetenbuch* (Kommentar zum Alten Testament 12), Leipzig: Deichertsche.

Simonetti, Manlio (1994), *Biblical Interpretation in the Early Church: An Historical Introduction to Patristic Exegesis*, Edinburgh: T. &.T. Clark.

Smith, D. M. (1995), *The Theology of the Gospel of John*, Cambridge: Cambridge University Press.

Smith, R. L. (1984), *Micah-Malachi* (WBC 32), Waco, TX: Word Books.

Soares Prabhu, G. M. (1976), *The Formula Quotations in the Infancy Narrative of Matthew: An Enquiry into the Tradition History of Mt 1–2*, Rome: Biblical Institute Press.

Sollamo, R. (1979), *Renderings of Hebrew Semiprepositions in the Septuagint* (AASF Diss Hum Litt 19), Helsinki: Suomalainen Tiedeakatemia.

Sperber, A. (1992), *The Bible in Aramaic. The Later Prophets according to Targum Jonathan*, Leiden: Brill.

Stade, B. (1881), 'Deuterozacharja. Eine kritische Studie. I.' *ZAW* **1**, 1–96.

— (1882), 'Deuterozacharja. Eine kritische Studie. III.' *ZAW* **2**, 275–309.

Stanley, C. D. (1992), *Paul and the Language of Scripture* (SNTSMS 92), Cambridge: Cambridge University Press.

Steck, O. H. (1967), *Israel und das gewaltsame Geschick der Propheten: Untersuchungen zur Überlieferung des deuteronomistischen Geschichtsbildes im Alten Testament, Spätjudentum und Urchristentum*, Neukirchen-Vluyn: Neukirchener Verlag.

Stendahl, K. (1968), *The School of Saint Matthew and its Use of the Old Testament* (ASNU 20; 2nd ed.), Lund: Gleerup.

Strauss, D. F. (1973), *The Life of Jesus Critically Examined*, London: SCM.

Sweeney, M. A. (2000), *The Twelve Prophets. Vol II Berit Olam*, Collegeville, Minnesota: Liturgical Press.

Telford, W. R. (1980), *The Barren Temple and the Withered Tree* (JSNTSup 1), Sheffield: JSOT Press.

Thomas, D. W. (1932), 'A Note on מחלצות in Zechariah 3:4', *JTS* **33**, 279–80.

— (1956), 'Haggai, Zechariah', *The Interpreters' Bible* 6, New York – Nashville: Abingdon, 1035–1114.

Thompson, M. (1991), *Clothed with Christ. The Example and Teaching of Jesus in Romans 12.1 – 15.13* (JSNTSup 59), Sheffield: JSOT Press.

Tigchelaar, E. J. C. (1996), *Prophets of Old and the Day of the End. Zechariah, the Book of Watchers and Apocalyptic* (Oudtestamentische Studiën 35), Leiden: Brill.

Toombs, L. E. (1962), 'Clean and Unclean', *Interpreters' Dictionary of the Bible* 1, New York – Nashville: Abingdon, 641–8.
Tromp, J. (1993), *The Assumption of Moses. A Critical Edition with Commentary* (SVTP 10), Leiden – New York – Köln: Brill.
Tuckett, C. M. (1983), *The Revival of the Griesbach Hypothesis* (SNTSMS 44), Cambridge: Cambridge University Press.
— (1999), 'The Historical Jesus, Crossan and Methodology', in Maser, S. and Schlarb, E. (eds), *Text und Geschichte* (FS D. Lührmann), Marburg: Elwert, pp. 257–79.
— (2001a), 'The Son of Man and Daniel 7: Q and Jesus', in Lindemann, A. (ed.), *Q and the Historical Jesus* (BETL 158), Leuven: Peeters, pp. 371–94.
— (2001b), *Christology and the New Testament: Jesus and His Earliest Followers*, Edinburgh: Edinburgh University Press.
Van den Berghe, P. (1962), "ANI et 'ANAW dans les psaumes', in De Langhe, R. (ed.), *Le Psautier: Etudes présentées aux XIIe Journées Bibliques*, Louvain, pp. 273–95.
VanderKam, J. C. (1991), 'Joshua The High Priest and the Interpretation of Zechariah 3', *CBQ* **53**, 553–70.
— (2000), *From Revelation to Canon. Studies in the Hebrew Bible and Second Temple Literature*, Leiden – Boston – Köln: Brill.
Van der Kooij, A. (1989), ' "De tent van David". Amos 9:11–12 in de Griekse Bijbel', in Becking, B., Van Dorp, J. and Van der Kooij, A. (eds), *Door het oog van de profeten. Exegetische studies aangeboden aan prof. dr C. van Leeuwen* (Utrechtse Theologische Reeks 8), Utrecht: Faculteit der Godgeleerdheid/Franeker: T. Wever, pp. 49–56.
— (1998a), *The Oracle of Tyre. The Septuagint of Isaiah 23 as Version and Vision* (VTSup 71), Leiden: Brill, pp. 112–22.
— (1998b), 'Perspectives on the Study of the Septuagint: Who are the Translators?' in Martínez, García and Noort, E. (eds), *Perspectives in the Study of the Old Testament and Early Judaism. A Symposium in Honour of Adam S. van der Woude on the Occasion of His 70th Birthday* (VTSup 73), Leiden: Brill, pp. 214–29.
— (2002), ' "Coming" Things and "Last" Things: Isaianic Terminology as understood in the Wisdom of Ben Sira and in the Septuagint of Isaiah' in Postma, F., Spronk, K., Talstra, E. (eds), *The New Things. Eschatology in Old Testament Prophecy. Festschrift for Henk Leen*. (Amsterdamse Cahiers SS 3), Maastricht: Shaker Publishing, pp. 135–40.
Van der Toorn, K. (1990), 'The Nature of the Biblical Teraphim in the Light of the Cuneiform Evidence', *CBQ* **52**, 203–22.
— (1997), 'Ein verborgenes Erbe: Totenkult im frühen Israel', *TQ* **177**, 105–20.
Van der Woude, A. S. (1984), *Zacharia* (De Prediking van het Oude Testament), Nijkerk: Callenbach.
Van Hoonacker, A. (1908), *Les douze petits prophètes*, Paris: Gabalda.
Vaux, R. de (1961), *Ancient Israel*, London: Darton, Longman & Todd.
Verseput, D. (1986), *The Rejection of the Humble Messianic King: A study of the composition of Matthew 11–12* (EHS Ser. 23.291), Frankfurt am Main: P. Lang.
Vögtle, A. (1994), *Der Judasbrief/Der 2. Petrusbrief* (EKK XXII), Solothurn und Düsseldorf: Benziger Verlag; Neukirchen-Vluyn: Neukirchener Verlag.
von Rad, G. (1975), *Old Testament Theology, volume 2*, London: SCM.
Wade, M. L. (2000), 'Evaluating Lexical Consistency of Greek Translations and Compositions', *Bulletin IOSCS* **33**, 53–75.
Walton, S. (2000), *Leadership and Lifestyle: The Portrait of Paul in the Miletus Speech and 1 Thessalonians* (SNTSMS 108), Cambridge: Cambridge University Press.
Weis, R. (1986), *A Definition of the Genre* Maśśa' *in the Hebrew Bible* (Diss.), Claremont Graduate School.

Weissert, D. (1973), 'Alexandrinian Analogical Word-Analysis and Septuagint Translation Techniques', *Textus* **8**, 31–44.

Wellhausen, J. (1898), *Die kleinen Propheten*, Berlin: Reimer.

Wenham, D. (1984), *The Rediscovery of Jesus' Eschatological Discourse*, Sheffield: JSOT Press.

Wilcox, M. (1988), 'Text form', in Carson, D. A. and Williamson, H. G. M. (eds), *It Is Written. Scripture Citing Scripture* (FS B. Lindars), Cambridge: Cambridge University Press.

Williams, A. L. (1930), *Justin Martyr: The Dialogue with Trypho. Translation, Introduction, and Notes*, London: SPCK; New York – Toronto: Macmillan.

Williamson, H. G. M. (1985), *Ezra, Nehemiah* (WBC 16), Waco: Word.

Windisch, H. (1930), *Die katholischen Briefe* (2nd edn; HNT 15), Tübingen: Mohr Siebeck.

Winter, S. C. (1994), 'Jude 22–3: A Note on the Text and Translation', *HTR* **87**, 215–22.

Wright, B. G. (1989), *No Small Difference. Sirach's Relationship to its Hebrew Parent Text* (SCS 26), Atlanta: Scholars Press.

Ziegler, J. (1943), *Septuaginta. Vetus Testamentum Graecum*. Vol. xiii: *Duodecim prophetae*, Göttingen: Vandenhoeck & Ruprecht.

— (1971), 'Die Einheit der Septuaginta zum Zwölfprophetenbuch' in *Idem*, *Sylloge. Gesammelte Aufsätze zur Septuaginta* (MSU X), Göttingen: Vandenhoeck & Ruprecht, pp. 29–42.

Index of Biblical References

Index of Modern Authors Cited